G

THE COMMONWEALTH AND INT
Joint Chairmen of the Honorary E
SIR ROBERT ROBINSON, O.M., F.R.S., LONDON
DEAN ATHELSTAN SPILHAUS, MINNESOTA

MENTAL HEALTH AND SOCIAL MEDICINE DIVISION
General Editor: HUGH L. FREEMAN

HUMAN GROWTH
and the Development of Personality

SECOND EDITION

HUMAN GROWTH

and the Development of Personality

SECOND EDITION

by

JACK H. KAHN, M.D., F.R.C.Psych., D.P.M.

Community Psychiatrist and Medical Director of The Child Guidance Clinic,
London Borough of Newham

Foreword by

G. M. CARSTAIRS, M.D., F.R.C.P.Ed., D.P.M.

Professor of Psychological Medicine, Edinburgh University

PERGAMON PRESS

OXFORD · NEW YORK · TORONTO
SYDNEY · BRAUNSCHWEIG

Pergamon Press Ltd., Headington Hill Hall, Oxford
Pergamon Press Inc., Maxwell House, Fairview Park, Elmsford,
New York 10523
Pergamon of Canada Ltd., 207 Queen's Quay West, Toronto 1
Pergamon Press (Aust.) Pty. Ltd., 19a Boundary Street,
Rushcutters Bay, N.S.W. 2011, Australia
Vieweg & Sohn GmbH, Burgplatz 1, Braunschweig

First edition 1965
Reprinted 1967
Reprinted 1968
Second edition 1971
Library of Congress Catalog Card No. 74–178681

Printed in Great Britain by A. Wheaton & Co., Exeter

BF
70 1
K33
1971

08 015817 X (flexicover)
08 015818 8 (hard cover)

And one man in his time plays many parts . . .

AS YOU LIKE IT

Contents

Foreword

EVERYONE who is engaged in one of the "helping professions", whether they are teachers, social workers, clinicians or clergymen or simply members of a voluntary social service agency, must encounter the recurrent problem of having to decide whether a client's experiences are truly abnormal or whether they fall within the range of common (or uncommon) occurrences. This holds true at every age and stage of human growth. Pregnant women often have to be reassured about the normality of their pregnancy, and an important function of post-natal clinics is to teach young mothers what to expect of their growing child. Nurses and doctors are quite familiar with this role, although not all of them appreciate that the time spent in this simple form of health education is just as important as their more usual therapeutic activities.

All this implies that we, the "helpers", know the range and sequence of normal human development, but rather often this is not the case. In our modern small family units it is possible for a young doctor or nurse to become quite out of touch with the domestic realities of living with babies, with teenagers or with ageing relatives. As a result, the constant promptings of experience which formerly were supplied by the large extended family have now to be replaced by deliberate study : but hitherto there have been few books to which one could turn. Dr. Kahn's work will prove invaluable for this purpose. He presents the reader with a well-informed account of human growth in which the matura-tion of the body plays an important part, but one which is over-shadowed by the development of intellectual and social accomplish-ments and by the patterns of expectation and response in human relationships which underlie each individual's personality.

This book does not deal, except incidentally, with sickness or psycho-pathology, but it provides an invaluable basis for the understanding of all the vagaries of normal human development. It will help all those who are confronted by perplexed or anxious parents, patients or clients, to recognise their problems more clearly and so to offer them informed guidance : it can therefore be recommended not only to practitioners and students of the helping professions but also to every intelligent citizen who would like to have a better understanding of human nature in general and of his own personality in particular.

G. M. Carstairs

Acknowledgements

The author is glad to express his indebtedness to Tavistock Publications for permission to quote from Dr. Winnicott's *Paediatrics and Psychiatry* and "Prevention of Mothering Breakdown" by John A. Rose in *Prevention of Mental Disorders in Children* (ed. G. Caplan); Her Majesty's Stationery Office for a section from M. D. Sheridan's *The Developmental Progress of Infants and Young Children*; Faber & Faber for quotations from *The Confidential Clerk* by T. S. Eliot; and the National Association for Mental Health for permission to quote material from the author's paper to the Inter-Clinic Conference 1963, "A Wider Concept of Deprivation". Acknowledgement is also due to the writers to whom reference is made in the text.

The author owes gratitude to numerous colleagues, past and present, and amongst these is glad to mention Miss Marion Whyte, Senior P.S.W. and Lecturer in the Leeds University Department of Psychiatry, who shared in the teaching of the first of the courses which provided the basis for this book, and Dr. A. T. Ravenette, Educational Psychologist, alongside whom the author is working in West Ham. He is also especially grateful to the students who took part in various courses and who may recognise in this book ideas and phraseology which were their own contribution to discussions.

The diagram on p. 152 was designed and drawn by Dr. A. T. Ravenette.

Introduction to Second Edition

THE topic of human growth and the development of personality is now a recognised part of the syllabus in the training courses for social workers. It also features, although not so uniformly, in the curriculum for medical students, psychology students, and the students at colleges of education. The purpose of study has to be seen in relation to the tasks undertaken by the different professions. Teachers work with children who are at some particular stage of development, and have to be aware of what went on before; and they need to have a picture of the stages still in front of the child who is at present a pupil. The helping and healing professions need knowledge of development as an aspect of diagnosis.

There are some disorders which are recognised as specific departures from the normal, and in this case the treatment is directed to the pathological process. The aim is cure. There are other disorders that are best seen as a dysfunction, and here the treatment is directed towards helping, or compensating for, the capacity which is affected. In this dimension of diagnosis, treatment may be a multi-professional affair, with the main responsibility falling upon the particular profession with specialised knowledge of some particular human function. Another dimension again is that of a deviation from a notional norm, where what is normal or abnormal is relative to the culture. The legal and social aspects are as important as the clinical ones; and, in this dimension, there is a responsibility of the helping professions to take part in the public discussions on the amount of deviation that should be tolerated. There is still a further dimension of the study of disorder which is to be thought of in terms of the provision or deprivation of the material and non-material necessities for development. At this level, the treatment would be to provide what has hitherto been omitted.

In all these dimensions, the disorder can be thought of either in terms of the individual or as the interaction of members of a group such as the family.

The choice between these different dimensions of diagnosis will depend upon the value which is subjectively attached by members of different professions to the study from one or other of the possible viewpoints.

The author's aim in this book is to call the reader's attention to a number of available viewpoints and possibly to enlarge the repertoire of methods of approach.

It is hoped that this would not lead to indecision. In fact, a diagnosis in any one of the dimensions is a decision for action. The knowledge of several dimensions is the justification for constructive co-operation between members of different professions who may be officers of the same department or of different departments, and it can allow for the organisation of a treatment plan for an individual or a family on a multi-disciplinary basis. Teamwork, of necessity, involves the joint understanding of the range of knowledge, skills and responsibilities, belonging to members of different professions who all have their own kind of training and experience. It permits them to join together in ground which is common to all and yet to maintain their separate responsibilities in the areas which are exclusive to any particular one. This theme has not been dealt with explicitly in this book, but it has determined the approach to a large number of the topics which have been discussed.

In this second edition a number of additions and alterations have been made. In the chapter on adolescence the author is grateful for having been granted permission to reproduce tables on the maturational sequence, in boys and in girls, which were published by the Excerpta Medica Foundation for the International Congress on Adolescence in 1966.*

The chapter on infantile sexuality has also been enlarged and it has been thought worth while to extend the description of the Oedipal situation. In order to avoid vague allusions to the original legend, the

---

* International Congress Series 108: *Psychiatric Approaches to Adolescence* (edited by G. CAPLAN and S. LEBOVICI), 1966. *Physical Aspects of Adolescence Development* by D. J. DUCHE and W. A. SCHONFELD and S. TOMKIEWICZ, pp. 19 and 21.

story is given in full, and comparisons are made with the Bible story of the intended sacrifice by Abraham of his son Isaac.

For permission to quote Freud's letter to Fliess in which he made his first reference to Oedipus, the author offers grateful thanks to the Hogarth Press Ltd., London,* and Basic Books Inc., New York.† The full-length account of the Oedipus story is taken from *A Classical Dictionary* by J. Lempriere, D.D., 1864.

There are many other quotations and references added to this edition and acknowledgement is made within the text or in footnotes.

Neither the references themselves nor the acknowledgements can ever be adequate or complete, as the subject, like the object of study, is in a continuous process of growth and change.

J. H. KAHN

* Hogarth Press Ltd., Sigmund Freud Copyrights Ltd., The Institute of Psycho-Analysis and The Hogarth Press Ltd. : Volume I of the Standard Edition.

† *The Origins of Psycho-analysis: Letters to Wilhelm Fliess, Drafts and Notes:* JAMES STRACHEY, 1964.

‡ *The Origins of Psycho-analysis: Letters to Wilhelm Fliess, Drafts and Notes: 1887–1902* by SIGMUND FREUD, edited by MARIE BONAPARTE, ANNA FREUD, ERNST KRIS, translated by ERIC MOSBACHER and JAMES STRACHEY, 1954.

Introduction

THIS book is based upon several series of lectures for training courses for child-care officers, social workers, probation officers, and nurses, and upon courses of in-service training for health visitors, assistant medical officers of health and mental welfare officers.

The lectures followed a pattern. The first part of each session was devoted to the presentation of a theme forming part of an agreed syllabus but with a certain amount of flexibility. The remaining part of the session was devoted to questions and discussions. The freedom given to the lecturer for digressions from the main themes became reflected in the subsequent discussion, which contributed fresh material to the topic, and which created new ideas which were carried into later parts of the course.

Every course of lectures was, therefore, different. There is some difficulty in capturing the spontaneous spoken word in a printed version which remains fixed. My intention, however, is that the book should be used by the reader as a starting point for associations of ideas. These associations in the reader's mind will be his own, and will become linked with previous reading and with his experiences in his personal and occupational life.

In this way a book can become a living interaction between author and reader. It has a beginning, but we do not know the end. It has also, as its accompaniment, the ideas that *might* have been written down if there had been enough time and enough thought. Everything that one ever says is said as an alternative to something else that one *might* have said, and is listened to against the background of some other thought in the listener's mind. A new arrangement of a familiar melody may contain phrases which are very different from the source, but which owe their impact to the accompanying original sound images. The variations are created with the original theme in mind, and, at times, the theme itself is deliberately recalled in all its well-known detail. Harmonies and discords are found in the mental associations as well as in the actual performance.

Writers, like composers, sometimes wittingly or unwittingly adopt this technique. I write this in the hope of disarming criticism when either the divergence from traditional themes, or the too literal use of familiar ideas, becomes obvious and jarring to the reader.

My own conscious theme is the constancy and the repetition of basic processes in human relationships. Parent and child, teacher and pupil, professional worker and patient, all have interactions which have something in common. The transactions are two-way. Whenever someone gives, something is received by him; and sometimes the traditional roles and unexpectedly reversed. The parent suddenly finds himself dependent on the child, the teacher learns from the pupil, and the therapist receives from the patient something that is healing.

Some acknowledgements of sources are made within the text. Countless other sources remain unrecognised or unremembered. Even when I quote the origin of ideas, however, I must take personal responsibility for the particular selection, and for the inevitable distortion which does injustice to the creations of others. The sources are referred to in order that the reader may make his own independent study of them.

This is not intended to be a book which tells people how to do things. The aim is to help readers to become sensitive to the dissatisfactions of themselves and others in a constructive way, and to learn to examine problems from new points of view.

J. H. KAHN

CHAPTER 1

Human Needs

ONE of the reasons for the study of human development is the wish to make provision for human needs in sickness and in health. It is necessary to understand how normal growth proceeds, and also to find out what takes place when something unsatisfactory is experienced, if we are to create satisfactory services for the individual growing up in the community.

The main emphasis in this particular book is on the emotional experience of individuals in their various interactions with one another. Meaning has been sought for normal and abnormal behaviour within the framework of the theories of psycho-analytical and other dynamic schools of psychology.

There are many other pathways through which the study of human development can be approached. Some of them are delineated below. Every human problem can be discussed in more than one of these ways, and it may be necessary to bear in mind the alternative approaches that are possible whenever one particular method is selected for some special need.

METHODS OF STUDY

First, we could consider the development of a single individual from birth (or from conception) to death, taking in turn different stages in the life of that individual, and dealing in each stage with the physical and mental life of that individual.

Secondly, we could consider the development of an individual in relation to the community. No individual exists alone; each child begins life in a physical union with his mother, maintains a close relationship

1

with her after birth, and develops a succession of relationships within the family, and later with a widening circle of others. When we study in this way, we can trace the manner in which the parents bring to the child their representation of the community within the home, and how the child passes through stages within the family to life at school and in the outside world, and later to life in the community as a whole, while at the same time developing personal relationships which can lead to marriage and the beginning of a new generation.

Thirdly, we could study the structure of the community as something existing in its own right, and then we should be concerned with the organisations and institutions of society, and this study would need the techniques of the sociologist. From this viewpoint, we should think of society as moulding an individual who was born into its existing systems, at the same time being aware that, at some stage, the individual contributes to the structure of society, and that he may occasionally be the agent of change in that structure.

Fourthly, there are those who find it useful to study individual personality in terms of a variety of patterns of culture which are available for mankind. Anthropologists such as Ruth Benedict think of different cultural groups as having selected, from the range of patterns available, certain aspects which give individuals in that group their particular characteristics.

Fifthly, we could study in more general terms the evolutionary development of mankind from historical records and prehistoric remains. Historical studies might be extended to include the development of political and economic aspects of progress, using comparisons of the present with the past.

Sixthly, we could study the physical environment in which man lives, and take into account the limitations of climate and natural resources which determine the capacity of man to maintain his existence. We could study the particular circumstances and elemental combinations which made life possible on this planet, and perhaps on other worlds. We could study the way in which man manipulates his environment and how in doing so he enables himself to extend the areas capable of supporting human life. We might observe, also, the way in which man has added extensions to his body in the form of machines which are created in his own image—mechanical cranes bigger than his arms, computers bigger than his brain (if less complicated), and vehicles which move faster than his legs are able to and which are now able to carry him beyond the boundaries of this planet.

VARIETIES OF APPROACH—PATTERNS OF HEALTH AND DISEASE

Any one of these approaches produces results which are valid within the framework of that particular study. The standpoint from which we make the observation determines the nature of our findings. The direction of the studies may in turn arise out of the purposes of our enquiries. Studies have a purpose which is sometimes a utilitarian one. We often study a process in order that we may control it or alter it. Thus, interest in anatomy developed partly out of people's desire to know enough about the body to be able to deal with diseases of the body. Such an approach is based on the assumption that disease processes can be understood when studied in terms of structure. If illness were looked upon as being of supernatural origin—as a punishment for sin or a testing process for virtue—there would be no purpose in attempting to study physical origins, and it would be impious to attempt to control the process by physical means. The assumption that disease is understandable is merely an alternative to an assumption that disease is not understandable. If we assume it is understandable, we can proceed with our studies, even when some types of disorder do not yield to our investigations, and still maintain our belief in the eventual subjugation of disease to our science.

The assumption of the existence of understandable processes within the human body in health and disease has developed into a concept of man as a kind of machine. This is a concept which has brought valuable results. There has been the discovery of recognisable patterns of change in body-structure which are associated with different experiences of illness. *Anatomy* is the name given to the study of body-structure; *Physiology* to the study of the workings of living tissue; *Pathology* is the study of the departures from the normal in structure and in chemical and other types of interchange, thus corresponding to both the anatomy and physiology of the normal. The study of pathology becomes the basis of classification of disease on the results of clear-cut observations. The understanding of disease processes has given rise to rational processes of treatment which aim at helping to repair the disease, or at dealing with the causes of the changes which have been discovered.

Aetiology is the study of the causes of illness, and these causes can include infections with organisms from outside, injuries, degeneration or wear and tear, and new growths. There are other diseases which are caused by deficiencies of essential factors in food. When we have satisfactory observations of causal factors and pathological effects we have a rational basis on which to develop our ideas of treatment.

This structural approach to the study of the human body and to the treatment of illnesses has had remarkable success. Procedures, based on these structural studies in this century and the latter half of the previous century, have added to the expectation of life of our present generation, have reduced the incidence of many diseases, almost completely wiped out others, and, to a lesser extent, have increased the effectiveness of treatment of disorders of mental life—i.e. of behaviour, and of thoughts and feelings. Some such disturbances are explainable in terms of physical change, yet many seem to elude explanation in terms of physical processes. Many people still hope that eventually all human activity, including mental processes, will be explainable (and controllable) on a physical level, yet there seem to be many aspects of human life for which physical explanations do not seem appropriate. For these disturbances, another kind of intervention would seem to be necessary for treatment, and another language to describe the process.

If we wish to study the mental life of human beings as a rational process, we must make assumptions similar to those for the study of physical aspects—namely, these too are understandable—that our thoughts, feelings and behaviour, and even our mental illnesses, make sense. Thus, we have a *psychology* of the normal which corresponds to the physiological, and a *psycho*pathology, which is the study of abnormal mental processes. In this field we become aware, too, of the importance of other aspects of life, some of which have been mentioned earlier. We become aware that a description of events is a preliminary to therapeutic intervention when disorders are apparent to the individual who suffers or to those with whom the individual lives. The description becomes the equivalent of diagnosis, and the terms in which a situation is described will often determine the type of intervention which takes place.

LEVELS OF DESCRIPTION: DIAGNOSIS

It is possible to summarise these general considerations from the point of view of the practical consequences of the study and description. Thus, human activities and problems can be said to be able to be experienced and expressed :

1. *In environmental terms*—referring to material resources, such as finance and housing, or to occupational, recreational, and cultural activities.
2. *In individual terms*—(intra-personal) referring in physical aspects to constitutional and organic factors, and in mental aspects to the psychology and psychopathology of the individual.
3. *In relational terms*—(inter-personal) referring to relationships with significant individuals in the marital and family situation. A description in these terms requires a study of family groups as if these were single units, and therefore the object of the study would be the family process, and not the separate individuals within the family group.

It is necessary to recognise that every disturbance or problem of individuals or families can be explained to some extent in terms of any or all of the above three categories.

INCOMPLETENESS OF PROVISION FOR ESSENTIAL NEEDS

The development of individuals or of family groups within a community depends upon the provision for their needs, but this provision is never complete. Problems therefore arise, and may be experienced or observed in one of these aspects. Thus, one aspect may be chosen as the one in which helpful intervention is desired. This means that the level of intervention which is decided upon will depend, not on any absolute standards, but on a choice based upon the state of knowledge, the resources available, and upon the degree of acceptability of a particular approach to both the recipient and the agency applying the help. An individual who feels distress might conceivably describe his problem as being entirely due to shortage of money, bad housing, or to unsuitable employment. At another time the same individual might feel that his physical health was below par and, with justification, seek medical help at a clinical level; or he might explain that everything would have been all right but for a disturbed relationship with his wife which had made him ill and left him unable to change his job, improve his financial position, and get a better house. He may be led to the conclusion, in the course of treatment, that he himself had contributed to the disturbed marital situation, and that the problem might be dealt with either as an emotional disturbance that concerned himself, or as a process which also involved his wife. In the latter case the inter-relationships will be the subject of treatment. One alone of these solutions might be accepted by the professional worker whom he consults. The professional worker, however, may try to help the man to restate the problem in terms of one or more of the other factors. It is a matter of choice, as well as of the state of knowledge, that determines the level at which the problem will be treated, and the choice is sometimes determined by the social class of the person concerned.*

ORGANISED AND UNORGANISED HELP

So far, it has been an assumption that the problems are to be studied scientifically, and that help is to be given professionally. Yet human problems have always received varying degrees of help from fellow human beings, in unorganised as well as organised channels. Professionally trained workers differ from untrained workers in that they apply their help within a disciplined framework, which is based upon the kind of knowledge of the problem which is expressed as a diagnosis. Untrained workers may be personally gifted and do good work with the goodness of their personality. They are unable to transmit their techniques to other people unless they have studied the process of what they do, scientifically. This is why many good organisations die with the death of a very talented and devoted founder. It is the professional self, not the personal self, which immortalises the work of an organisation.

If the diagnosis is in *environmental* terms, as described above, the intervention may be legal or administrative, and in some cases there may be a need for a social worker to formulate the needs in these terms, to guide the individual to the social services, and to enable him or the family as a whole to utilise the appropriate provisions.

* A. B. HOLLINGSHEAD and F. C. REDLICH, *Social Class and Mental Illness*, New York, 1959.

When the diagnosis is in *clinical* terms, the intervention required is a medical one and, although in preventive services a process may be applied to large groups of individuals, curative processes are usually directed towards single individuals. This applies to problems which are recognised as having an explanation in organic terms, and equally to mental illness when this can be described as a disturbance in a single individual. The professional discipline is thus mainly a medical one, but social workers may have a role as ancillary workers, or they may have an independent case-work function in relation to other members of the patient's family but acting in the patient's interests.

When the diagnosis is in *inter-personal* terms it is important to recognise that the intervention needs new developments in the study of human relationships. This is the process of intervention which has been given the name "case work". It is this field in which unorganised intervention is still likely to occur, as every member of the public feels himself to be an "expert" in human relationships.

No community can ever deny its members the benefit of giving and receiving support and understanding on a voluntary basis, but the professional work which is to be organised by the social service departments of local authorities has far-reaching responsibilities, including activities which require the enforcement of statutory obligations.

A unique function of voluntary organisations is to explore new areas of need which are given insufficient recognition by governmental and local authority services, and to provide facilities which have not yet received official authorisation. They may fill the gaps between existing services and apply pressures for the directing of resources to neglected sections of the community. What voluntary organisations, however, cannot do is to perpetuate the standards which are brought into being by the originators of the movements they represent. It is the fate of voluntary organisations to have their successful movements taken over and incorporated into official services; and the enthusiastic pioneer is succeeded by those who learn to formulate the ideas in a way which can be communicated to new entrants who can develop and maintain professionalised skill. There always remains an area of human endeavour that goes beyond theory and training and which has to be preserved by the renewal of inspiration, often by private individuals, in each generation. Professionalism and training become specially important wherever the services are intended to be applied comprehensively to the community as a whole, and where the worker has to be answerable for his standards, and where the consumer does not have an easy opportunity to refuse what is offered.

Some facilities are looked upon by individuals as being provided on their behalf. Some provisions are looked upon as obligations that are imposed upon them. The image of the social worker or administrator who is concerned with these provisions depends upon the public image of the particular service involved.

PROFESSIONAL HELP AT DIFFERENT LEVELS:
POINTS OF GROWTH

Some professions have long traditions and the image is well established. Doctors, teachers and nurses receive a professional education, pass qualifying examinations, and acquire great experience in their profession. They work in their own field with the authority of their professional background. Nevertheless they are consulted by people on matters outside the range of their training and professional experience. In such matters, then, if they are to respond at all to the call for help, the response is with the untrained part of their personality, and the value of their response depends upon qualities which have no relation to their professional skill. When one deals with problems of human interaction, new knowledge must compete with the general level of untutored understanding in the general population, and there is need also for recognition of the fact that the same untutored processes will accompany the attitudes of the trained professional worker in this field, even in spite of his training. Every professional worker must learn to recognise the times when he responds to people's needs with his professional skill and understanding, and he must beware of confusing these with the occasions when his response is no different from what it might have been if he had never received his training. At any moment he must be prepared to ask himself by what authority he acts. He must also be prepared to recognise that he may develop a habit of seeing all problems as having an answer in one particular dimension.

Once again, we have to recall that our observations are always limited to what can be seen from one viewpoint. Our enlightenment is partial, and, even though it seems to be appropriate to a particular problem, the usefulness of any level of intervention depends upon the degree to which it can become acceptable to those to whom it is to be applied.

We must remember the other possible lines of enquiry which were referred to at the beginning, and the various levels of intervention referred to immediately above, when from time to time we may find ourselves talking about *the* "cause" or *the* "treatment needs" of some particular illness or aspect of behaviour, and when some other viewpoint might be equally relevant. We must realise that at times we are all inclined to claim the whole truth in a particular explanation of living events, yet our observations have relevance only within their own framework. Different groups of professional workers examine the problems and pursue truth in their own way, yet absolute truth and standards appear to be something that we are destined to pursue and never attain.

When there is only one *right* way we feel secure. Doubts and uncertainties are a luxury that sometimes we feel we can do without. We need a few certainties for our daily bread and our ordinary work. We choose professions through which we direct ourselves to the helping of some particular individuals with specific problems. Professions have their boundaries and their limitations.

Sometimes we feel that the problem is not in the patient or client but in society. Professionally we have no means of influencing society. We may try to alter conditions, but we continue to work within the framework that exists. We may question the Law and try to alter it, but it is only in exceptional circumstances that people feel any option other than to obey it.

Professions have their rules, and their skills are based upon training which uses as much knowledge as is available. It is also necessary to know something about the principles and techniques in other professions, but one worker keeps within his own field.

It is when we become dissatisfied with our knowledge and our certainties that we may be ready to take the next step in personal and professional growth. Perhaps it is at the point of growth that different professions have something in common. At this growing point we meet members of other professions who are having the same struggles, and who may be seeking the company of others in their ventures into unknown territory.

CHAPTER 2

Definitions of Personality

SCIENTIFIC observations need theories and definitions in order that the observers may communicate with one another in some common language. The ordinary individual has theories of personality even if the theories are not formulated in precise words. People assume that it is possible to understand another individual's feelings in certain circumstances, and they are prepared to explain, or even predict, someone else's behaviour with some degree of confidence. This implies that behaviour, thoughts, and feelings follow some kind of pattern that is regular enough to justify the making of predictions. When explanations or predictions are not expressed precisely, they cannot be checked, and perhaps it is by forgetting wrong predictions, and remembering correct ones, that the ordinary individual retains his faith in his capacity to put himself in another individual's place. Scientific theories are at a disadvantage against ordinary beliefs in having to be expressed in terms that can be challenged.

CATEGORIES OF DEFINITION

A scientific study of personality must start with a definition of terms, and there is no shortage of definitions of personality which can be used as a starting point. G. W. Allport in his book *Personality—a Psychological Interpretation** devotes the entire second chapter to definitions, and there are fifty of them, and introducing these definitions he casually refers to personality as "The total manifold psycho-physical individuality". The definitions are grouped under the following head-

* Henry Holt, New York, 1937. Revised, 1963.

ings : Etymology, Theological, Philosophical, Juristic, Sociological, External Appearance (Bio-social Definitions), and Psychological Meanings. His final definition is that "Personality is the dynamic organisation within the individual of those psychophysical systems that determine his unique adjustment to his environment".

Etymologically the word "personality" has been considered to be derived from *Persona*, which denoted the theatrical mask used in Greek drama to indicate the character which the actor was portraying. Another possible derivation, of Latin origin, is the phrase *per sonare*, which applied to the device in the mask through which the actor projected his voice. In one case, the emphasis is on the assumed role; in the other, there is reference to what is revealed of himself by the person behind the mask. There are other meanings of the word person, derived from the same source; emphasis on his importance ("quite a person"); representative, e.g. parson of the Church; and a special use of the word "person" is applied to part of the (male) body.

Theological meanings are concerned with the inner nature rather than the assumed manner. Philosophers are concerned with definitions of self in terms of emotional qualities or attributes, and some of them lay emphasis on rationality or on self-awareness of the subjective core of a man's being.

Juristic meanings refer to the status of an individual and include his claim to the protection of his rights by law. This concept includes his possessions which have become known as his "personalty".

Sociological meanings refer to the person as the unit of the mass or the social group. The role and status of the individual in society becomes important, and therefore personality is thought of as the social effectiveness of an individual.

The External Appearance of Bio-social Definitions link with the original etymological derivation. This is because it is the extensions of personality that add to the external appearance by which impressions are made on other people.

Psychological definitions are grouped in many classes, some referring to mental organisation or to patterns of behaviour, and others to mental structure as described by adherents of various psychological schools. There are also omnibus definitions such as the one by Morton Prince who defined personality as "The sum-total of all the biological innate dispositions, impulses, tendencies, appetites, and instincts of the individual, and the acquired dispositions and tendencies—acquired by experience".

Each definition has a value for a particular purpose in a particular setting. We must continually refer to the limitations of the scientific observations. We might illustrate this pragmatic approach by a passage in one of George Birmingham's novels of nineteenth-century Ireland at a time when there was great economic distress in Ireland. The British Government put forward a succession of schemes for financial relief. On one occasion grants were offered to townships where conditions were such that they were without resources of their own. A certain village applied, producing convincing figures, and received a grant. A year later another scheme was put forward where the qualifying conditions were the existence of resources which could be developed with more capital. The same village put forward an application with equally convincing figures on those grounds. When it was pointed out that these figures contradicted the earlier ones, the local council did not give the answer which the author thought an English local authority would have given, such as that the original grant had changed the circumstances— they merely stated that the earlier figures were produced for a different purpose! Although this story was told lightheartedly, it is a fact that our findings are always influenced by our approach and our purpose. It is a fact that we actually need different definitions for different aspects of our study of personality.

This idea is expressed in a more formal way in William James's description of "What Pragmatism Means" : *

> The pragmatic method is primarily a method of settling metaphysical disputes that otherwise might be interminable. Is the world one or many?— fated or free?—material or spiritual?—here are notions either of which may or may not hold good of the world; and disputes over such notions are unending. The pragmatic method in such cases is to try to interpret each notion by tracing its respective practical consequences. What difference would it practically make to any one if this notion rather than that notion were true? If no practical difference whatever can be traced, then the alternatives mean practically the same thing, and all dispute is idle. Whenever a dispute is serious, we ought to be able to show some practical difference that must follow from one side or the other's being right.

* W. JAMES. *Pragmatism: A New Name for Some Old Ways of Thinking,* Longman, Green & Co., 1907.

The pragmatic approach is not the haphazard selection of ideas in quick succession for "trial and error", as some of the "error" can be avoided by doing the "trying" in imagination. This requires an awareness of different methods that could be tried. The exercise, then, is to ask "if we use this approach, rather than another one, in which direction will it take us?" Touchstone in *As You Like It* had the same idea which he expressed in the words ". . . much virtue in If".

PERSONALITY AS AN ASSEMBLAGE OF QUALITIES

Here I shall use or imply two or three definitions and, although they will have links with those quoted by Allport, they may be expressed somewhat differently. The first one is selected and slightly adapted, not from psychological sources, but from the large number which is given in the *Oxford English Dictionary*. Personality is

"an assemblage of qualities which makes each individual unique".

This definition is sufficiently vague to include a large number of factors, and makes it possible to discuss separate qualities and to refer to them in turn as we trace an individual's development at each stage of his life. We can describe the separate qualities in a variety of categories, but purely for convenience we shall use as headings *Physical, Intellectual and Emotional* qualities. It will be recognised that these headings cannot be discussed entirely separately; each one of them is linked with the other two. The separation is for the convenience of description and for the communication of ideas, and we need to recall that the description of separate qualities cannot include the idea of the wholeness of personality.

PERSONALITY AS DYNAMIC INTERACTION: EXTENSIONS OF PERSONALITY

Another definition of personality refers to the popular use of the word when it is taken to describe the effect of an individual on other people. This type of meaning is applicable when it is necessary to emphasise the *social* aspect of personality and, if we take into account the image that an individual has of himself as a result of the impression that he makes on others, we can speak more precisely of personality as "a dynamic interaction between an individual and his environment".

The qualities mentioned in the first definition are relevant to this second one, but the social aspect is important when we wish our descriptions to go beyond the range of what is included within the skin of an individual. Thus it is easy to recognise in terms of the second definition that an individual's personality can be different in different company. It is also possible to recognise that there are extensions of personality which go beyond the physical constitution, appearance and colouring, and include clothes, a man's pipe, a woman's perfume, the spectacles an individual wears, wallet or handbag, and such possessions as the motor-car, the house, furniture, and books on the shelves in the home. These are items by which people are recognised or which give them their own image of themselves.

When considering the effect of an individual on others, there is a popular usage of the word personality, in a quantitative sense, as when people say of an individual that he has "lots of personality" or even that he "has personality". It is rather reminiscent of the use of the word blood-pressure, only to *have* blood-pressure is a bad thing and to *have* personality is a good thing!

A third definition of personality is concerned more directly with the relationships of individuals with one another, and with the emotional life in individuals in groups. This class of definition includes various psycho-analytical and psychological theories of personality dealing with the mental organisation of individuals and of groups. For some purposes, processes of inter-personal relationships between individuals in a family or larger groups are more important than observations in terms of the mental life of a single individual. We may find it possible to describe the family processes dealing with the family as a single unit and not separate individuals.

For the purpose of description—the most useful definition is the one which refers to personality as an assemblage of qualities.

DESCRIPTION OF THE PHYSICAL, INTELLECTUAL AND EMOTIONAL ASPECTS

The preliminary descriptions will deal with the three classes of quality mentioned above, i.e. physical, intellectual and emotional. The *physical* aspects of personality include body-structure—height and weight, physical appearance, colouring of eyes and hair. Some of these features (such as colouring) are determined at conception and are inherited in a manner that follows the regularities which we describe as genetic laws. Other factors are inherited in the form of potentialities or limitations. An individual's capacity for growth may be an inherited quality, but the reaching of the limits of that capacity depends upon the good fortune of receiving a diet which will satisfy optimum requirements.

Body-structure in relation to other aspects of personality has been studied by Sheldon,* who made a large number of measurements and described physical types in correlation with types of emotional reaction and predisposition to particular types of mental disturbance. These results favour the idea that body shape is related to inherited constitutional factors which link structure with temperament. Mental processes also are linked with physiological factors such as the *metabolic* processes, i.e. the chemical interchange which follows the absorption of food, and which results in the production of energy. Different people think in different ways, and their bodies work in different ways—there is a difference in body chemistry in different individuals.

Inherited factors are obviously important, but the effect of nurture has also to be taken into account when we are estimating the contribution of nature. Higher standards of food and of care have led to an increase in the average height and weight of children of comparable age during the last thirty years. On a nation-wide range, the population as a whole is reaching a standard which once applied exclusively to the richest sections of the community. In times of economic distress the average height and weight decreases. Individual deficiencies may be partly determined by individual experience of deprivation of care. The same result may occur when, as a result of some types of illness, there is a failure to absorb an adequate diet even when one is available.

Furthermore, some characteristics which had been thought to be racial, and therefore inherited, may be altered when individuals of a race are moved to a different environment. For instance, the short stature of the Japanese becomes altered when individuals from Japan are brought up in a European or American culture. This is happening

---

* *The Varieties of Temperament*, Harper, New York, 1942.

even in Japan itself following the gradual adoption of diets introduced from other cultures.

Thus in studying the physical aspects of personality we have to recognise a wide range of differences within what is accepted as normal in any setting, and the existence of differences that are considered to go beyond the normal. We have also to recognise that at different periods or in different countries the standards of the normal are likely to vary. We are sometimes left with the conclusion that *that which is normal is that which is considered to be normal in any particular setting*, and that the idea of normality can alter in the course of time in any of the different settings.

By the *intellectual* aspect of personality we mean the capacity for conscious thought and the ability to direct thoughts for a particular purpose. We think of *intelligence* as a capacity in which inheritance is thought to play the major part, and in contrast we think of *educational attainment* as referring to the amount of knowledge that an individual might have at any one moment. The importance of the role of environmental influences, going far beyond the formal educational process, has recently been stressed alongside that of inheritance in relation to the development of intelligence.* Burt, however, upholds the view that heredity is the major determinant.

Intelligence grows along with the growth of the body, although not precisely at the same rate. There is an approximate constancy of the level of intelligence as compared with that of other individuals during the course of growth, and therefore it is possible to arrive at a measure which indicates the relationship of an individual's intelligence with other individuals of the same age. This is not measured by an absolute figure, as height is, but by a relative figure, known as a "Quotient", which is used to compare an individual's intelligence with that of a notional average individual of the same age. The mental age is derived from the standardisation of responses to a battery of tests applied to a very large child population. The child whose pattern of response is

---

* A. H. HALSEY, Genetics, Social Structure and Intelligence, *Brit. J. Sociol.* **9**, 15–20 (1958).

B. BERNSTEIN, Social Structure, Language and Learning, *Educational Res.* **3**, 173–6 (1961).

similar to that of the average of 8-year-old children has attributed to him a mental age of 8 whatever his chronological age.

The intelligence quotient was originally derived by taking the mental age divided by the chronological age, and multiplying by 100 (MA $\div$ CA $\times$ 100 $=$ IQ). The calculation is based on the use of the figure 100 to represent the average. It will be obvious that a child with a chronological age of 10 and a mental age of 12 will have an IQ of 120. A child of the same chronological age with a mental age of 8 will have an IQ of 80. Modern tests by-pass the elucidation of a mental age.

The use of the concept of *mental age* is one way of describing the intellectual capacity of children whose intelligence is far above or far below the average, and has been used for communications with other professions. The use of the *quotient* is necessary when we want a figure to represent the intelligence of the same individual at different ages; and it is particularly necessary with adults as the measurable aspect of intelligence stops growing at some point between 15 and 18 years (in a way similar to that in which physical growth in height ceases at about the same time). It would not make sense to describe an adult of average intelligence as having a mental age of 16.

For statistical purposes description in terms of the *standard deviation* is more adequate, but this is a sophisticated approach, and its use requires familiarity with statistical methods; the standard deviation is indicated in Diagram 1. See p. 152.

Sometimes it causes surprise when it is stated that the growth of intellectual capacity ceases in adolescence, yet strangely enough it is not so disturbing to recognise that physical growth stops at the same time. Adults seem to need some reassurance that they maintain an intellectual superiority over the growing adolescent, boy or girl! They may find this reassurance in the fact that the *use* of the capacity can develop continuously through some of the succeeding stages of adult life. Experience and maturity (which includes emotional factors) add new qualities to intellectual life.

Estimations of adult intelligence suggest a peak in young adult life and a decline with regard to some aspects taking place gradually from the age of 40 and more rapidly in old age. Nevertheless, the loss of speed in some mental processes, which is the index of the deterioration, is compensated for by the range of experience within a lifetime which enables problems to be placed in perspective. Some potentiality for growth remains (see p. 224) and is revealed in tests of vocabulary and imagination.

The intelligence tests which are used for measurement of intelligence differ according to the purpose for which they are required. There is no test which can measure the full range of mental life, and no test can measure any quality which does not find expression in some kind of external observable performance. Psychologists used to try to devise tests for what was postulated as the inborn capacity or potentiality. The best, however, that is possible, is to aim at avoiding the use of tests which are unduly influenced by the particular educational or cultural background of individuals, unless indeed they are examining the educational or cultural background. No test can completely exclude such influences, and different tests are effective, more or less, for the purpose for which they are used. Tests used in the educational setting are intended to differentiate the types of educational needs of different children. Other tests are used clinically as part of the investigation of mental life in relation to the treatment of some mental disorder.

Educational tests usually are *group tests* which demand responses to a set of questions on paper, and the results are examined afterwards. *Individual tests* allow the psychologist to take into account the attitude of the child as well as the content of the response, although this is necessarily a subjective process. All tests must be affected in some degree by the previous experience of the individual, but there are many tests which give results which are considered to be satisfactory enough for the making of comparisons between individuals who have been brought up in similar cultures and conditions. Mostly they are thought to have a predictive value which is accurate enough for conclusions to be drawn as to the type of education or occupation to which an individual can successfully apply himself, and some are useful enough in the clinical field as part of the information on which a diagnosis is made. Every test has its limitations and its value within some practical field.

Intelligence tests at best give a snapshot view. The process of growth of intelligence as described by Piaget* is a regular definable sequence of successive stages. Piaget's concepts enable us to regard a child as being

* J. PIAGET, *The Child's Construction of Reality*, Routledge & Kegan Paul, 1955.

at some particular stage of the mental development which is marked out by functions which have now become possible.

As an abstract quality, intelligence has many definitions, and a generally accepted one is that of "the capacity to extract the relevant information, in order to draw conclusions when dealing with a problem with some purpose in view".

The usefulness of intelligence tests as a measure of intelligence for educational decisions has become a controversial issue, and there has rightly been some resistance to the original concept of the intelligence quotient as a factor as unchanging as the blood group. It is necessary to recognise that in the growth of intelligence, the inborn aspect is a potential or capacity which determines limitations rather than the actual value which might eventually be reached. In this it resembles physical height, and it resembles physical height also in that the reaching of the limits of the capacity will depend upon the provision of the appropriate food. The material for the growth of intelligence consists of the experiences of a child at home and at school; the general cultural background and the quality of education both link up with the progress of intellectual development. Children will differ in their intelligence level at any age just as they differ in height, and just as there are those who are tall and those who are short in height, there are some children with high intelligence and some children with low intelligence. In physical height there are some who are beyond the range of normal, and this is recognised more readily in adults. There are those who are giants and those who are dwarfs. There are likewise those with intelligence so high, and perhaps so uneven in its distribution, that they are outside the normal, and there are people whose intelligence is so low that they are unable to fit in with normal living, in some of its activities, or they may be even so limited as to be unable to take any part at all in the ordinary life of the community.

These wide differences in intelligence may depend upon genetic variations within or beyond the normal range, or upon genetic differences which are qualitative rather than quantitative and which are associated with other abnormalities. Some of the abnormal processes of development of intelligence may occur in individuals of normal inheritance as a result of post-natal experiences. Deprivation of experience inhibits growth of intelligence in the same way as an insufficient diet prevents physical growth. Children who are brought up in institutions, or who are otherwise denied close and continuous contact with adults who are interested in them, show such slow development that they may be mistaken for those with congenital deficiencies in intelligence. If the deprivation is continuous, they actually *become* defective notwithstanding their original normal potential.

There can be also deprivation of a cultural kind—even the vocabulary which is available in a home or a district affects the growth of intelligence. Words are the means by which we communicate and through which we express our mental activity. Words are also the material out of which we are able to build up our thought processes and through which we perceive the world. A limited vocabulary will limit the capacity for the development of some aspects of mental life, e.g. the lack of words in which to express abstract ideas hinders the development of abstract thought.

The *emotional* life of an individual encompasses the basic feelings and moods which are the product of internal mental processes, and which are the links between an individual and other people. It is concerned with the elemental feelings of love and hate, and the derivatives of those experiences, tenderness and aggression. It seems probable that the intensity with which these feelings are expressed may be an inherent quality, and that different individuals have a different capacity for emotion, but there are emotional differences between people which are the result of events in the formative years in their childhood.

Thus the emotional aspects of personality may be a resultant of natural endowment and the experiences after birth. We could imagine an emotional quotient similar to the intelligence quotient if only we had data which were measurable. The food needed to develop the emotional capacity of a growing child is relationships of the right quality within his family. We can imagine emotional growth which is normal, and we can accept that there are variations which would still come within the range of normal. Normality would not depend upon absolute standards but upon what is considered healthy in a particular community at a particular time. We cannot escape the making of value judgements which are implicit in our norms, but these, also, differ in different communities.

We could also recognise that in any community some people have emotional development which is deficient, perhaps because of some inborn lack, or perhaps because of starvation of the requisite kind of relationship.

We have to consider the requirements for what we would regard as normal or optimal development. At this stage we could just refer to the idea that the emotional life includes opposing feelings at all stages, and that there are aspects which are unconscious as well as others which are conscious. There can be simultaneous love and hate, in which case one component can be hidden from awareness at one particular moment. The love of a parent for a child can be accompanied by resentment at some of the burdens that the care of the child entails; or the rejection of a child, however openly expressed, can be accompanied by the opposing feelings of love and the wish to keep and to nourish the child whose presence seems so much undesired. This conflict of feelings or *ambivalence* underlies all relationships. Maturity can be considered to be the awareness of both components, the acceptance of the universality of conflict, and the readiness to take personal responsibility for the control of these feelings.

The description of physical, intellectual and emotional qualities leaves out a good many other aspects of personality. All three are concerned in the *social* development of an individual, but in describing separate qualities we do not give a picture of a complete personality in a social setting.

THE IMAGE AND THE SOURCE

Whatever method we use in observing an individual, the result of our study is incomplete. Nevertheless, human beings have a knack of filling out a complete picture from fragmentary observations. We build up some idea of a wholeness which may be accurate, or not, even when we use a medium which leaves out everything but that which can be observed during a single moment of perception. We can see a photograph of an individual which has captured a fleeting glimpse, and yet we feel that we know how the individual will behave. We receive a little more information when we see a film at the cinema, but if it is a silent film we have observations just of actions and gestures. A sound film adds the voice, and with this further material we can recognise an individual who was seen previously in another film, and feel that we know more about him. We recognise the disembodied voice of a person on the radio, and a "personality" in a television programme may appear to us as if he were a familiar visitor to our home. The actor whom we see in the flesh, but at a distance, appears to us even larger than life because we fill out in our imagination the parts of his personality which are not observable. We often feel disappointed when we meet in person someone whom we have known only through a medium which has its limitations.

If we read a book and later see a play or film based upon it, frequently it happens that we are disappointed because our own imaginings are more satisfying to us than those of the artistic interpreter who was responsible for the production. This also happens to us with people we know when, because we have built up a fantasy of them from the limited ways in which they have appeared to us, we are disappointed by later experience of them which makes them more human and fallible. Sometimes this appears to us to be the result of their deterioration, and we may say "they have let us down".

Parents do something like this with their children, comparing them at various stages with an image which has no relation to the real child. Teachers do something similar with their pupils, doctors with their patients, case-workers with their clients, and, in ordinary social relationships, people judge their friends by an image which they themselves have created. The first impression borrows something from previous experience of other people, and this provides a number of categories into which each new acquaintance is grouped. We add in our minds something more than we can see in those with whom we are in contact. We may feel it as a personal injury whenever we are forced to alter the first mental picture.

Bearing in mind the fact that our observations always contain some distortion, it is part of professional work and of scientific observations to minimise the distortion. It is with the knowledge of these limitations that we trace the development of an individual through certain maturational stages of life, and discuss the innate qualities and the subsequent provisions which are necessary for development in each of the stages to which we shall refer.

CHARACTER AND TEMPERAMENT

There are a number of consistent features of personality that survive in each individual throughout the vicissitudes of the processes of development.

Character is the term used to describe the effective organisation of an individual's capacities. The word sometimes carries a moral implication, referring to the way in which an individual is in control of his activities.

Temperament refers to the prevailing moods of an individual and is dependent upon inborn factors which determine the balance of endocrine secretions. It is associated with the type of response and the degree of susceptibility to emotional stimulation. The concept is related to the postulation by Hippocrates of the four humours (blood, phlegm, yellow bile, and black bile) which, in different proportions, were thought to be responsible for the constancy or changing nature of the moods of different individuals. This idea has been given fresh life within the framework of the physiological concept of *homoestasis*. The cells and fibres which constitute the central and peripheral nervous systems include two main sub-divisions which are anatomically distinct and which are physiologically in opposition. These maintain the balance and influence the stability or equilibrium of the activities of vital organs and of the body as a whole. This balance, when slightly disturbed, may be restored without conscious sensation.

Psychological evidence of the existence of different basic temperaments is being provided by work such as that of Schaffer referred to in Chapter 4.

CHAPTER 3

Developmental Stages

INDIVIDUALITY OF THE BABY AT BIRTH

Descriptions of a baby as a separate individual usually refer to his helplessness and dependence and, in descriptions of his relationships with the mother, it is stressed that the baby needs the mother (or substitute for her) for his very survival. All this is true, but it is equally important to be aware of the fact that even at birth the baby has a vigour and an assertiveness which gives him a life of his own. In the image that a mother has of a baby, even in the stages before she becomes pregnant, there may be a picture of a plump, happy but helpless child lying contentedly on a soft pillow. The strength of her unborn baby may be surprising and at times alarming.

A mother's image of the baby is not a snapshot but a moving picture, yet it may omit some of the essential sequences. One mother might envisage the infant exclusively as a grown-up, pursuing a career with independence and with an ability to take some of the burdens that the older parents can no longer carry. To another, the main picture of the child might alternate between a passively dependent chubby baby and a later edition who would have the ability to separate, but who would still prefer to keep in contact with her. One could hypothesise also on the tensions of the child who might have need for someone who can give comfort at his frequent moments of discomfort or distress, alternating with a need for self-assertiveness and for a freedom from the imposition of conditions which limit his activity.

DEPENDENCE AND INDEPENDENCE

During pregnancy the mother becomes aware of something that is within her but which has a separate life. The baby is cushioned within

24

the mother from many of the discomforts of extra-uterine life. He receives the benefits of the chemical interchange in the mother's bloodstream, and there are some variations in his body processes which depend upon the changes in the mother's metabolism. The child has his own circulation of blood with a barrier between his and his mother's circulation, but some of the constituents, which are in solution in the plasma of the bloodstream, pass through this barrier and provide the child with nourishment and with oxygen.

There is a separateness as well as a union. In the later stages of pregnancy the child has physical movements which the mother cannot control. The kicks which she experiences are as independent of her as they would be if she were kicked from outside.

The process of birth still leaves the child dependent upon the mother, but it emphasises the processes of separation which becomes more complete with each further stage of the child's development.

At birth the child has some physical accomplishments in his own right. Within seconds he takes in air with what seems to us to be a struggle, and then he breathes in and out. He can cough and sneeze in a way which helps to clear his air passages when mucus threatens to obstruct them. He can wriggle and thus prove that his muscles give him the power of movement, and he can grip with considerable strength a finger put into the palm of his hand. He can cry, and thus call attention to his needs for relief of physical discomfort or to the distress of loneliness. Most important of all, he can suck.

These accomplishments are necessary for survival. There are other qualities which, at this stage, are merely potentialities to be developed later. Some of these would seem to be patterns of behaviour which are already laid down, and which merely await physical maturation for their full expression. Other potentialities depend for their fulfilment upon the physical, intellectual and emotional experiences which are the material for their growth.

At all stages we have the mysterious phenomenon of a single process serving simultaneous and opposing functions, e.g. the intra-uterine movements which give notice of separate existence and, at the same time, provide a communication between unborn child and mother.

NATURE AND NURTURE

We have those capacities and accomplishments which are due to nature and those which are due to nurture. Sometimes it is difficult to distinguish between the influence of one or the other, and some qualities may have a contribution both from inheritance and from post-natal experience.

The *physical* characteristics in the various stages of development are described in terms of body-structure and capacity for movement. *Intellectual* life is represented in the learning in general about the outside world and the more formal learning which is called education. The stages of *emotional* development are more difficult to define, and our descriptions depend more upon inference than on direct observations in measurable terms. Each physical and intellectual stage has its counterpart in emotional development, but the different aspects may develop at different rates in any one individual.

DEVELOPMENTAL NORMS

Many workers in different professional fields have made observations on developmental stages regarding the behaviour patterns and responses of the child week by week and month by month. A. E. Gesell has written extensively, alone and with collaborators, giving the results of an enormous number of recorded observations of many aspects of infant development. He describes "norms", which are averages, against which any individual child can be measured in what is called "Developmental Diagnosis",* and it is maintained by Gesell and his co-workers that "it is possible to diagnose in the first year of life nearly all cases of amentia, cerebral injury, many sensory and motor defects, and severe personality deviations". They state that "the human organism is a complicated action-system, and an adequate developmental diagnosis requires an examination of four fields of behaviour representing different aspects of growth. These four major fields are :

(1) Motor behaviour.
(2) Adaptive behaviour.

* A. GESELL and CATHERINE AMATRUDA, *Developmental Diagnosis*, Paul B. Hoebner Inc., 1960.

(3) Language behaviour.

(4) Personal-social behaviour."

The detailed description of the infant's growing capacity, supplemented in some publications by illustrations, gives a good background of knowledge for the precise diagnosis of the present capacity of the child, and this has been shown to have some predictive value of future progress. R. S. Illingworth, who supplements some of Gesell's findings with his own extensive paediatric experiences,* summarises the literature, and describes stages of normal development and its variations including the mental development associated with various physical defects. Illingworth discusses reasons for the demand for "norms" in child development :

"To satisfy the intellectual curiosity of parents about their children especially after a previous stillbirth or a family history of mental or physical handicap."

"In cases of adoption and to estimate the possibility of some inherent handicap."

"Following injury or infection in a new born baby, to be able to follow the development made in later stages."

"In cases where there are problems of behaviour or food difficulties to be able to take into account mental and physical defects."

Parents sometimes come under criticism for using the timing of the developmental landmarks of the child for the purpose of competition with other parents. A point is scored when one's child sits up, talks and has achieved toilet training in advance of the neighbour's child. It is the game of keeping up with the Jones's baby. Rather than criticism there should be understanding of the anxiety about the progress of their babies when parents are cut off from the traditional sources of knowledge and reassurance that used to come from the older generation in large families. This lack of background information applies especially to parents of handicapped or defective children. They do not know what to expect when the child's development is delayed and even the professional workers, whose help they seek, often seem to be without a framework within which they can discuss a particular child.

* R. S. ILLINGWORTH, *The Development of the Infant and Young Child, Normal and Abnormal,* 2nd ed., E. S. Livingstone, 1963.

In the case of adoption we have the controversial point as to whether adoptive parents have the right to the exclusion of deficiencies in the children they adopt.

Yet there is every reason, as Illingworth says, to consider it to be a double tragedy for a husband and wife, who have been unable after several years of marriage to satisfy the normal desire to have a child, to adopt a child who subsequently appears to be mentally defective. Some adoptive parents deliberately choose a handicapped child, and there are others who are prepared to take their chance along with natural parents, but it seems to be justifiable to attempt to protect the ordinary range of adoptive parents from the burden of handicap that could be detectable at the time when placement is arranged.

DESIRE TO DIFFERENTIATE: ORGANIC AND EMOTIONAL CAUSES OF DISORDERS

Where injury or infection or problems of behaviour call for investigation, professional advisors and parents alike are often anxious to be able to distinguish between those disturbances which are due to inherent causes and organic factors, and those which are due to emotional ones. Any theory of causation leads to inferences which are either satisfying or disturbing to the parents. If the condition is inherent it is nobody's "fault", but is likely to be thought of as uncorrectable. Of acquired disturbances, the organic ones are thought of as less blameworthy than the emotional ones. If relationships within the family are thought to be responsible for emotional disturbances, the parents feel guilty and seek confirmation of their fear that their behaviour towards the child is responsible, and may even attract blame in order to refute it.

These comments are made because of the doubts as to the advisability of the use of "norms" as standards *by parents in order to judge their child, in such a way that they feel that the child is good when he is level with, or in advance of, the norm, and bad if he lags behind.*

Emotional attitudes with regard to the use of developmental tests are somewhat similar to those with regard to the use of intelligence tests. Individuals who do not get a particular desired result from tests feel that it is the test itself which threatens the future of their child. The validity of the tests is challenged, and the purpose often misunderstood.

For this reason one requires to know their limitations and special values. As with intelligence tests, it can be held that no assessment should be made for the information of a parent unless there is the opportunity for discussion of the results with the parent by a worker who is familiar with the child as well as with the standards.

With this proviso it can be said that professional workers who deal with children will find it invaluable to have knowledge of developmental norms, and Illingworth gives ample evidence for the statement that the developmental tests "can detect mental retardation and neurological conditions with a considerable degree of certainty". He adds "There is little evidence that mental superiority can be detected in infancy."

CHARTING THE STAGES

Dr. Mary Sheridan, who carried responsibility within the Ministry of Health in relation to the special provisions for handicapped children, has produced a very clear chart of observations on "The Developmental Progress of Infants and Young Children".* The categories that are given under the headings Posture and Large Movements, Vision and Fine Movements, Hearing and Speech, Social Behaviour and Play, seem to be more related to the everyday activities of children than the headings used by Gesell.

The work covers the age range of 1 month to 5 years, and an extract covering the period from 1 to 6 months is reproduced by permission (pp. 44/45). It will be noted that the records of progress are arranged under the four headings in vertical columns. It is therefore possible to read expected average performance at any one age by reading across the pages, and the progress in one quality by reading vertically downwards. It is the experience of many students that it is easier to comprehend the developmental progress by following one quality at a time rather than by attempting to maintain the picture of the relative progress of each quality at any one time. Perhaps this is partly because of the knowledge that the different qualities grow at different rates (the child may grow in physique at a greater rate than in intellectual performance), and partly because of the fact that our span of attention

* *Reports on Public Health and Medical Subjects,* No. 102, H.M.S.O., 1960.

is limited. An individual's personality is a complete whole, but the capacity to study it seems to be limited to observations on a very narrow range of his activity. Having got a picture of each quality in turn, it may then be possible for the student to turn back occasionally and to attempt to bring two or three different aspects into relation with one another. This limitation in our capacity to observe when trying to understand any subject will accompany us and hamper us in all our studies.

There are other ways of describing developmental stages. *Biological stages* are those which depend upon maturation of inborn capacities, *cultural stages* are patterns imposed upon the individual in each particular society, and the two are superimposed. Psychoanalysts describe *stages of psychosexual development* under the headings of *Oral, Anal* and *Genital* in accordance with the successive predominance of sensitivity of different areas of the body during the early years.

Walking marks the division between the stage when the infant is carried about from the stage when he has freedom to move independently, and thus serves both physical and social needs. *Talking* is the stage when the child, who had previously been able to communicate with his mother in a private language of gesture and inarticulate sound, learns a code which allows him to communicate with a wider world. Each of these new capacities marks a stage in which there is opportunity to form relationships within a widening circle of other individuals.

TRANSITION BETWEEN STAGES AS A CRISIS OR STEPPING STONE

Some stages such as school entry are a further mark of the progress from life in the family to life in the outside world. There are a succession of further stages in each individual life where there is a transition from one stage to another. These include transfer from one school to another, puberty, school examinations, school leaving, entry into occupation, courtship, marriage, moving house, illness, deaths of relatives and close associates, and the changes in middle and old age.

Every change is to some extent a crisis. Early methods of satisfaction are outlived, but the desire for them may remain as accompaniments to later satisfactions as we pass through each separate stage. The various landmarks have been spoken of as "crisis events",* and there may be emotional disturbance of greater or lesser intensity at each stage. There can be regret, anxiety, or depression during the crisis of giving up an old status and an old satisfaction, and there is a point of instability between the two phases of life. This is literally true in the process of learning to walk. A child who has learnt to stand, holding on to someone's hands or a piece of furniture, has to take a few steps into the unknown before reaching the safety of another hand or another piece of furniture. Inevitably he falls, yet it is rare for him to show anxiety unless that anxiety is conveyed to him by the adult who is with him. He falls and falls again, picks himself up with great determination, and begins to walk again. The new accomplishment and the new freedom is sufficient reward.

Sheridan has spoken of the landmarks as "stepping stones", and this imaginatively refers to the passing to the new level of satisfaction of the next phase. The keeping in mind of these two separate ways of looking at the developmental landmarks serves the practical purpose of calling our attention to the fact that some individuals and some families need special help on these occasions.†

* E. LINDEMANN, Recent Trends in Preventive Child Psychiatry, in *Emotional Problems of Early Childhood* (ed. GERALD CAPLAN), New York, 1955.
* Ecological Ideas Regarding Mental Health and Mental Ill-Health, and Mental Health Consultation.
Both from G. CAPLAN, *Concepts of Mental Health and Consultation*, U.S. Department of Health, Education and Welfare, 1959.

CHAPTER 4

The Suckling

BREAST FEEDING AS A REUNION WITH MOTHER

It is a traditional custom to put a baby to the mother's breast immediately after birth. The process of birth may have been distressing to the mother. In some cases the mother accepts labour in its literal sense as a job of work in which she actively participates, and looks upon each pain as the product of her own activity which is bringing the desired result nearer. Sometimes intensity of pain or the anxiety of the mother calls for active intervention on the part of the medical attendant. Anxiety increases, and yet almost invariably after completion of the birth processes, which is marked by the expulsion of the placenta or afterbirth, there is a look of tranquillity and satisfaction on the mother's face which is something that goes beyond mere relief.

The baby has been subjected to considerable pressure in the process of birth, and has had the abrupt ending of the supply of oxygen and food from the mother's blood. He has to make an initial struggle for the first breath of air. Feeding comes later, and the feeding re-unites mother and baby at a new level. Imaginatively we can picture the baby in his first distress wishing for something to relieve and comfort him, and what he wishes for then materialises—almost as if she were the creation of his need. Ever after, in distress, we reach out for comfort, and hope to match the kind of realisation of that first re-union of baby and mother.

The feeding process begins, and this satisfies a multiplicity of needs of both the mother and the child. The mother needs to give suck as the child needs to suck, but there can be many reasons why a mother may not be able to feed her child at the breast, and why she may not even wish to. The inauguration of the flow of milk is slow. For the first three days after the birth of the baby the fluid which comes from the breast is not milk but colostrum. It is a thinner fluid and there is less of it than of the milk which will come later, but the baby has enough reserve of food for this period. The sucking of the nipple at this stage stimulates the flow of milk, and is thought also to help the process of involution of the muscles of the uterus which had become enlarged during the months of pregnancy.

ESTABLISHING THE FLOW OF MILK: SIGN RELEASE PHENOMENA

The establishment of the milk supply is now thought to depend upon a precise mechanical stimulus which occurs when the size of the baby's mouth and the size of the nipple have a certain relationship, and a measurement of these relative sizes was carried out by Mavis Gunter* in relation to the success or failure of breast feeding. This is thought to be one of a series of phenomena where something is set going by a mechanical process which is important in the tie between mother and child. These processes were first discovered in the study of the behaviour of animals with their young, and the science in which there is an attempt to correlate observations on the nurturing of young animals with that of the human infant is called "Ethology".

Lorenz, in a book called *King Solomon's Ring*,† was one of the earlier writers on this subject. (The book was so named because of the legend that King Solomon wore a ring which enabled him to understand the language of animals.) Lorenz kept a number of different animals within his home and observed their behaviour, and then studied it by altering the circumstances. For example, the young geese follow the mother immediately after being hatched from the egg. It is a behaviour pattern which has survival value. Lorenz noticed that the pattern of following was set going by the sight of the first moving object which, in fact, was usually the gosling's mother. Lorenz found experimentally that the goslings would follow any other moving object which came into the line of vision immediately after hatching. A dog or even a moving rubber ball would be treated by the goslings as if it were the mother.

---

* Instinct and the Nursing Couple, *Lancet* **1**, 575 (1955).
† KONRAD LORENZ, *King Solomon's Ring*, Methuen, 1952.

When Lorenz arranged that he himself became the first moving object to be seen, the goslings followed him and continued to do so even into their adult life.

It would seem that there are certain processes which set going a kind of behaviour, and other processes which inhibit them when the behaviour is no longer appropriate. The substitute mother is lacking in some of the processes including that which later sets the offspring free.

Another example is the opening of the beaks of young nesting birds at the moment that the mother (or father) arrives with a worm. This occurs not on the sight of the mother or even of the worm carried in its beak, but as a result of the vibration caused when the parent bird alights on the side of the nest, and it can be reproduced experimentally by touching the edge of the nest.

These processes are called "*Sign release phenomena*". Different forms of behaviour depend upon a particular stage of maturation in the young and upon the appearance of some outside stimulus or sign. They are "species specific", i.e. there are different kinds of behaviour and different signs in different kinds of animal.

These phenomena occur in the behaviour of the human infant and mother, and have been described by John Bowlby.[*] The sucking at the breast is one only of these phenomena. In addition, the baby's smile, the baby's cry, the baby's clinging with the hand around the neck of the mother, are all activities which arouse something in the mother for which she is ready, but which needs a stimulus for it to be released.

There is a level of mothering which exists as a potential in every individual which is part of the general sympathy and compassion for other human beings, and there also is mothering which is intellectual and which can be studied. In addition to all this, there are the built-in processes, described above, which need some particular occurrence for development and release. Successive stages of mothering are roused by the developing activities of the baby : not just what the baby is doing, but the fact that what the baby is doing is changing from day to day. It is the *rate of change* in this case that is the stimulus and not the behaviour of the baby at a particular time.

The process takes place in stages. A stimulus brings part of the

[*] The Nature of the Child's Tie to his Mother, *Int. J. Psycho-Anal.* **39**, 350 (1958).

mothering process into being, further development reinforces the tie, and still further development on the part of the child is the stimulus to release the tie and permit the child to separate.

This kind of explanation enables us to understand the mother of the child who suffers from some handicap and who does not develop at the normal rate. The mother of such a child may not be able to develop some of the normal responses, or to release her child from herself at later stages, because the necessary stimulus never arrives. The inappropriateness of the tie at different stages may be what we refer to when we say that she rejects or over-protects him.

This particular topic was introduced at this point in order to explain the fact that some failures to establish breast feeding have purely mechanical causes. A mother may wish to feed the baby and fail, and then she feels inadequate. There are other mothers who do not want to feed their babies, and it has become known that it is possible for the wish not to feed the baby to lead to failure in the production of milk. Thus it is often implied by the professional attendant (doctor or midwife) that a mother who fails *could* feed the baby if she only wanted to. A feeling of guilt is thus added to the feeling of inadequacy. It is said that she "rejects" her baby, but perhaps it is the professional attendant who is rejecting (towards) the mother.

MECHANICAL AND EMOTIONAL FACTORS

When breast feeding is first established, difficulties can arise from lack of knowledge of the simple mechanics of holding the baby to the breast. Most mothers have had no experience of seeing other mothers breast feeding their babies—families are small and breast feeding in other homes is private.

Sometimes a baby is held at the breast in such a way that the baby's nose is embedded in the breast,* and the baby has to let go of the breast with the mouth in order to continue to breathe. Sometimes such a baby will pummel the breast in his effort to get his mouth free while still wanting to suck, and the mother will say he is "fighting the breast", or more simply that he is "refusing" the breast. Such a mother feels deeply hurt, by what she feels to be the baby's deliberate behaviour. Breast

* There is a similar effect if the baby's upper lip is pressed against his nostrils.

feeding is broken off and, although the mother blames the child, she just as unfoundedly feels guilty herself.

Breast feeding has become one of the topics which arouse partisan feelings. Most studies of the baby's mental life are conducted on the assumption that the baby's feeding takes place at the breast. Most writings for the lay public state the value of breast feeding for the infant, and sometimes make reference to the value that the mother herself receives from the process. Reference is made to the universality of breast feeding in primitive races. It has recently been suggested that this universality is achieved only at the expense of high infant mortality, which means that where breast feeding is not established, the infant simply dies!*

ARTIFICIAL FEEDING: RATIONAL AND IRRATIONAL REASONS

Bottle feeding remains prevalent, in spite of teachings to the contrary, in any country where facilities for artificial feeding exist. Perhaps bottle feeding is like contraception. It seems to be practised wherever the techniques are available. It seems to be inevitable that where the opportunity occurs, people separate off certain biological aspects of sexual and reproductive life that are unwanted, and retain those which seem at the moment to be considered essential, valuable, or satisfying.

Professional attitudes are influenced by the personal self as well as the professional self of the doctor or nurse in charge of the family. Sometime the professed attitude is that of supporting breast feeding, but the attitude which in practice comes in response to the mother's enquiry is the personal one which supports that part of the maternal feelings which finds breast feeding difficult. In a recent study† of reasons given by mothers for their adopting artificial feeding, many of the reasons given by mothers for taking the baby off the breast were explanations which they hoped would be acceptable, and which would answer implied criticism.

* M. MEAD, *A Cultural Anthropologist's Approach to Maternal Deprivation—Deprivation of Maternal Care*, p. 50. W.H.O. Public Health Papers 14, 1962.

† L. J. NEWSON and E. NEWSON, Breast Feeding in Decline, *Brit. Med. J.* 5321 (1962).

Among the large number of unspoken reasons, there is the undoubted convenience of bottle feeding which permits the mother some freedom from the constant tie in that it is a process which can be carried out by other people. Moreover, a mother may take the baby off the breast because of her fears that her milk is not good enough for her child, and often this erroneous view is supported by professional attendants. In small drops all milk looks thin compared with the opaque liquid seen in depth in the bottle, and perhaps human milk is in any case less opaque than cow's milk. The belief of milk "not being good enough" or not "suiting" baby is part of every woman's fear of not being quite good enough, or of being in some way inadequate. There are also the associations of breast feeding (involving the nipple in a mouth) with sensuality; and women who feel that *any* deep sensations are bad will feel frightened by the association of this experience with sexuality.

Other women are afraid that breast feeding will alter the shape of the breast, and so it does, to some extent; and, if a woman's image of herself is that of the profile in which youthful breasts are a prominent but delicate feature, she will find herself unable to accept the next stage of her development.

A more recent factor in bottle feeding has been the medical emphasis on hygiene and sterility of everything brought to baby's mouth. Bottles can be boiled, powdered milk comes out of tins and is free from bacteria. The composition of the feed can be modified according to the prescription of the revered doctor, and the mother actually sees the level of milk in the bottle going down, and knows that it is passing into the stomach of her baby. It has the right composition, and the right quantity, the right temperature with a guarantee of freedom from infection.

All these latter reasons can justify those feelings in her which favour her wish to discontinue breast feeding, but some of the wish for close contact with the baby remains. Even when the baby is fed with the bottle, the baby may be held close to the mother's body and feel her heartbeat, be sensitive to her confident embrace, and smell her presence. There is an abundance in mothering which spreads into the feeding of the baby whether at the breast or with the bottle. We need to recognise that in this country breast feeding is now the practice of the minority.

VIGOUR OF BABY'S SUCKING

The baby's part in the feeding process is studied by direct observation, and inferences are drawn from what we see in the light of our ideas regarding the development of personality. A baby feeds at the breast or at the bottle with the mouth, and the baby is an active participant in the taking in of the milk. A baby sucks vigorously. This fact is responsible for both the satisfactions and the anxieties that mothers have about breast feeding. The fantasy that a mother might have had about her baby in the days before her marriage or during the time of her pregnancy is likely to be of a passive and helpless child, and the feeding process is pictured as the milk passing peacefully into the baby's mouth and down the throat. The baby's sucking, however, is a very vigorous process, and at this early stage it emphasises the conflict between dependence and separateness.

The sucking process serves many purposes for the baby. The baby *feeds* with the mouth, the baby also *feels* with the mouth. He experiences a sensation which is stimulating and pleasurable within the act of feeding. Sensation is at its most intense level in a young baby with regard to objects which touch the mouth. The mouth is the point at which the baby makes contact with the outside world and, if that contact is with the nipple, it is the mouth which is the point of union of the baby with another person. It is at this point, therefore, that the baby becomes aware of the limits of his body, and of the distinction between what belongs to him and what is outside him. This sensation would seem to be the first area through which the baby is able to perceive, and, for some considerable time afterwards, any object which is put into a child's hand is taken immediately to the mouth, presumably to distinguish it by its shape as well as by its taste.

The contact of mouth with nipple—or with the teat which is the substitute of the nipple—is associated with the pleasure of feeding. It is the sensation of loving contact with another individual. It is a means of getting satisfaction which can be recollected in dreams, and you may see a baby continuing with sucking movements when falling asleep. It is a sensation which can be reproduced by self stimulation when a baby sucks his thumb, or the stimulation can be provided by someone else who puts a dummy teat in the baby's mouth. Sucking gives the sensation of love which can be experienced with another individual, or as something deriving from stimulation of the recollection of it.

This capacity to derive sensual satisfaction with the mouth becomes partly superseded, as people grow, by other satisfactions, but it remains with us as an essential core. We celebrate important occasions with meals or with drinks; and we give ourselves comfort when we smoke or when we continue to suck our thumbs, our pipes, or our pencils, or when we chew gum which has no nutriment but merely taste. The word "companion" implies someone with whom one has shared bread.

PRIMITIVE LEVELS OF SATISFACTION AND FRUSTRATION

The vigour with which feeding takes place provides another aspect of the activity which is concentrated on the mouth. The baby sucks vigorously and assertively. The mother feeding the baby at the breast who is unprepared for this, may even feel that the baby is attacking her. There is good evidence, in the reconstruction of infant life which takes place when older children or adults regress in mental illness to infantile levels, that babies themselves have some awareness of fantasy of destructive power in the process of emptying the breast. It is also true that there are primitive levels of thought and feeling in all of us in which there is a wish to make reparation for the attack which we make on the source of our feeding and of our satisfaction.

To summarise simply, *the baby feeds with the mouth, feels with the mouth, loves with the mouth, and attacks with the mouth.* There are various stages of mental life which can be described in different terms according to the particular theory of personality development which is held by the person making the observation. This stage, where the feeding process plays such an important part in the physical, perceptual and emotional life of the baby, is called *The Oral Stage* by those who adopt psycho-analytical viewpoints.

There are further stages described within this framework, and many different mental processes are attributed to each stage. It is possible, however, to find the rudiments of all the later processes in this early stage. The stage includes fundamental biological drives which serve the function of maintaining life and of giving satisfaction. The process is also linked with the contact between human beings and with the fantasies that we have about these contacts as well as the realities of them. The process is also linked with the restrictions which are imposed upon human beings from the earliest stages after birth. We begin to live in a world which is ordered and arranged by other people who are guided by custom. Feeding is provided sometimes according to the child's needs and demands, and sometimes according to ideas conveyed through the mother as to when the child should be fed and when food should be withheld. Babies may develop a rhythm which is satisfactory to them, and which fits in with the framework provided for them.

FEEDING ROUTINES

There has been a change in feeding patterns. Differences of feeding patterns of different races or different cultures have been noticed by anthropologists, and these have been equated with different types of personality in the adult members of the community. There have been changes in feeding patterns in the last few generations in this country. It has been suggested that there is a pendulum swing from rigid feeding schedules to on-demand feeding. The rigid pattern held sway particularly in the 1930's.

Possibly the changes are more complicated. The feeding pattern prevalent a couple of generations ago, according to descriptions and recollections, depended upon the proximity of the baby to the nursing mother who fed the child at the breast. The child was fed at irregular intervals on his demand or at the whim of the mother. Rigid schedules perhaps began with the opportunity for regularity which was provided by artificial feeding. Regularity became associated with the goodness of mothering and with virtue in the baby. Regular hours and regular amounts were prescribed, and mothers were forbidden to feed even a crying (and presumably hungry) baby if there was still half an hour to go before the time of the next feed. Night feeding was prohibited, and mothers were told "Once you give a feed to a baby in the night, you will have to go on doing so." Good mothers were terrified to give way to what they were told were their baby's improper demands.

A reaction from this has been, in more recent years, the system of "on demand" feeding, which was considered to be a return to the feeding processes of a previous generation. Perhaps the difference in the mother working to this system is her complete subordination to the baby's cry.

It might be possible to describe variations of this "on demand" system which would make a fourth level, namely, a fairly regular rhythm of feeding which allows for variations of the individual baby's needs, and variations of any particular baby's needs on different days. It is surprising how, under some such regime, both baby and mother become adapted fairly quickly to a regularity which is convenient, but which is sufficiently flexible to make allowance for variations in the appetite for food and comfort.

It is thus evident that in this period of early feeding of the child we have all the variations of problems which can occur in the search for satisfaction and for approval, or of the need to love and be loved, even when it involves accepting the restrictions and the accompanying feelings of rebellion against having to conform.

On the mother's part, this period includes a miniature representation of the conflicts which she will continue to have about having a child who is dependent upon her and at the same time trying to separate; and of her own feelings about wanting simultaneously the incompatible rewards that come from another creature's dependency and independence.

Feeding has been described in detail because it is the most important activity in the development of the child, and because in it can be concentrated every possible pattern of personal adjustment and interpersonal interaction. The baby is in the meantime acquiring experiences of the outside world, and learning to distinguish through his perceptions the difference between what goes on within him and what goes on in the outside world of objects and people. He makes attachments to the mother and to other individuals, and these depend upon different stimuli—the mother's face in full view with both eyes visible to him, stimulates his smile—the profile is not sufficient. The mother responds to the baby's smile as does everyone else. The baby's cry is a particularly important communication, and is perceived as such. It can be a signal of discomfort to which the mother or some other individual responds. It can be a call for a feed, or it can be interpreted on occasions as "temper". Many people become abnormally sensitive to the baby's cry, having been led to believe that babies spend their time feeding or sleeping, and, if he is awake and crying between feeds or in the night, they feel that something is wrong, either with the baby or with themselves. It should be noted that the young baby has no way of communication other than by crying.

PATTERNS OF INFANT CARE

The baby's cry becomes another activity which, like the feeding, is an issue between parents and children. Parents are told to ignore the baby's cry in order that he should not become "spoilt". The importance of regularity of feeding and sleeping is that from the early stages it is thought that the baby should be forced into a pattern of behaviour which is acceptable. Mothers even fear that the child who cries for comfort, or who refuses his feed, will become delinquent if she gives in and becomes indulgent. Others fear equally terrible consequences if the baby's needs are not anticipated in such a way that he never has reason to cry.

Some mothers are at the mercy of the latest professional pronouncement. Some mothers cheat a little and find an excuse for responding to the baby's needs for food or comfort. In a recent study of infant care in Nottingham,* what was reported to health visitors was different from what was reported to university staff who had no professional relationship with the mothers. They could admit giving a night feed or comforting the crying baby to a non-professional person, but tended to tell the health visitor what they thought she expected them to do.

The baby develops other needs. He is happier in the pram when propped up so that he can see outside objects; and moving shadows of the leaves of a tree are more satisfying than the fixed outlines of walls, and still less satisfying is the emptiness of the visual field when the baby lies flat in the pram.

An active baby makes demands for food, warmth and many other stimuli, but there seems to be a tradition in describing the baby as "good" when his demands are minimal. They are described as "easy" and "content". If someone asks mother about a baby "Is he good?"

* J. and E. NEWSON, *Infant Care in an Urban Community*, Allen & Unwin, 1963. (*Patterns of Infant Care*, Penguin, 1965.)

the expected answer, quoted in this study, is "Yes, he is very good. I hardly know I have got him." This is somewhat reminiscent of the idiom of some wives in describing the absence of sexual relationships. They say "My husband is very considerate"!

Schaffer,* who studied the behaviour of babies in the temporary separations which occur when left for short intervals in their prams, records the comment of one mother whom he interviewed. "When I take him out for a walk in the park he just will not lie in his pram like other babies. He has to be propped up so that he can see everything that is going on. The hood has to be left down in case he misses anything, and the moment the pram stops he begins to cry."

Schaffer suggests that there is an optimal amount of stimulation which differs from infant to infant, and that it is a function of mothering to supply this optimal amount. But mothers, too, differ in their sensitivity to the infant's call, and some say "I cannot bear to hear my baby cry, and have to pick him up the moment he starts".

Schaffer† also reported the wide differences in the reporting of the liking and disliking of physical contacts in the form of cuddling, hugging and kissing. Mothers varied in their needs for these contacts, and babies in their response to them.

An important study of individual differences, covering work over a span of twenty years, has been recorded by Sibylle K. Escalona.‡

She found it possible to distinguish between active and inactive infants. Active infants are those whose behaviour involves the whole body; they require little in the way of background stimulation and are able to respond at their most mature level to the routine caretaking contacts of maternal figures. The mere presence of objects and toys within reach and sight can draw responses from the active infant. Inactive babies draw their stimulus and satisfaction from part activities of their own bodies; they overcome distress unaided by sucking their fingers, by rocking, and they begin to scan the immediate environment for visual and auditory stimuli. This capacity to find comfort can lead to a vicious circle. The inactive infants need more stimulation than the

---

* *Determinants of Infant Behaviour II*, Methuen, 1963.

† H. R. SCHAFFER and PEGGY E. EMERSON, *The Development of Social Attachments in Infancy*, Child Development Publications, Indiana, 1964.

‡ SIBYLLE K. ESCALONA, *The Roots of Individuality*, Tavistock Publications, 1968. Review article, J. H. KAHN, *Mental Health*, 1970.

1 month

Lies on back with head to one side; arm on same side outstretched, or both arms flexed: legs flexed, knees apart, soles of feet turned inwards. Large jerky movements of limbs, arms more active than legs. At rest, hands closed and thumb turned in. Fingers and toes fan out during extensor movements of limbs. When cheek touched, turns to same side; ear touched, turns away. When lifted head falls loosely. Held sitting, head falls forward, with back in one complete curve. Placed downwards on face, head immediately turns to side; arms and legs flexed under body, buttocks humped up. Held standing on hard surface, presses down feet and often makes reflex "stepping" movements.

Stares expressionlessly at brightness of window or blank wall. Shuts eyes tightly when pencil light shone directly into them at 1–2 inches Follows pencil flash-lamp briefly with eyes at one foot. Notices dangling toy or rattle shaken in line of vision at 4–6 inches and follows its slow movement with eyes from side towards mid-line on level with face through approximately quarter circle, before head falls back to side. Beginning to watch mother's nearby face when she feeds or talks to him.

3 months

Now prefers to lie on back with head in mid-line. Limbs more pliable, movements smoother and more continuous. Waves arms symmetrically. Hands now loosely open. Brings hands from side into mid-line over chest or chin. Kicks vigorously, legs alternating or occasionally together. Held sitting, holds back straight, except in lumbar region, with head held erect and steady for several seconds before bobbing forwards. Placed downwards on face lifts head and upper chest well up in mid-line, using forearms as support, and often scratching at table surface; legs straight, buttocks flat. Held standing with feet on hard surface, sags at knees.

Visually very alert, particularly preoccupied by nearby human face. Moves head deliberately to look around him. Follows adult's movements near cot . Follows rattle of dangling toy at 6–10 inches above face through half circle from side to side, and usually also vertically from chest to brow. Watches movements of own hands before face and beginning to clasp and unclasp hands together. Recognises feeding bottle and makes eager welcoming movements as it approaches his face. Regards still objects within 6–10 inches for more than a second or two, but seldom able to fixate continuously.

6 months

Lying on back, lifts up head from pillow. Sits with support in cot or pram and turns head from side to side to look around him. Moves arms in brisk purposeful fashion and holds them up to be lifted. When hands grasped, pulls himself up. Kicks strongly, legs alternating. Can roll over. Held sitting, head is firmly erect, and back straight. Placed downwards on face lifts head and chest well up supporting himself on extended arms. Held standing with feet touching hard surface bears weight on feet and bounces up and down actively.

Visually insatiable: moves head and eyes eagerly in every direction. Eyes move in unison: squint now abnormal. Follows adult's movements across room. Immediately fixates interesting small objects within 6–12 inches (e.g. toy, bell, wooden cube, spoon, sweet) and stretches out both hands to grasp them. Uses whole hand in palmar grasp. When toys fall from hand forgets them or searches only vaguely round cot with eyes and patting hands.

Startled by sudden loud noises, stiffens, quivers, blinks, screws eyes up, extends limbs, fans out fingers and toes, and may cry.
Movements momentarily "frozen", when small bell rung gently 3–5 inches from ear for 3–5 secs with 5 secs pauses: may move eyes towards sound.
Stops whimpering to sound of near-by soothing human voice, but not when screaming or feeding.
Cries lustily when hungry or uncomfortable.
Utters little guttural noises when content.
(*Note.*—Deaf babies also cry and vocalise in this reflex way, but if very deaf will not show startle reflex to sudden noise.)

Sucks well.
Sleeps most of the time when not being fed or handled.
Expression vague, but tending to become more alert, progressing to smiling at about 5–6 weeks. Hands normally closed, but if opened, grasps Examiner's finger when palm is touched.
Stops crying when picked up.
Mother supports head when carrying, dressing and bathing.

Sudden loud noises still distress, provoking blinking, screwing up of eyes, cry and turning away.
Definite quietening or smiling to sound of mother's voice before she touches him, but not when screaming.
Vocalises when spoken to or pleased.
Cries when uncomfortable or annoyed.
Quietens to rattle of spoon in cup or to bell rung gently out of sight for 3–5 secs at 6–12 inches from ear.
May turn eyes towards sound; brows may wrinkle and eyes dilate, may move head from side to side as if searching vaguely for sound.
Often licks lips in response to sounds of preparation for feeding.
Shows excitement at sound of approaching footsteps, running bath water, etc.
(*Note.*—Deaf baby, instead, may be obviously startled by M's sudden appearance beside cot.)

Fixes eyes unblinkingly on mother's face when feeding.
Beginning to react to familiar situations—showing by smiles, coos, and excited movement that he recognises preparations for feeds, baths, etc.
Responds with obvious pleasure to friendly handling, especially when accompanied by playful tickling and vocal sounds.
Holds rattle for few moments when placed in hand, but seldom capable of regarding it at same time.
Mother supports at shoulders when dressing and bathing.

Turns immediately to mother's voice across room.
Vocalises tunefully, using single syllables e.g., ka, muh, goo, der.
Laughs, chuckles and squeals aloud in play.
Screams with annoyance.
Shows evidence of response to different emotional tones of mother's voice.
Responds to baby hearing tests at 1½ feet from each ear by correct visual localisation, but may show slightly delayed response.
[Tests employed—voice, rattle, cup and spoons, paper, bell; 2 secs. with 2 secs. pause.]

Hands competent to reach for and grasp small toys. Most often uses a two-handed, scooping-in approach, but occasionally a single hand.
Takes everything to mouth.
Beginning to find feet interesting and even useful in grasping.
Puts hands to bottle and pats it when feeding.
Shakes rattle deliberately to make it sound, often regarding it closely at same time.
Still friendly with strangers but occasionally shows some shyness or even slight anxiety.

active ones in order to reach the same level of social awareness, but they are the ones that get the least attention.

An important generalisation was made from analysis of the conditions under which infants first show visual attention to their surroundings. A moderate degree of stimulation favours development; too strong an arousal leads to regression.

The mother, in particular, varies her response at this early stage to the infant's changing needs. She introduces variation and intensifies those actions which, at one moment, are pleasing to him and reduces her activity when the stimulus is too great. Social encounters with siblings and fathers are less accommodating; the infant may be '. . . bounced, tickled, tossed, or teased by the offer of toys withdrawn just before they are grasped . . .'. It is the non-maternal contacts which provide the growing infant with the experience of having to accommodate to an unaccommodating world.

CHAPTER 5

Toilet Training

DIVISIONS in the developmental stages are made under different headings by observers who have different standpoints. There is a difference in the outward behaviour between an infant who has to be carried from place to place and the toddler who can move on his own initiative. There is a difference between the baby who babbles in a manner intelligible only to those who communicate with him in the same baby language, and the young child who has acquired the speech which is understood even by strangers.

Walking is a *physical* landmark, talking an *intellectual* one even though it depends upon physical maturation and emotional relationships.

TOILET TRAINING AS A SOCIAL DEMAND

The acquisition of control of bladder and bowel is a step in the *social* life and implies conscious conformity to rules laid down by others. Control of bladder and bowel functions also has *physical* and *emotional* aspects. Control of bladder and bowel function becomes important wherever mankind lives in large communities. The excreta can carry infection, and indiscriminate passing of urine and faeces and careless handling can be a danger to the community. Excreta become associated with dirt, disease and danger.

Control of the process of elimination marks the stage when the child begins to take responsibility for carrying something out which is not a personal need but a duty imposed upon the individual because of the needs of the group in which he lives and the needs of the larger community which contains the group.

The attitudes to the products of elimination are always complex. Separate from the body they may be looked upon as carrying danger, but the process of elimination itself can carry with it a feeling of goodness and of healthiness and, at the moment of elimination, the products themselves can be regarded with satisfaction as a sign of healthy body activity. Health is often judged by the regularity and the quantity of urine and faeces.

MATERNAL ATTITUDES TO PRODUCTS OF ELIMINATION

In early infancy the baby's urine and motions are looked upon benevolently. They are so close to being a part of the baby's body that the mother handles them without fear or distaste and often with a considerable amount of affection. The first motions after birth are called meconium, and they are different from the faeces which are formed later in that the substance is completely free from bacteria. Shortly after birth when the child is fed with milk at the breast or from the bottle the bowel products change in character and begin to contain some of the fat from the milk. The motions are often a pale yellow in colour and quite sweet to smell, and mothers handle the napkins with satisfaction and without fear when changing a napkin which contains the child's motion or which contains the urine.

Digestive disorders may alter the character of the "stool" (as it is sometimes called). Green, loose and scanty motions may be a sign of underfeeding the baby. A hungry unhappy baby with loose stools soon produces an unhappy mother who becomes anxious about the child's feed, and the mother may even be tempted to dilute the feed in the belief that the milk is too strong for her baby. This is where the mother needs reassurance as to the goodness of her milk if she is feeding at the breast, and of the goodness of her mothering if she is feeding the child with the bottle, and she may need practical information about some of the processes of feeding.

Gradually, as the child is given mixed feeding, the motions change in colour and character, and begin to resemble the more adult faeces. They begin to have the characteristic smell of motions, due to the activity of bacteria which become the normal inhabitants of the bowel.

The mother may still feel safe in handling these more mature stools but begins to feel that it is necessary to be more careful of her disposal of them and in her cleaning up of the baby, of herself, and of the utensils. Gradually her attitude to these products alters, and as the baby shows signs of physical development and intellectual awareness, she is able to give him some of the responsibility for the disposal of the motions and urine and is able to seat the child on the W.C. The little boy is able to stand and direct his urine into the W.C., if the W.C. is low enough, and the little girl is able to choose a time to sit on the W.C. for the passing of urine or for her bowel action.

MATURATION OF NERVOUS PATHWAYS

There are steps of physical development which have to be reached before a child can be said to acquire this kind of control. It apparently depends upon maturation of nerve fibres which go to the muscles which control the "sphincters" (the name given to the muscles around the openings of the bladder and the bowel).

The nerve fibres in general are able to work efficiently when they acquire a myelin sheath, and this maturation takes place at different times in nerves to different parts of the body. The fibres to the muscles controlling elimination mature somewhere around the eighteenth month of life, and then the child is able voluntarily to initiate contractions in the abdomen which set going the process of relaxation of the sphincters and expulsion of the excreta. Previous to this the emptying of bladder and bowel is reflex and involuntary.

Reflex contraction of bladder and bowel muscle tends to take place throughout life whenever a certain degree of distension is reached. Voluntary contraction of muscles assists this natural and more primitive process, and voluntary control inhibits the process. In the early months of life the reflex emptying of bladder and bowel may appear to be unpredictable, and therefore there are wet and soiled napkins. There are, however, some patterns of regularity, and some indications that the process is about to take place can be observed. There is a tendency to empty bladder and bowel as the result of a series of reflexes when food enters the stomach. The contents of the different parts of the bowel are, in turn, passed on a stage further in a kind of shunting process. The bowel is thus likely to expel some of its contents, and simultaneous bladder contractions lead to a passing of urine.

The mother who places a child on the "potty" shortly after feeds may succeed in catching the products, and take pride in the dry and clean napkins. On other occasions she may notice the beginning of the elimination when the baby flushes and the rate of breathing alters. Quick recourse to the potty saves the napkin. Sometimes mothers who in this way train themselves, rather than the baby, take a pride in what they think is the baby's achievement, and equate it with the goodness of the baby. The danger here is that the inevitable accident becomes badness in the baby. Another danger is that there is a difficulty in the mother's adaptation for the transition to the stage when the baby has the capacity to control the passing and the withholding of urine and faeces. The pattern of the baby's behaviour has changed, and yet the mother is still seeking the same result.

BATTLES OF WILL

If regularity has become an issue, and if the mother feels that it is necessary for her rather than the baby to control the regularity of the passing of the urine and motions, the baby is likely to get satisfaction from resisting her demands as soon as he is capable of doing so. Battles begin over toilet training in the same way as they can occur when food is offered too rigidly in timing and quantity.

The young infant learns to retain his motions even when laxatives are given up to the point when the motions become so loose that they have the consistency of diarrhoea and can no longer be controlled. Alternatively, the infant may pass the motion at an inconvenient time and place at the very moment that the mother has given up the struggle.

TENSION, RELIEF, AND GRATIFICATION

During the end of the second half of the first year, or during the second year, the baby has learned to distinguish sensations in connection with the passing of urine and faeces, and there is a pleasure in the relief of the distended bowel and bladder with the emptying at what seems to be the right time. There is a pleasure in the sensation of the passing of urine and motions, and these sensations begin to rival those of the mouth as a source of gratification.

Psycho-analysts refer to the *anal* period of psychosexual development and also they pay attention to the importance of sensations and fantasies in connection with the urethra. These orifices (anus and urethra) become, for the time being, an important focus of emotional experience. There is a sense of gratification when elimination is satisfactory, or of discomfort and pain when the timing or the nature of the product has altered in some way—such as when the urine is too concentrated or infected, or when the motions are too hard or too loose.

The thoughts and fantasies about the actual products are complex because the action of elimination is thought of as good and sometimes the products themselves are thought of as good or, alternatively, actions and products are thought of as bad and dangerous.

The products are a part of the child's body and the goodness or badness is of himself. These products are an extension of the personality into the outside world. While the child was first experiencing the sensations of feeding and learning the limits of himself, it must have been hard to distinguish where his mouth began as there was a continuous passage of milk between the mouth and the nipple or bottle. When sensation first develops at the bowel orifice, it must have been difficult to determine where the body ended as the products passed outwards. Moreover, just as feeding is not entirely a personal activity but a relationship between the child and the mother, elimination also is a kind of relationship because the mother communicates approval or disapproval of the child by her attitude to it. According to folk-lore, this approval is reciprocal, and a baby will wet in the arms of someone who can give him sufficient confidence as to permit him to relax.

BOWEL ACTIVITY AS BASIS OF PERSONAL EXPERIENCE

Thus, elimination serves a biological function for a child, and it can also be part of the loving contact between the baby and the one who is caring for him. Fantasies about the products themselves enter into the structure of the later mental life in terms of goodness or badness, and even shape delusional feelings which are present in some degree in the normal individual and in more intense form in the mentally disturbed. Many people continue to think of urine and faeces as poisonous even when they are in their body, and they seek to find medicines of physical procedures such as washouts to cleanse themselves. More fancifully still, they can think of these products as dangerous to other people, and slang in some circles includes the use of the names of products of elimination as epithets applied to other people who are the subject of verbal attack. Alongside these attitudes there is pride in the achievement of urination and defaecation, and boys in particular take pride in quantity and direction in the passing of urine! These are features of which every individual has some knowledge. Such ideas become exaggerated in mental illnesses when social controls are removed.

There are some who are not mentally disturbed but who derive character traits from the degree of importance given to the toilet care during this period of training. Cleanliness is next to godliness, and dirtiness is sin; and the close anatomical association of bladder and bowel with sexual organs connects the sin of dirtiness with sexual guilt (and incidentally, links sexuality with the toilet). Some people react to this so strongly that cleanliness and orderliness become their chief virtue. They are tidy in their appearance and in their work and often put these characteristics to good use. Sometimes individuals carry the tidiness and carefulness into every field of activity and become miserly, or the same process may take more abnormal forms when the individual is so fearful about the power to damage people by dirt or untidiness that he develops obsessional rituals to protect others from the consequences of his hidden powers of evil.

There are milder degrees of these processes which find justification in various cults concerning food and the control of movements of the bladder and the bowel. Many people regard regularity as a sign of health and go to great lengths to ensure it for themselves and their children, and, as mentioned above, the more that attention is paid to the activity, the more it can become an activity in which battles are fought between child and parent. Thus, bladder and bowel activity can succeed oral activity in providing individual gratification, and in addition, communication both of a loving and of an aggressive nature.

CONTROL AS STAGE OF DEVELOPMENT

Bladder and bowel control serves the further function of marking a stage of maturity, and temporary or permanent regression to more infantile states can be indicated by a return to the uncontrolled infantile habits. Enuresis (wetting) and encopresis (soiling) can have many explanations when they occur at different stages of an individual's life, and it is always necessary to take into account that such a symptom can have a meaning as part of the interaction between the individual and his family as well as a purely personal or clinical significance.

ENURESIS

This is one of a type of problem which deals with control in the individual, and in which the symptom resembles immaturity. The change from immaturity to maturity is one about which parents are seriously concerned and yet, at the same time, a child's lapses into greater degrees of immaturity are looked upon partly as humorous. Grown-ups refer to their own occasional loss of control in temporary illness, or following indiscretions, with good-humoured tolerance which sometimes conceals intense anxiety. Loss of control is a serious insult to one's image of oneself, and the ideas are important symbolically—we speak of a "leak" of official secrets.

Parents sometimes look upon enuresis in children as an indication of their own failure, or as inherent defectiveness in the child. Professional people tend to look upon it as a disease entity and look for a single causal factor. Enuresis, however, is a condition which is best looked upon as (to adapt a phrase of Sir Aubrey Lewis's) "a patch of *family* biography".

We should not give the name enuresis to bedwetting at too early a stage. There are many reasons for the failure to acquire control, or for the loss of control after it has been acquired :

(1) *Low intelligence.* This is the equivalent of continued immaturity. Mental handicap does not inevitably lead to continued enuresis, but the process of acquiring control should be expected to proceed more slowly than with a child whose intelligence is within the normal range.

(2) *Unsatisfactory social conditions.* For example, in overcrowded

homes where several children sleep together in one bed with inadequate bedding, if one or more of the children is enuretic, there is no incentive for any of the others to acquire control. In such homes there may be inadequacy of parental care, and a lack of consistent control of any kind. The cause of enuresis here is inadequate training and care.

(3) *Excessive training.* Undue attention to the activity of processes of evacuation causes increased sensitivity of the bladder to its contents. The bladder requires a lower threshold of capacity and has to be emptied more frequently than normally. If a child is afraid of punishment for wetting the bed, or if he is told in the day-time not to ask to go too frequently to the W.C., the effect of his anxiety may increase the need to go. People are familiar with this even as adults in social situations and within the normal range of familiar activities. An example of this is of the child who develops the habit of asking to go to the W.C. as soon as he arrives at a strange house on a visit with his mother. After several instances of this behaviour the mother gives strict instructions before setting out that he is not to ask to go immediately on arrival. The extra precaution is taken of a last visit to the W.C. just before leaving home, but before he has arrived at the bus stop he needs to go once again! This type of anxiety can set a pattern in a more serious way when the occasional inevitable lapse is taken as a serious fault.

(4) *Temporary regressions.* Children return to infantile behaviour patterns during emotional stress of any kind or during physical illness. This can occur at times of school examinations or disturbances affecting other members of the family. The birth of a younger child can cause a return to bedwetting in an older child either as a result of unconscious rivalry, or even as deliberate imitation of the baby who shows no signs of control yet receives lavish attention.

(5) *Fixation at infantile level.* Some children remain immature in a way that partly satisfies unconscious wishes of their own and of their parents. Often this is an interaction, particularly between mother and child, and occasionally both father and mother are closely linked together with the child in an over-protecting relationship. One example of this was of a 13-year-old girl who had been enuretic since the age of 3. At that time the parents had been advised to lift the child at night to pass urine, and up to the age of 13 this was still being carried out by

mother and father together each night. Napkins were fixed and refixed by father and mother together as part of the attention to this girl.

More frequently the close relationship is one between child and mother alone, and in some cases the bedwetting is a call for attention from the child to its mother. It has been said that some children cry with their eyes and some cry with their bladders.

(6) *Aggressiveness.* Although as described above the symptom can be partly satisfying to the parent and child, it could also be an outlet for anger against the mother, or an expression of conflict. It is the mother who has to wash the sheets, and, in some cases, this is discussed bitterly within the family and with the child, and sometimes the child is asked to wash the sheets and to make his own bed. Occasionally the child who wets the bed regularly at home is perfectly dry at the home of a favourite aunt (this, incidentally, proves the fruitlessness of a continued search for the cause of enuresis in the mechanics of micturition). Sometimes enuresis proves a necessary safety valve in a disturbed family relationship, and an illustrative case is that of a child of 9 brought to a clinic for continued nocturnal enuresis. She was a shy, pretty, only child of middle-class parents in a pleasant suburb of an industrial town. Enuresis was the only symptom. Her intelligence quotient was 85, and she was being coached by her mother for the Secondary Selection Examination which was to take place in eighteen months' time! She had to get up at seven each morning and do an hour's arithmetic with her mother before going to school. All this she did obediently but without apparent benefit. She and the mother attended the clinic three times, but visits were stopped because they interfered with attendance at school. Supposing some treatment had been available which could have "cured" the enuresis, the effect might have been disastrous. The bedwetting was the one way in which this girl could allow herself to rebel.

(7) *Orgastic.* The passing of urine has its own pleasure which is related to sexual sensation. Some children openly admit that they like the sensation of warm urine at the moment that it is being passed. Moreover, a boy approaching puberty may pass urine for the resemblance of the sensation to that caused by seminal emissions, and sometimes to conceal an emission which has occurred.

There is a wide range of types of treatment in current use. Some of the methods are based on theories which are in direct opposition to theories on which others are based. Many children have had a number of these very different methods of treatment and, therefore, before coming to any particular method, have already had a history of the trial and failure of other methods. Each method must have its successes, and one could ask what proportion of cases get better, and at what stage? One might also ask whether recovery at any particular stage is directly related to the remedy being applied.

Successful results coming from a variety of different kinds of treatment may have one thing in common, and that is the arrival by the individual concerned at a particular developmental stage when control becomes possible or acceptable. Treatment thus becomes related to maturation. It is not a process where something that went wrong has become remedied, but rather a process which helps development which has been delayed in that particular respect.*

* J. H. Kahn, Enuresis, Causes and Treatment, *Nursing Mirror*, 9 and 16 Oct. 1964.

R. F. Barbour *et al.*, Enuresis as a Disorder of Development, *Brit. Med. J.* 5360 (1963).

CHAPTER 6

Infantile Sexuality

DESCRIPTIONS of sexuality which are entered into for the purpose of marking out stages in the development of emotional life usually deal with the topic as a phase in infancy which follows oral and anal phases. The importance of sensation in different areas or zones of the body is linked with gratifications, frustrations, and with fantasies. Theories of infantile sexuality were built up within a framework which assumed the existence of instincts which link psychic experience with the physico-chemical economy of the body.*

SEX DIFFERENCES: PHYSICAL BASIS

The physical nature of the sex differences requires more attention than is usually given to it, and the sex of the infant has its importance, to both parents, long before the time when the infant has even the most shadowy consciousness of sexual identity. Notwithstanding jokes about "la différence", it is too often taken for granted that human beings can be referred to with a male pronoun while making occasional acknowledgements of the existence of the female. I cannot absolve myself from this fault, but at least in this section it can be pointed out that there are differences in the rate of development of physical and intellectual performance, in the time of reaching maturity, senescence and death; and these differences have a personal and social importance. The sex difference exists in the first single cell resulting from the union of the ovum with the spermatozoa. It continues to exist within the constitution of the chromosomes in every cell of the mature body. Each human cell has forty-six chromosomes, of which forty-four are in identical pairs,

* EDWARD GLOVER, *Psychoanalysis*, Staples Press, 1939.

57

the remaining two determining the sex of the individual. These special chromosomes are designated 'X' and 'Y'. Where the cell contains two 'X' chromosomes the individual is female. Where there is one 'X' chromosome and one 'Y' chromosome the individual is male. While still within the womb, the development of the foetus proceeds in directions determined by this chromosome constitution. The embryo with an 'XX' constitution gradually takes the characteristic shape which includes ovaries, a uterus, and the female external genitalia connected with the vagina. An embryo with chromosomes having an 'XY' constitution begins to develop testicles and a penis.*

The body tissue which carries both primary and secondary sexual characteristics shows very little development until the time that puberty is reached, but there is no period of life in which the sexual characteristics do not affect the totality of personality, including the process of growth.

RATES OF GROWTH

Measurements of the comparative maturity of development as between the sexes are based on examination of the bone structure, and it has been stated that "girls are on the average ahead of boys in skeletal maturity from birth to adulthood".† At birth, boys are about four weeks behind girls in skeletal age, and girls maintain their lead and reach adolescence and final mature size some two years before boys. The longer and later adolescence of boys gives them a final advantage in height and weight at the adult stage.

CULTURAL AND BIOLOGICAL FACTORS

Differences have been noted in the rate of intellectual development between boys and girls and in the responses to the teaching of different subjects at school. There is a tendency to attribute these differences to

---

* Some chromosome anomalies are associated with congenital diseases. For example, some cases of Mongolism are due to what is called "trisomy", i.e. one chromosome in a pair has at some stage been sub-divided, making three chromosomes instead of two in that position. Some other anomalies are linked with abnormalities of the sex chromosome structure where, for example, there is a genetic constitution of XXY, XXX, or XYY. In some of these cases there are abnormal shapes of sexual organs and doubtful sexual identity, but in some instances there appears to be a normal sexual identity, including fertility.

† G. A. HARRISON et al., Human Biology, Oxford University Press, 1964.

cultural factors, including that of the forward look, on the part of all concerned, to the feminine adult function in our society. It scarcely seems likely, however, that the vital biological distinction is, in itself, not without its effect on the potentiality of the male and female to respond in a different way to similar stimuli.

The sexual differences inevitably lead to differences in the experience of the infant within the family and the social setting. Parents frequently would choose for their first child a boy rather than a girl and, less frequently, a girl rather than a boy. They may vary their preference for subsequent children. Even when there is no apparent preference, and when the child of either sex receives full acceptance, there seems to be some kind of response from the child that carries approval according to its sex. Vigorous feeding is more readily approved in a boy than in a girl. Mathematical failure at school carries less disapproval in girls than in boys; and, in boys, maladaptations to family standards is more likely to find expression in undesirable behaviour than it is in girls.

These brief references to the basic differences between the sexes tend to emphasise that sexuality is something which enters into every aspect of life, and that it is something which has consequences for the interactions within the family from the very moment of birth. Having said this, we can now take up again the sequence in the stages of psychosexual development within the framework of psycho-analytical theory, which assumes that adult behaviour has its roots in infancy.

SENSUAL PLEASURES: INTENSITY OF SENSUAL EXPERIENCES AT DIFFERENT STAGES

It takes a considerable time before a child has a complete sense of his identity and of the limits of his body. Each movement that the baby is able to make is repeated until it is mastered and then, as if to increase the satisfaction, it is made more complicated. Each sensation is recaptured in the attempts to repeat the experience or to enjoy it in fantasy; and the child learns how to explore his own body. He has learned that pleasure comes to his lips from contact with other individuals, with the mother's nipple or the mother's face, and from the kiss that he is encouraged to give to members of his family. He is able to enjoy the contact of food and to revive the pleasure by sucking his thumb or the dummy teat. He has also learned that denial of the desired pleasure is possible, and that some of the pleasurable sensations seem to be disturbing because they are so overwhelmingly intense. He has discovered that there is both gratification and anxiety in the contacts between himself and his mother or nurse at the moment that he becomes aware of the sensation of the passing of urine and faeces. He may experience some satisfaction in the feel of a wet or soiled napkin against his skin, or he may learn to think of it as bad and dangerous. The sensations become partly a personal property and partly a communication between himself and others.

GENITAL SENSITIVITY

The next stage in the exploration of his personal and inter-personal experiences is the discovery that the genital organs are especially sensitive. Boys and girls alike learn that there can be a kind of pleasure from the touching of the genital organs. Pleasure can be produced or enhanced by movements of the body which cause rubbing of these parts. This pleasure reaches a height during the second year of life and the accidental discovery leads to a deliberately produced pattern of pleasure and excitement. The nature of the sensation has the quality of overwhelming intensity to a greater extent than in any other previous experience. The accompanying anxiety can be increased when the activity is noticed and disapproved by the parents.

COMMUNICATION OF GUILT

Mother and father alike are disconcerted by the sexual nature of a young baby's play with himself or herself. It seems so inappropriate and so out of keeping with the ideas of childhood innocence. The residues of guilt which the adult has with regard to sexual enjoyment seem to be justified when the parent is confronted with this activity in a young infant. Disapproval is conveyed to the baby boy or girl in looks, words, or physical punishment. The primitive guilt which the baby has already begun to experience in his or her abandonment to the depths of sexuality becomes reinforced by the parents' attitude.

Perhaps the sexual stimulation has already followed the pattern of oral and anal sensations in appearing both as a personal gratification and also as a process of communicating with others. The satisfaction can become associated, therefore, with fantasies in which other individuals are involved. Stimulation can be produced by the child alone; but stimulation also occurs during toilet care and cleansing when the same parts are handled by the mother or the individual who does the nursing. The individual who condemns the pleasure is also the individual who takes a share in stimulating it. Gratification and frustration become associated with the love and hostility with which child and adult communicate with one another.

The sexuality differs from the oral and anal (and urethral) activities in having no immediate biological function at this stage. Fantasy reigns supreme, and the adult to whom sexuality has a more physical fulfilment, finds the infantile sexuality to be incomprehensible. The adult, however, father or mother, is aware of the sexual role of the baby girl or boy and the response of baby to parent is affected by the parental attitudes which are based on this knowledge. The girl or boy learns to recognise that girls and boys are treated differently, and each learns to recognise the personal sexual role.

The sexual sensation in the genital organs has so far followed the previous pattern of sexuality. Oral, anal and genital phases follow one another in sequence at separate periods, but sensations in these three areas can be experienced simultaneously. Freud described the infant as "polymorphous perverse", implying that in a way that is similar to the perversions of abnormal adults, the normal infant can derive sensual satisfaction from many different parts of the body.

MASTURBATORY ACTIVITIES

The deliberate seeking of sexual sensations becomes a form of masturbation, and this can occur in baby boys and baby girls. Each can continue to stimulate the genitals with the hand until a stage is reached where there is a flushing of the face and a holding of the breath similar to that in adult orgasm. Sometimes the rubbing is continued without a climax ever being reached. Occasionally the child learns that the use of the hand is disapproved but is able to get a similar sensation by rocking the body, and this can occur even to the extent of shaking the cot. A more remote displacement of the activity is head banging. A child may bang his head for long periods and continue even when this produces pain. Perhaps pain serves the purpose of satisfying guilt feelings by giving an inbuilt punishment for the activity which is also a pleasure.

Some degree of masturbatory activity is universal in the second year of life, and it persists into later stages of childhood. Parents are naturally worried by these activities. Some parents succeed in denying that it ever occurs, some try to distract the child by giving the child some other activity, but most babies or infants lose the habit spontaneously when the world becomes a more interesting place and when they no longer need to find their solace from their own body.

Children who are severely punished, or children who are left too much alone, are more likely to continue with the habit. *Very* severe punishment or withdrawal of love may, equally, have the effect of inhibiting sexual activity to such a degree that subsequent sexual maturity is never achieved. It is understandable that parents should be concerned about the persistence of masturbation as they themselves have recollections of adolescent sexual fantasies which seemed to serve no immediate biological purpose, but perhaps the sensations and the fantasies do serve a purpose as a blueprint for the more mature sexual activities that are part of normal adult life.

CHAPTER 7

The Oedipal Situation

STAGES in the emotional development of an individual, as revealed in psycho-analytical studies, are given names which depend upon the area of the body which at any one time is predominantly sensitive during the child's expanding experience of himself and of the outside world. The early stages are labelled *oral, anal* and *genital.* Satisfaction and frustration are localised successively in the mouth, excretory organs and the genitalia.

The historical progress is referred to as "Psycho-sexual development". The word "sexual" is used in a general sense, and this use is justified by the continuing nature of the sensuality in the separate stages. The sensations may appear overwhelming at times, and at all stages there can be tension followed by gratification, with disturbing as well as pleasing overtones.

The three stages are usually described separately, but they are not clearly divided from one another, and early kinds of satisfaction survive as a central framework for each successive stage.

When the infant first becomes aware of the complex sensations around the genital organs, these become associated with the primitive recognition of his or her sexual status. The child begins to interact, in fantasy, in a different way with each parent. In general, the child develops a specific and intense attachment to the parent of the opposite sex. The parent of the same sex becomes a rival.

This stage has been described as the *Oedipal Situation.* Originally it was referred to as the *Oedipus Complex*, but the word *situation* appears preferable when the process takes the normal course, complicated though that may be. Freud used this label in order to refer to the Greek legend which was the subject of the play *Oedipus Rex* by

Sophocles. In this drama, it was prophesied at the time of the birth of Oedipus that he would kill his father and marry his mother. He was, consequently, to have been put to death, but, being abandoned instead, he was brought up in the belief that his foster parents were his real parents. The means adopted to avert the prophesied fate led to its fulfilment. When Oedipus came to adult life he met, quarrelled with and killed his father, and married his mother, in ignorance of their true identities.

MYTHS AS PATTERNS OF REGULARLY OCCURRING HUMAN SITUATIONS

The use of the label "Oedipus complex" is a familiar part of psychological language and, for that matter, of present-day humour. The first mention of it appeared in a letter written by Freud to Wilhelm Fliess in 1897. Freud was a somewhat reluctant discoverer of the contents in the hidden depths of the human mind. Fliess was a Berlin physician and biologist with wide interests and it was to Fliess that Freud turned as someone to whom he could unburden himself in letters which gave day-to-day record of his work and his thoughts about it. It became a painful experience to Freud that each new patient made him the recipient of childhood memories of scenes of seduction by grown-up persons—most frequently by the parent of the opposite sex. At first he had taken the memories as clear evidence of historical fact, but later he learned of instances where there was independent evidence that the incidents could not have taken place. He was so shaken by this discovery that his immediate thought was that he must now abandon his methods and his theories, but afterwards it occurred to him that there must be some reason for the fact that human mental processes could consistently produce these fantasies in almost identical patterns. He had begun to conduct his own analysis, making private records of his own apparently undirected thoughts, communicating the basic ideas to the distant and idealised personality of Fliess. He wrote :

> So far I have found nothing completely new, but all the complications to which by now I am used. It is no easy matter. Being entirely honest with oneself is a good exercise. Only one idea of general value has occurred to me.

I have found love of the mother and jealousy of the father in my own case too, and now believe it to be a general phenomenon of early childhood, even if it does not always occur so early as in children who have been made hysterics. (Similarly with the "romanticism of origins" in the case of paranoiacs—heroes, founders of religion.) If that is the case, the gripping power of Oedipus Rex, in spite of all the rational objections to the inexorable fate that the story presupposes, becomes intelligible, and one can understand why later fate dramas were such failures. Our feelings rise against any arbitrary individual fate such as shown in the Ahnfrau,* etc., but the Greek myth seizes on a compulsion which everyone recognizes because he has felt traces of it in himself. Every member of the audience was once a budding Oedipus in phantasy, and this dream-fulfilment played out in reality causes everyone to recoil in horror, with the full measure of repression which separates his infantile from his present state. . . . †

Freud had turned to the Greek myths for his literary prototype of the complex and turbulent tangle of family relationships. The original story of Oedipus is not of the delicate family romance in which a 4-year-old boy says to Mummy, "When I am big I am going to marry you"—not even when the boy adds that at that time Daddy will be a little boy or that Daddy will go away. The Oedipus story is of incest, murder and rape, and it is not lacking in details of basic human situations which are relevant to problems of personal identity, of parentage and the special case of adoption.

PRESENT-DAY IMPLICATIONS

There are some hidden or unexplored depths of the story. One of these is the tacit assumption that, because of the prophecy, the parents of Oedipus had the right to put Oedipus to death in order to avert the prophecy. This part of the story usually passes almost unnoticed. Even today, in many parts of the world a child may be murdered for being the wrong sex or being one child too many. In this century and in this country babies were murdered in the big cities for the sake of a few pounds of an insurance policy taken out with this in mind. The laws regarding life insurance had to be altered.

---

* *Die Ahnfrau*, the title of a play by Franz Grillparzer.
† Origins, pp. 223–4.

THE OEDIPUS LEGEND IN FULL

At the time when Freud was formulating his theories, scholars of all countries were united by knowledge of classical literature. Today this knowledge can no longer be assumed and it may be possible to understand some of its implications better if a fairly full account of the story is given. The following is quoted from *A Classical Dictionary* by J. Lempriere, D.D., published in 1864.

ŒDIPUS, a son of Laius, king of Thebes, and Jocasta. Being descended from Venus by his father's side, Œdipus was born to be exposed to all the calamities and persecutions which Juno could inflict upon the posterity of the goddess of beauty. Laius, the father of Œdipus, was informed by the oracle, as soon as he married Jocasta that he must perish by the hands of his son. Such dreadful intelligence awakened his fears, and to prevent the fulfilment of the oracle, he resolved never to approach Jocasta; but his solemn resolutions were violated in a fit of intoxication. The queen became pregnant, and Laius, still desirous of averting the evil, ordered his wife to destroy the child as soon as it came into the world. The mother had not the courage to obey, yet she gave the child as soon as born to one of her domestics, with orders to expose him on the mountains. The servant was moved with pity, but to obey the command of Jocasta, he bored the feet of the child, and suspended him with a twig by the heels to a tree on mount Cithæron, where he was soon found by one of the shepherds of Polybus, king of Corinth. The shepherd carried him home, and Peribœa, the wife of Polybus, who had no children, educated him as her own child, with maternal tenderness.

The accomplishments of the infant, who was named Œdipus on account of the swelling of his feet (*oidéw tumeo nous pes*), soon became the admiration of the age. His companions envied his strength and his address, and one of them to mortify his rising ambition, told him that he was an illegitimate child. This raised his doubts; he asked Peribœa who, out of tenderness, told him that his suspicions were ill founded. Not satisfied with this, he went to consult the oracle of Delphi, and was there told not to return home, for if he did, he must necessarily be the murderer of his father, and the husband of his mother. This answer of the oracle terrified him; he knew no home but the house of Polybus, therefore he resolved not to return to Corinth where such calamities apparently attended him. He travelled towards Phocis, and in his journey, met in a narrow road Laius, with his arm-bearer, in a chariot. Laius haughtily ordered Œdipus to make way for him. Œdipus refused, and a contest ensued, in which Laius and his arm-bearer were both killed. As Œdipus was ignorant of the quality and of the rank of the men whom he had just killed, he continued his journey, and was attracted to Thebes by the fame of the Sphynx. This terrible monster which Juno had sent to lay waste the country (vid. Sphynx), resorted to the neighbourhood of Thebes, and devoured all those who attempted to explain without success the ænigmas which he proposed. The calamity was now become an object of public concern, and as the successful explanation of the ænigma would end in the death of the Sphynx, Creon, who, at the death of Laius, had ascended the throne of Thebes, promised his crown and Jocasta to him who succeeded in the attempt. The ænigma proposed was this : What animal in the morning walks upon four feet, at noon upon two, and in the evening upon three? This was left for Œdipus to explain; he came to the monster and said, that man, in the morning of life, walks upon his hands and his feet; when he has attained the years of manhood, he walks upon his two legs; and in the evening, he supports his old age with the assistance of a staff. The monster, mortified at the true explanation, dashed his head against a rock, and perished.

Œdipus ascended the throne of Thebes, and married Jocasta, by whom he had two sons, Polynices and Eteocles, and two daughters, Ismene and Antigone.

Some years after, the Theban territories were visited with a plague; and the oracle declared that it should not cease till the murderer of king Laius was banished from Bœotia. As the death of Laius had never been examined into, and the circumstances that attended it were never known, this answer of the oracle was of the greatest concern to the Thebans; but Œdipus, the friend of the people, resolved to overcome every difficulty by the most exact inquiries. His researches were successful, and he was soon proved to be the murderer of his father. The melancholy discovery was rendered the more alarming, when Œdipus considered, that he had not only murdered his father, but that he had committed incest with his mother. In the excess of his grief he put out his eyes, as unworthy to see the light, and banished himself from Thebes, or as some say, was banished by his own sons.

The Oedipus story contains elemental themes which are repeated amongst the great by the prudent slaughter of the young who might grow up to be rivals, and by the usurping of power by the young who could not afford to wait to inherit it. The rivalries across the generations are matched by those between siblings. Stories of brotherly love are told side by side with the story of Cain and Abel. Freud might have used Bible stories had he known them as well as he knew the Greek myths.

ABRAHAM, ISAAC, ISHMAEL AND SARAH

The Bible story of the readiness of Abraham to sacrifice his son, Isaac, has some of the same elements as the Oedipus legend, including Divine intervention into human affairs.

In the authorised version (Genesis 22, 1 and 2) the story begins, "And it came to pass after these things that God did *tempt* Abraham, and said unto him, Abraham : and he said, Behold here I am. And he said, Take now thy son, thine only son Isaac, whom thou lovest, and get thee into the land of Moriah; and offer him there for a burnt offering upon one of the mountains which I will tell thee of."

The story continues with the account of the preparation for a sacrifice. When the altar was complete, Abraham "bound Isaac, his son, and laid him upon the altar, upon the wood". When he stretched out his hand and took the knife to slay his son, an angel of the Lord called on him to stop, saying "Now I know that thou fearest God, seeing thou hast not withheld thy son, thine only son, from Me".

This story is usually quoted as an example of Abraham's willingness to sacrifice to God what was dearest to him. It could equally well be told as the turning away from human sacrifice. There is, however, yet another meaning to be found. The first words of the chapter were, "And it came to pass *after these things*".* One should, therefore, turn to the preceding chapter which deals with the birth of Isaac in Sarah and Abraham's old age, and the casting out of Ishmael and his mother. Sarah had believed herself to be barren and had offered her handmaiden, Hagar, to Abraham so that he could have offspring. As so often happens following adoption of a child by an infertile couple, they subsequently had a child of their own. At the time that Isaac was weaned and when Abraham made a great feast, Sarah "saw the son of Hagar, the Egyptian, which she had born unto Abraham, mocking". She asked Abraham to cast out the bondwoman and her son so that, "for the son of this bondwoman shall not be heir with my son", "and the thing was very grievous in Abraham's sight because of his son". During the night, Abraham received reassurance from God that from the seed of Ishmael He would also make a nation, "because he is thy seed". Yet Hagar and Ishmael were cast out into the desert and only survived by miraculous intervention.

In the description of the preparations for the sacrifice of Isaac, it is said that "and Abraham rose up early in the morning . . .", presumably before Sarah was awake.

Could the hidden meaning of the story be that Abraham was, in effect, saying to Sarah, "You made me get rid of *my* son. Now I shall get rid of yours"?

* Our italics.

MATURATION AS AN HISTORICAL AND AS A
PERSONAL PROCESS

Myths and legends provide metaphors which help the understanding of nuclear situations that are repeated throughout history. We like to believe that the modern civilised man has acquired control over passions that found freer expression in the early history of the human race and in the infancy of present-day human beings. Thus the behaviour of parents of "battered babies" can be better understood in terms of extreme immaturity, in which the demands of the new-born infant are in competition with those of the adult, but at the level such as that of the rivalry of a slightly older infant sibling. At a more mature level, the competition between the adolescent and the adult generation could be said to represent the search by youth for answers to riddles of the universe in dimensions which still seem to be forbidden by and to the older generation.

EMPHASIS BY OMISSION

All these myths, legends and metaphors add meaning to observations of human behaviour because they select a salient element for particular emphasis. For that reason these special descriptions always leave something out. At first what is left out is that which is so obvious that it is taken for granted, but new knowledge sometimes takes us into dimensions which exclude the original level of understanding. The stories selected for psychiatric enlightenment leave out consideration of the tender love of parents for each other, and for their children, and of brotherly love as a reality.

We can turn once more to the Bible (Jeremiah 31. 19)* for an illustration of parental love :

> Is Ephraim a darling son unto Me?
> Is he a child that is dandled?
> For as often as I speak of him,
> I do earnestly remember him still;
> Therefore My heart yearneth for him,
> I will surely have compassion upon him,
>   saith the Lord.

* Soncino Press 1949, English Text by the Jewish Publication Society of America.

The Biblical quotations and interpretations given above provide an attempt by the author to place the descriptions of the Oedipal situation in a wider context of human thought and levels of maturity. It is intended to emphasise that explanations can exist in different dimensions, using different assumptions, and arriving at different conclusions. The usefulness of any particular metaphor is to provide a theory which is internally consistent and coherent. Sir Denis Hill* pointed out that Freud attempted to treat neurotic symptoms by discovering that the neurotic symptom had meaning. He quotes Medawar,† who stated that scientists are constantly building explanatory structures, telling stories, which are scrupulously tested to see if they are stories about real life.

We can therefore return to the Oedipus story as the drama selected for the psycho-analytical explanation of some aspects of living.

ACTING THE DRAMA IN FANTASY

The kernel of the drama is enacted in fantasy in the lives of young children when they become aware of the sexual differences between the parents. For either boy or girl, the mother is the first object of love, but subsequently the situation develops in different ways according to whether the child is a boy or girl.

A boy is fed, fondled, gratified and denied by the mother. The sensations of his own body become related to her activities as well as to his own. He prolongs the sensations by reproducing her actions in his imagination, and elaborating them. He begins to desire exclusive possession of her, and these desires seem to become fulfilled whenever his father is absent. His father's presence becomes a threat to his claim for sole rights. He resents the contacts that he notices or imagines between father and mother. He may try to come between them by pushing the father away, or even, in desperation, seeking the company of his father if that will separate father from mother.

With a girl, this interaction takes a different course. She too is at first dependent upon, and closely attached to, her mother. As she develops, she becomes aware of her own feminine role, and so do her

---

* SIR DENIS HILL, On the Contribution of Psychoanalysis to Psychiatry: mechanism and meaning, *Brit. J. Psych.* (1970).

† P. B. MEDAWAR, *The Art of the Soluble*, 1967.

parents. She turns from her mother and claims her father as her special property and future husband.

The fantasies find words in which they can be expressed towards the end of the second year and during the third year of the child's life.

REPRESSION OF SEXUAL COMPONENT

The mental experiences become associated with tension in the sexual organs which by now have become sensitive. By this time, the child will have noticed disapproval, and sometimes will have experienced punishment, whenever any interest or excitement is shown in connection with the sexual organs. Feelings of guilt are aroused, and these become associated with the desire for possession of the mother or father respectively.

The sexual nature of the feeling becomes repressed. The boy who wished to destroy his father gradually invents games of make-believe in which he pretends to *be* his father. Later still, he is content to model himself for future development on the reality of his father. Similarly, a girl begins to imitate her mother when she no longer wishes to usurp her.

The process is more complicated still when there is more than one child. Two children of the same sex cannot have exclusive possession of one parent. Even in infancy, the second one has to take the parent who is still unclaimed—whatever the sex. When there are many children, there are a variety of possibilities, and an older child might become a subsidiary mother or father, and enter into interactions with the younger children in a way that is reminiscent of the rejecting and accepting attitudes of a parent with a child.

PARENTS AS PARTICIPANTS: ABNORMALITY

The process becomes truly abnormal when parents enter actively into the situation as a result of their own abnormal needs. Parents may be rivals of each other, and they may encourage the love and jealousy which the child may show respectively towards them. There is a play-off of love and hate, and there may be envy of any preference shown to one parent or the other.

Normally the child is partly aware of the fantastic nature of his feelings. If these feelings are fostered and nurtured by the attitudes of the parents, the child may begin to think of them as both real and frightening. A boy inflates himself in fantasy to adult size, makes a brave show, and finds himself inadequate. There is terror under his grotesque assumptions. Worse still, the parents may enlarge their own image of the child, and deal with him as if he were offering a serious threat. Parents sometimes present a ready-made fantasy to a child, and, when he accepts it in a literal way, they are as dismayed as the child is.

Sometimes when a father dies, a well-intentioned adult will say to a boy of, say, four years "You will have to look after mother now." The boy expects himself to have an adult masculine strength, and fails according to his own standards. When a living father is considered to be unsatisfactory, a mother may turn to her infant son for male comfort. The child may then model himself on the very qualities of his father that his mother rejects. The mother then says "He is out of control." He defies her and shouts back at her, and she is afraid that he will overwhelm her. The child, meanwhile, has also drawn upon himself the criticisms of neighbours and perhaps his teacher, but within himself he is terrified because he well knows that he is playing a part which is beyond his real capacity.

Parents sometimes fear the sexuality that is revealed in the words and the behaviour of their young children. Some good parents fear the assertiveness that is culturally associated with masculinity. A boy is described as ". . . lovely when he was a baby. He was so cuddly." At the age of 3 or 4 years, his normal curiosity and vigour is thought of as an abnormal and undesirable aggression. His masculinity is deliberately attacked, and he may even develop feminine qualities in order to propitiate one of his parents.

In similar fashion, a girl may respond to her parents' unspoken wish for a boy, and adopt a sexual role on masculine models.

Normally, however, the early emotional interaction which is based on the unequal relationship of child and adult is given up. The repression of this kind of sexual imagery begins to shape a system of internal controls which is called the *Superego*. Freud stated "The Superego is the heir to the Oedipus Complex."

LATENCY PERIOD

The historical description of stages of psychosexual development, in classical psycho-analytical terms, includes a *latency period*. This begins at around the age of 5 years, following the resolution of the oedipal situation and (in Freudian concepts) the formation of the superego. It ends with the onset of puberty, which brings biological reproductive capacity and the re-activation of sexuality. Puberty is the stage where either further repression or conscious control of sexuality becomes necessary, but it is implied that during the latency period sexual fantasies are in abeyance.

The latency period is thus, approximately, the stage between the age of 5 years and a point between 11 and 15 years when sexual maturity becomes apparent. It corresponds to the early school life when the child's mental activities are becoming roused by experiences and perceptions of the world of ideas and of material objects. It is implied that the child's mental life is predominantly conscious and intellectual.

One wonders whether the postulation of a latency period was the last concession that the early analysts felt compelled to make to the myth of childhood innocence! It is true that so much of the child's waking life is spent within the school that there is less opportunity than before for the emotional turmoil of family relationships. The inner fantasies, whenever they are revealed, are nevertheless shown to be rich in elaboration of ideas about birth and death, and about the complicated physical interaction between the individuals of different sex.

If we insist upon assuming the existence of a latency period, it should perhaps be postponed to that stage of life which was referred to in an epitaph on the tombstone of a woman who had died at the age of 80 years. "During the last ten years of her life," it stated, "she was the model of virtue."

PSYCHO-ANALYTICAL FORMULATIONS

The historical or developmental framework, as outlined above, is one aspect only of psycho-analytical formulations regarding mental life.*

* A fuller account is given in KAHN and NURSTEN, *Unwillingly to School*, 1964, Pergamon Press, in the chapter headed "The Psychopathological Basis of Treatment".

The mind is also described in *structural* terms, as if it were in separate parts, under the names of *Ego, Id* and *Superego*. "Ego", which means "I", refers to the conscious self in action. "Id", which means "It", is the impersonal unconscious reservoir of mental activity which is with us from birth or before; and "Superego" is the creation of our need to make an adaptation of compromise between our internal desires and external demands.

Dynamic explanations refer to the active forces in mental life, deriving from the instincts which serve for self-preservation of the individual, reproduction of the species, and the complexities of communal life. Conflicting forces, which are related to incompatible desires, are the origin of *ambivalence*. Anxiety is the result of the irreconcilability of opposing attitudes, and *defences* include *repression* of one of the aspects, *projection* of some idea or feeling on to some other person instead of oneself, or *displacement* from one person or object on to another. There may be temporary or long-standing *regressions*, during emotional disturbances, to earlier patterns of feeling or behaviour, or *fixations* at some immature stage.

Another explanatory model of mental organisation is in *economic* terms. An imaginary substance called *libido* is postulated as representing the springs of the capacity to live and love. This corresponds to the "Life force" or *"Elan vital"* described by some philosophers. There is an assumption that the libido can become attached (or cathected) to the idea of certain objects of persons. When the distribution is unsatisfactory, there will be a tendency for the libido to become redistributed in ways that will reduce tension. This is the pleasure/pain principle, and symptoms of emotional disorder are formed when the distribution continues to be faulty.

Melanie Klein built up another explanatory system on the foundation of ideas originally expressed by Freud. This is the *object-relations theory*, which has been still further elaborated by Fairbairn. Personality is looked upon as if it were built up by the incorporation of what are called good and bad objects. The objects are mental representations of persons or parts of persons. Melanie Klein placed some of the developmental phases at earlier stages in the child's life than did Freud. According to her, the formation of the superego begins within the child's experiences at the breast. To the infant, the nipple (or breast) is the only part of the mother which he can experience in his early contacts. The part represents the whole, and the goodness of the contacts of the breast becomes incorporated into a child's mind as a feeling of goodness within himself. The goodness of the breast becomes his own property. This process is described as *introjection*, and is a figurative swallowing of mental representations. The vigour of the child's feeding may, at the same time, give him the feeling that he is attacking the breast. In the uncertainty of the limits of the body, this can be felt as badness of the breast, and this is the beginning of the process of *projection*. The badness, too, becomes his own by a further process of introjection, and it also appears that the badness outside him is attacking him in retaliation. An introjected object can be projected on to something in the outside world, and becomes a fresh object of introjection and so on to infinity.

Even in adult life, we can project either goodness or badness on to some previously unknown person, and receive back from him exactly what we have projected. In infancy, such fantasies are given reality when the threatening character of the projection coincides with harsh attitudes of a parent, or they can become corrected by more tolerant parental attitudes. Thus the real goodness and badness of the parent gives some substance to the primitive fantasies of the developing infant mind.

Some of the fantasies are more completely the creation of the child alone. There is an overwhelming and disturbing character about the desire for gratification, and sometimes a feeling of guilt accompanies its fulfilment. Many of the restrictions, controls and self-denials which govern people's lives are self-imposed rather than the result of external limitations and punishments.

The superego of some individuals can become more intolerant (and irrational) than the degree of strictness of the parent would appear to justify. There are some people, indeed, who punish themselves for every success, or who manage to achieve failure at the moment that success comes within reach.

The basis of envy, greed and gratitude as enduring character traits is laid down, according to Melanie Klein, in the satisfactions and frustrations at the breast.

The discoveries of mental processes, described in analogies for which this new technical language had to be created, have enlarged our understanding of a wide range of human activities. There are by-products of psycho-analytical studies which began with Freud with the purely utilitarian purpose of treating illness of the mind. The same disciplined process of search for meaning has been applied to the examination of poetry, drama, and other art forms, and also to economic transactions, politics, and to people's attitudes to their religious ideas.

Psycho-analytical terms have been referred to and briefly explained, but as a general rule these terms will be avoided. This is because many of the words have acquired widespread currency, and are used in an undisciplined way. When words are used in an undisciplined way it is for the purpose of *avoiding* understanding of the ideas to which the words are meant to refer.

CHAPTER 8

Rejection

THE use of a particular word to describe a process in human behaviour occurs whenever a new way of looking at a process has come into being. The word "Rejection", applied to an aspect of the relationship between mother and child, had shock value when first used. After the word came into common use it became so much a stock phrase that it has been used more to avoid thinking about the subject than to face the problems involved. Jargon is sometimes used in a way that is like putting labels on unopened parcels in order to have an excuse for not looking inside to see what is really there.

There can be good reason for not using the word rejection at all and to think rather in terms of breakdown of the parental process or of the parent/child relationship. The word, however, has some value if we first acknowledge that there is an element of rejection in all human relationships.

In order to make the problem more real, and to give it flesh and blood, here are extracts from two newspapers :

> The 25-year-old mother of three children, Mrs. . . ., wants to find a home for a fourth baby she is expecting in July.
> She would not part with her 7-year-old son . . . or her 3-year-old daughter . . ., but she said last night: "I don't like babies. I think they are terrible things. They all scream their heads off."
> Mrs. . . . and her husband insist that they could not afford another child. Their third child, a 21-month-old girl, is in the care of the . . . Council.
> Mrs. . . . said she had asked the Almoner at . . . Hospital if she could have this baby adopted. The Almoner replied that she was shocked but she would see what she could do.
> "Later the hospital said they were not prepared to help me. We wrote to an evening paper to see if we could get help through its columns. We would like the child to go to a good home where there are no other children—to someone who deserves a child."

As Mrs. . . . spoke her two children remained in the room watching television. Amid all the questions and answers, they kept their eyes on the television set. But they know about the child to be born and have been told that it will have to be "given away" or they will not be able to have a holiday this year.

"Babies are a full-time job. Two are quite enough, and this house is not made for a big family. Big families cause squabbling and the father goes off for a drink to get some peace," said Mrs. . . . "We are a very happy family and I do not want to have anything to spoil it."

2nd Article.

MRS. . . . WANTS HER BABY BACK
Decision to give child away regretted

Mrs. . . ., aged 26, the housewife who with her husband decided to give away their baby before the child was born, has refused to sign the adoption papers for the girl who is now with her prospective foster parents.

Mrs. . . . said yesterday "I never thought it would happen to me. But I keep on thinking about the baby and wishing I hadn't given it away. I can't sleep at night and I lie awake worrying whether she is all right. I suppose it is the mother instinct. After all, she is my own flesh and blood."

Such cases are fairly uncommon although similar stories are reported from time to time. Great indignation is aroused, and newspapers consider them worthy of report.

REVEALING THE BASIC ATTITUDES IN PROFESSIONAL WORKERS

This particular case is quoted because one of the newspaper accounts happened to appear on the morning of a lecture that I was giving as part of a course for social workers. I read it out to the group at the beginning of the lecture. The students had themselves read different versions in their separate newspapers and there were comments such as "She was a monster", "She was not fit to have a baby", and a discussion of this item continued to occupy the second part of the session following the lecture. The discussion became heated, and some of the participants, who had already had long experience of social work in various capacities, were unwilling to discuss the motivation of the person concerned in anything other than critical terms. Amongst explanations given was that it was a planned attempt to get money from newspapers who would be willing to pay for the story of her life. It was only the discussion of the reasons involved when a newspaper finds the topic worthy of space, and perhaps of payment, that enabled us to refer to our own feelings about such events.

HIDDEN ACCEPTANCE IN A REJECTING MOTHER

Is it possible to recognise that the rejecting mother, who shocks us by her attitude, is also partly a mother who has accepting feelings which are mainly hidden from herself, and that, conversely, the ordinary accepting mother has hidden rejection feelings? In practice there appear to be qualitative differences in behaviour, but the feelings behind the actions are part of something that is universal.

UNIVERSALITY OF REJECTION

Every mother who has a baby, has a baby instead of something else. There is always some sacrifice involved. There are physical burdens of pregnancy and childbirth; the responsibility that both parents have for the care of the young child; the sacrifice of leisure and recreational interests; the financial cost which could have gone to some material possession; the possibility that having the baby might mean that the mother has to give up the satisfactions of a career with its day-to-day enjoyments and its long-term ambitions. Yet all these may be gladly given up for the fulfilment that comes from parenthood.

It is easier to describe what a parent gives up in a material sense or in other personal satisfactions when having a child, than to describe the nature of the satisfaction which occurs in the interaction between the parents and the child whose changing responses give a new experience to the parent at each stage. Parents are more likely to tell their friends about the anxieties and burdens, the loss of sleep, feeding troubles, the sitting-in night after night, the worry about illness—these become topics of conversation. It is culturally acceptable to emphasise these points and also to delay marriage and to delay the having of children until certain material standards have been obtained. For many people there is a conventional list of possessions which may include a certain amount of capital, a house, particular articles of furniture and household equipment, and perhaps a car. When these have been acquired (and then only) do many couples permit themselves to turn to the thought of having a family. With some the postponement is for the purpose of enjoying a particular kind of social life. With others it is so that both husband and wife may continue a career for which they have prepared themselves and which gives other rewards as well as financial ones. The deferment of having a family may help to maintain mobility which permits professional advancement.

There are degrees of importance which different people attach to these gains against those of having children. In all these cases, however, the more intangible urge to seek the satisfaction of the new experience of the child, which is born out of their union with one another, is present even when it is unacknowledged. Thus we return to the thesis that rejection is a question of degree, and the important problem is to recognise those degrees which are so severe that we are entitled to call them pathological.

COMPETING NEEDS

It is necessary to call attention to the reality of external factors which increase the stress on some young parents of today as compared with those of a previous generation. At one time, the extended family of all social classes gave practical support, and those who could afford it had paid domestic help. The modern parents may be isolated, and domestic help is either unobtainable or too expensive for all but the wealthiest, and yet, more than ever before, husband and wife may have responsibilities which take them from their homes. There is a need for facilities for feeding and napkin-changing in public transport and waiting rooms. The offer of such services would obviate the necessity for criticisms of parents which are frequently made without sufficient understanding of the circumstances in which they have to live.

PATHOLOGICAL SITUATIONS

Situations which carry an unusually high probability of abnormal rejection can be classified as follows :

1. Factors Relating to the Marital Situation or Status

    (a) A pregnancy that is illegitimate. In such a case there may be an almost complete rejection, or, paradoxically, a most intensive degree of attachment with a mother who does not have to share a child with another parent.

(b) A pregnancy that is the cause of marriage. This is more likely to be a factor where the marriage would not have taken place at all but for the pregnancy. There may be much less disturbance where pregnancy merely brings forward the date of a marriage previously intended, but even here the recriminations between the parents and their respective families may add to the burdens during the pregnancy and early months of the child's life.

(c) A pregnancy, whether planned or unplanned, that causes the postponement or the end of a mother's career, leaves the child with the burden of responsibility for the unfulfilled ambitions.

(d) The existence of marital disharmony, where the pregnancy provides a tie to the marriage, either deliberately sought for this purpose, or occurring unplanned. Having the child for any other purpose than its own sake is a poor basis for parenthood, and, although it is sometimes "prescribed" as a way of healing a marriage, it is more likely to add to the total disturbance than to cure it.

(e) Mixed marriages. Differences of colour, race, religion, nationality, social class or intelligence level can occur, and such marriages may be well founded if they are entered into by the partners with some basis of identity with one another. There are, however, some such marriages which are entered into more *because of the differences* than because of anything that the partners have in common. It is as if the differences are sought as part of rejection processes which already exist, but which in the first place apply to the family of origin. A son or daughter who rejects some aspect of the personality of the parents or the family background may seek company with an individual who stands out in contrast to them. In such a case, the marriage may not be wholehearted on either side. The rejection process eventually involves the partners themselves. The having of a child brings to light the fear that the child may have an undesirable quality representing the marriage partner.

It may be worthwhile here to recall the universality of all these processes, and to remind ourselves that there is always, even in the "normal" marriage, some degree of rejection of the partner. How often do we hear in our ordinary lives, when the child misbehaves : "How like your mother!" or "How like Uncle Jim!"

2. Factors Concerning the Child

(a) A child of the wrong sex—particularly after two or three children of the same sex.

(b) A child of the wrong intelligence level, either below or above the parental level.

(c) A child with some hereditary defect. This applies to handicapped children with all kinds of defects—physical, sensory or intellectual.

(d) A child who has some crippling illness occurring after birth.

All these instances represent, to some degree, a failure of the child to become the fantasy child of the parent. This process can be even more intense if one child has died. The parents may immediately seek another child to replace the one that was lost. Any shortcomings of the living child are met with the belief that these would never have been present in the child which had died and, in fact, where one child out of a number is lost, it is often felt, and sometimes said, to the others, that "the best one went" and that any of the others could have been more easily spared.

Adoption brings in problems of its own, but the problems have a resemblance to those I have just outlined. It is the wish that the adopted child should be a special child of the parent's fantasy. Parents of adopted children expect trouble. They are advised to enlighten the child regarding the facts of adoption and a formula is sometimes suggested "that other parents have to take what God sends them, but we chose you out of a lot of children". In my view this, far from being reassurance to the adopted child, is an attempt to tell him that he should be as special and outstanding as the parents expected when they chose him out of so many. Enlightenment should be given, not as something separate, but as part of the explanations of the facts of birth. The child cannot know what it is to be adopted unless he also knows how babies ordinarily become members of a family by being born to the mother in the family. A second point with regard to adopted children is that they should not be deprived of standards of behaviour or of the punishments that are applied to ordinary children within the family; an adoptive parent might say "I could have chastised him if he had been my own." A third point is that such children should no more be expected to show gratitude for being in the family than a child who is born into the family.

The processes of rejection which are so universal include the begrudging to the child of the results of the parents' personal efforts. The baby is competing with the parents for the limited resources available. It is conceivable that this begrudging is more likely to apply to a child of another father and another mother who is taken into the house and adopted as the family's own. Such children, born of other parents, become heirs to the adopted parents and sometimes the adoptive parents question their wisdom of having embarked upon a course which leaves most of the accumulation of their life's work to be enjoyed by someone not of their own blood. It is no wonder that there are special problems in adopted children when they become adolescent and express the kind of rebelliousness which most adolescents go through. The marvel is that so many adoptions work successfully and give happiness to both parents and child.

3. Factors Concerning the Pregnancy and Delivery

(a) Physical illness affecting the mother's health—toxaemias, threatened abortions.

(b) Complications during the confinement necessitating surgical attention at the time or later.

4. Factors Relating to Deep Emotional Disturbances of Either Parent

(a) Fears in the mother regarding the confinement including fantasies of physical harm to her body. These are sometimes increased by the exchange of old wives' tales which touch on fundamental fears.

(b) Fear of loss of attractiveness due to alteration in the figure—particularly with regard to the abdomen and breasts.

(c) Fears associated with the repudiation of sexuality, the pregnancy providing evidence to the world that sexual contact has taken place.

(d) Fear of having an abnormal child which in some degree is universal, but more intense where the mother is overwhelmed by feelings of inadequacy or of badness within herself.

(e) Immaturity of either parent. There can be rejection of the pregnancy and of the child when either mother or father is immature and would therefore feel a rivalry with the child for the attention of the other parent.

(f) Deep feelings of sexual inadequacy in either the mother or father may be associated with guilt concerning masturbation, and they may be unable to accept the parental role.

REJECTION PROCESS

Methods of expressing rejection feelings can take many forms. There is the socially acceptable postponement of marriage or contraception within marriage. After conception has taken place rejection may be shown by attempts at abortion, either illegally or legally. Many illegal abortions take place, sometimes resulting in danger to the mother's health or even her life. Willingness to undergo such operations, knowing these dangers, is a measure of the depth of feeling involved. Termination of pregnancy is legal where it is considered that its continuation would lead to danger to the mother's life or permanently injure her health.* Such decisions may be difficult if the immediate position is balanced against the long-term possibility of subsequent guilt feelings and loss of self-esteem.

After the birth of the child the most extreme form of rejection is infanticide. This is or was accepted practice in some cultures, and in our own legal system it is recognised that a mother's reaction to her newborn child may be affected by factors not present in other periods in her life. The verdict of infanticide is different from one of murder and applies

* The Abortion Act, 1967, which became law in England, Wales and Scotland on 27th April 1968, allows for the consideration of social reasons for termination of pregnancy. See "Legal Abortion. The English Experience", HORDERN, A., 1971. Pergamon Press.

to cases where a woman causes the death of her newly born child at a time when she had not fully recovered from the effect of giving birth to such child.

The more usual ways of expressing attitudes of rejection are :

(1) *Open rejection*. The child is neglected, handled roughly, spoken to sternly, criticised for every action and sometimes openly blamed for change of family fortune or alteration in mother's health.

(2) *Over-protection*. Here the child is guarded from danger, from infection and from contamination by undesirable habits which other children at school or in the neighbourhood may have. The right food and the right medicines are forced down the child's throat. Attention to body process is maintained at a high level, but the normal activities of the child are restricted as being possibly dangerous. Education, recreation and social enjoyment all become limited. This process is even more dangerous to the child than open rejection because the child finds it harder to protest against what is done for his own good.

(3) *Indulgence*. There is a level of indulgence which is carried out out of love, which is relatively harmless; but there is another level which is carried out as the result of apathy and which is a form of deprivation. A child who is "bought off" with some material gift as a substitute for parental attention gets no satisfaction from the gift, and is deprived of the appropriate level of the restraint which parents offer as part of the standards of their families.

REJECTION FEELINGS : REALITY AND FANTASY

Rejection may be felt by the child in cases where it actually exists, and also it may be imagined in cases where there is no apparent reason. The death of a parent may be interpreted in the child's fantasy life as desertion of him by that parent. He may even feel in some ways guilty and responsible for the loss of his parent. Many mothers threaten that they will run away when the child is naughty, and some attribute their illness to the child's misdeeds. Divorce or separation of parents can have similar effects, especially if quarrels between the parent preceded either of these events.

The child who is left with just one parent is deprived of the benefits and support that he would get from the missing parent, but he has other deprivations too. The remaining parent is not able to fulfil his or her *own* role in attempting to fulfil both. The child who loses his father also loses his mother, because the mother, in attempting to be the head of the house, is unable to give him the relaxed and confidently affectionate mothering of which she might have been capable before. Sometimes a single surviving parent is too demanding of the child and seeks from him a level of companionship that would be appropriate in a marriage partner. The child then feels inadequate in that he fails to realise the parent's expectation.

When a child is taken to hospital he may interpret this as being deserted by the parent, particularly if he has not been given adequate explanation, and if he is not visited frequently in hospital. The effects of separation from the mother, or deprivation of maternal care, has been the subject of monumental work by John Bowlby.*

When another child is born into the family this may lead to actual or fantasy rejection of the older child. In some cases the parents concentrate all their attention on to the new arrival, and the first child is neglected. Some feelings of neglect and rivalry exist, however, even when parents make efforts to prepare the first child and share their concern between him and the younger one. The older child may still wonder why it was necessary for them to have had another child. He may come to the conclusion that it was because he himself was not good enough. There seems to be no escape from these feelings; and the only child who has not been supplanted may still have fantasies of other children being born in the family and taking *his* place in the family. The realisation of the actual experience of having a brother or sister generally is not so disturbing as the fantasy, and perhaps the greatest reassurance comes in a wider family network when the arrival of a new baby is not a rare and shattering event.

BALANCE OF REJECTION AND ACCEPTANCE;
MOTHERING BREAKDOWN AND DISTRESS

We must return to the recognition of the fact that concentration on processes of rejection and the outlets of its expression may divert us from recognition of the process of acceptance, which, like rejection, is always present. Acceptance shows itself in the provisions for a child's develop-

* J. Bowlby, *Maternal Care and the Mental Health*, W.H.O., 1958; *Child Care and the Growth of Love*, 2nd ed., Penguin Books, 1965; *Attachment and Loss*, Vol. I, Hogarth Press, 1969.

ment; the mothering or parenting process is a balance of rejecting and accepting attitudes. In this sense mothering or parenting can be looked at as quantitative. Rejection ceases to be an "all or none" process, and it becomes easier to understand that there are circumstances which temporarily affect the ability of the parent to make provision. John A. Rose compiled a series of contingencies* that seemed to be, singly or in combination, the critical stresses associated with mothering breakdown and subsequent pathogenic mother–infant interaction.

1. Multiple births.
2. Children born within ten to twelve months of each other.
3. Dislocating moves in pregnancy or the new-born period involving changing geographical areas and the need to find new ties.
4. Moving away from a family group or back to the group for economic reasons at a critical period for mother and child.
5. Unexpected loss of security by reason of job losses, to husband; to the pregnant woman.
6. Marital infidelity discovered in the pre-natal period.
7. Illness in self, husband, or relative who must be cared for at a critical period.
8. Loss of husband or of the infant's father close to the pre-natal period.
9. Role reversal if a previously supporting person breaks down and becomes dependent.
10. Conception and course of pregnancy related to the loss of a person with whom there was a deeply significant tie.
11. Previous abortions, sterility periods, traumatic past deliveries, loss of previous children.
12. Pregnancy health complications when occurring at a given time.
13. Experience with close friends or relatives who have had defective or injured children.
14. The juxtaposition of conception with a series of devaluing experiences.

All the contingencies listed above will be seen to increase the burden on the mother—or, alternatively, to deplete her of some of the resources

* *Prevention of Mental Disorders in Children*, ed. G. CAPLAN, Tavistock Publications, 1961.

from which she gives to her child. Thus rejection, and acceptance (which we shall discuss next), may be seen to be partial aspects of the transactions between parent and child, and these transactions are reciprocal.

RECIPROCAL REJECTION: CHILDREN'S FANTASIES ABOUT PARENTS

Children are accepting and rejecting towards their parents. Abnormal degrees of rejection from children may come at the point when a parent no longer sustains the image of perfection, and yet either he or the child refuses to part with the idealisation. The qualities of goodness or badness may be perceived separately by the child, and each quality projected on to one parent. One parent then appears as all good and the other as all bad. Later, when grown up, many individuals may begin to feel that perhaps they did an injustice to the parent who was rejected. Occasionally a child accepts all the badness of his parents as his own. Where there has been insufficient contact he perceives the lack of communication as a barrier between them and himself, and feels that he was responsible for creating it.

Fairy stories incorporate some of the familiar themes which recur transitorily in most people's minds. The child who no longer fulfils the parents' image becomes the changeling substituted by fairies. Children who find it hard to believe in their fleeting exalted fantasies cannot believe that these imperfect men and women can be their real parents. Was not the son or daughter of some king stolen away and placed in an ordinary home? At no situation of life are people entirely exempted from these fantasies. There is always a higher position which could have been one's own.

Lady Elizabeth in *The Confidential Clerk* by T. S. Eliot stated

> Do you know, Colby, when I was a child
> I had three obsessions, and I never told anyone. . . .
> The first was, that I was very ugly
> And didn't know it. Then, that I was feeble-minded
> And didn't know it. Finally
> That I was a foundling, and didn't know it. . . .
> I refused to believe
> That my father could have been an ordinary earl!
> And I couldn't believe that my mother *was* my mother.
> These were foolish fancies. I was a silly girl.

CHAPTER 9

Acceptance: the Basis of Infant Care

IN THE discussion of rejection it was emphasised that rejection is never complete. Whenever rejection processes are expressed there is the accompaniment of some degree of the opposite processes which we may call acceptance.

Any activity which is directed towards the care of the child implies some degree of acceptance, and there are unexpressed feelings of acceptance even when the evidence is hard to find. Ordinarily we might judge the level of acceptance by different kinds of provision, and these can be summarised as material needs and non-material needs. The material needs are those upon which life depends: food, clothing, shelter, protection from injury and disease, and treatment and care for any injuries or illnesses which might occur. Without these provisions no child could survive.

RAISING THE STANDARDS OF MATERIAL PROVISION

Within living memory the rejected child was likely to be neglected with regard to these provisions, and both neglect and ignorance as to the best methods for providing for the material needs were factors in the higher infant mortality of the last century. Higher general standards of material provision, which are associated with the higher standards of living, have reduced mortality and morbidity, and rejection is more likely now to become evident as deprivation with regard to the non-material needs of children.

We now emphasise the emotional needs of children, but we can only afford to do this when we can take it for granted that the material needs are met. We must never lose sight of the fact that physical care is the basis of life. At the beginning of this century the infant mortality, which is the number of babies in each 1000 who die before reaching their first birthday, was 160, and towards the end of the last century approximately one-fifth of all babies died before the end of their first year. Infant mortality varied between town and town, and between different social classes in the same town.

The present-day infant mortality is approximately 20,* but even today there are differences, although not such wide differences, between the infant mortality of local authority areas in different parts of the country. The higher infant mortality of sixty years ago was an index of lack of knowledge and sometimes of a failure to apply existing knowledge. It became recognised that more babies died amongst the poor and in the large towns than amongst the weathy and less crowded communities.

As in many other social reforms, the pioneer spirits were individuals in private or public life who began to arouse the social conscience of the community with regard to the unnecessary death of young babies. Gradually, as a result of the work of these individuals in this and other countries, various services were built up within the community to deal with the problem. One example was the Mayor of the town of Huddersfield in the year 1903, Alderman Benjamin Broadbent, who earned the nickname of "Baby Broadbent" because of his work in the publicising of ideas on infant care. He was inspired by Dr Moore, the Medical Officer of Health for the town. Being a rich man, he offered a gold sovereign to every baby born in his own parish during his year of mayoralty, but this was not to be given on the date of birth but on the first birthday. During that year the infant mortality went down by half! It would appear that a sovereign could buy a baby's life in the year 1903, but this would not be quite the truth. The gift was part of the publicity on infant care which was conveyed to the parents of young babies by the medical staff of the Health Department. The town adopted a scheme for notifications of birth in order to assist in the visiting of homes in which the babies were born. This was instituted on a voluntary

* The infant mortality rate, England and Wales, 1969, was 18 per 1000 live births. To this must be added the still-birth rate, which was 13 per 1000 births. Still-births and infant deaths occurring in the first week are combined to form the "perinatal mortality" for which the figure for 1969 was 23 per 1000 live and still-births.

basis at first and the scheme was taken up by other municipalities, and later was applied to the country as a whole.

Earlier efforts at provision for needs of infants included a scheme which was the forerunner of the Health Visitor who in some countries is called the Public Health Nurse. In Salford, Lancashire, in 1862, a Ladies' Committee was formed to employ "honest working women" to visit and teach mothercraft in the homes of young infants. In rural Buckinghamshire, in 1890, a Dr. De'Ath instituted a training scheme for such visitors.

Maternal and child health services, the staffs of which include medical officers and health visitors, are now an established feature of the local authority health services in all parts of the country. Community health services of various kinds have been built up by the drawing together of provisions of vastly different origin as well as by the establishing of entirely new projects.

The improving standards of infant care have been most effective with regard to the preservation of life and the prevention of physical illness. It is said that many of the children, whose lives have been saved, survive merely to suffer emotional neglect or, in some cases, children with some physical or other handicap may survive to a life which is limited by those handicaps. This may be partly true, and, if so, it pushes the frontier of our work a little further out, and we must continue to attempt to raise the level of living for those children whose lives are handicapped in any way.*

CULT OF HYGIENE AND REGULARITY

Material care and cleanliness, adequate clothing and protection from deficiencies in feeding have been emphasised, and, for a brief period in the advance of knowledge, attempts to give exactly calculated standards led to the fear of over feeding. Quantities of food and times of feeding were calculated so exactly that many a baby went hungry and frustrated. The reality of the dangers of infection led some people to attempt to reduce human contacts. Mothers were encouraged to wear masks

* CICELY D. WILLIAMS, Lancet, i, 346 (1964), points out the absurdity of the idea of "survival of the fittest" in communities with high infant mortality. The conditions which kill off the weakest also cause chronic sickness in those who survive.

when feeding their babies, and to hold their babies away from them so that the baby never enjoyed the comfort of the mother's arms, the feel of her heart beat against the body, the presence of her smell, and the sharing of inarticulate noises. There was a lack of logic about some of these ideas of sterility because the baby for whom the tap water had to be boiled would take an occasional drink of the bath water.

This kind of standardisation of care has been harmful to many children, and to many parents, who were deprived of the skin-to-skin contact and of the feelings of boundlessness in their contacts with each other. Yet many children who were brought up by parents who became devotees of these systems of infant care have survived and have done very well. They developed and retained good relationships with their families. Perhaps whatever the process might be, and whatever the essence of mothering is, the good mother who adopts a particular method because it is "the right thing" communicates her goodness to the baby through this process. The goodness of the mothering surmounts the badness of the process and we can say that "it is not what we do but the way that we do it which gets results"; and yet we can add that a good mother with good methods does even better.

In discussing the material care we have found ourselves referring at the same time to the non-material care which includes the love between parent and child.

WINNICOTT ON MATERNAL CARE

A beautiful statement of maternal care is provided by Winnicott in *Paediatrics and Psychiatry.** ". . . Let us attempt to study the mother's job. If the infant is to be able to start to develop into a being, and to start to find the world we know, to start to come together and to cohere, then the following things about a mother stand out as vitally important :

"She exists, continues to exist, lives, smells, breathes, her heart beats. She is *there* to be sensed in all possible ways.

"She loves in a physical way, provides contact, a body temperature, movement, and quiet according to the baby's needs.

"She provides opportunity for the baby to make the transition between the quiet and excited state, not suddenly coming at the child with a feed and demanding response.

* D. W. WINNICOTT, Collected Papers, *Paediatrics and Psychiatry*, p. 161. Tavistock Publications, 1958.

"She provides suitable food at suitable times.

"At first she lets the infant dominate, being willing (as the child is so nearly a part of herself) to hold herself in readiness to respond.

"Gradually she introduces the external shared world, carefully grading this according to the child's needs which vary from day to day and hour to hour.

"She protects the baby from coincidences and shocks (the door banging as the baby goes to the breast), trying to keep the physical and emotional situation simple enough for the infant to be able to understand, and yet rich enough according to the infant's growing capacity.

"She provides continuity.

"By believing in the infant as a human being in its own right she does not hurry his development and so enables him to catch hold of time, to get the feeling of an internal personal going along.

"For the mother the child is a whole human being from the start, and this enables her to tolerate his lack of integration and his weak sense of living-in-the-body."

NON-MATERIAL NEEDS

The non-material needs can be set out under categories of *love*, *opportunities* of expression appropriate to the child's individual capacity, and *standards*.

The *love* of which we have spoken is given to a child as a right and not as a reward for being a particular kind of child or for a particular kind of behaviour. When we speak of the mother's love for the child, we can recognise the general potential of mothering (or parental feeling) which is present in all human beings. There is an appeal which any infant has which calls up something in all human beings but with various degrees of intensity. That perhaps is the starting point. Some additional feelings are released by special responses or special activities of the child as described by ethologists. There is a further component which comes from the satisfying of the maternal image or fantasy which the mother has had of her child before the confinement, and sometimes even as a young girl before her marriage. The existence of the child partly embodies the image or fantasy, but the process of the confinement and the feeding of the baby at the breast may give the mother a new experience for which her fantasies have given her no preparation. The baby, as has been mentioned, is not passive in his feeding; he sucks with vigour, even with aggressiveness, and, at a very early age, the mother realises that the baby has a life of his own. The mother may find difficulty in accepting this real baby as a substitute for her own fantasy. She may find difficulty in accepting her own emotional role of the mother of a baby who is separated from her as well as depending upon her.

The whole process of acceptance and of the provision of non-material needs by the mother, and later by the father, and still later by those who represent the community, is influenced by the disparity between the image and the reality.

The *opportunities for expression* of a child's capacity should be those which are appropriate to the reality of the child, i.e. to his age, to his level of ability, and to the culture which is approved in the generation in which the child lives. The image may include factors which relate to the parent's concept of his own childhood which took place in a culture which has since been the subject of change resulting from rapid technical progress.

The opportunities or outlets for the child's activity apply to the child's physical, intellectual and emotional life. *Physically* he needs freedom of movement which will allow for the development of his muscular skill. The young infant is relatively more active than the older child and has lesser capacity for sitting still or for being quiet. As the infant develops, the emphasis on physical activity will depend on his total range of ability, and upon the valuation of some of his activities in his particular setting.

The *intellectual* life includes formal education in school and also the learning that accompanies all other activities and interests. There are problems when the child's intellectual capacity is higher or lower than that of the parents or of the rest of the family. The imposition on the child of levels that are inappropriate may lead to intellectual failure and, at the same time, may cause injury to emotional development.

In his *emotional* life the child needs freedom to express his feelings in relation to the individuals closely associated with him by family ties. The young infant is closer to awareness of the conflicts of love and hate than the older individual who has learnt what is and what is not socially acceptable.

The *standards* referred to are the moral or religious framework which is provided first within the family and then within the community. A child can feel that his actions within this framework are approved, and beyond it that they call for censure.

The framework which is provided in the first place becomes absorbed into the personality and needs to be appropriate to the age of the child and to the general culture. The framework should not be so severe that the child is inevitably bound to go beyond it.

All the above provisions should be at an appropriate level. The child should not be expected to respond or to perform in a manner beyond his capacity, and the capacity is the personal quality which may differ from that of other children of the same age. A child who is pressed to perform beyond his own level, or kept back from activities within his own capacity, may accept the inappropriate demands of others and build them into his own internal standards. He may thus continue to apply them long after those who initiated the process have ceased to be part of his life. This applies also to standards of morality. The capacity to absorb abstract standards, in the form of principles which can be generalised, is not present in children before a certain age. It is damaging to give even the *right* standards at the *wrong* time. The right standards are those which are observable in practice. No matter how good the standards may seem to be, they will prove wrong if it should be inevitable that they will be transgressed. Standards should not be too rigidly applied even when they are appropriate. A child needs the comfort of knowing that it is not the end of the world if he does something which his parents and he both agree is wrong. He may even need the comfort of knowing that he can do wrong and that his parents can check him.

RELATIVITY OF LEVELS OF PROVISION

All these provisions—the right kind of love, and the right kind of opportunities and the right kind of standards—vary somewhat with cultural changes. No child ever gets the ideal provision in all these categories. Rejection is relative and so is acceptance. The general provision for children today is at a higher level than it was a generation ago. It is true that there are still children who are grossly deprived of the appropriate love, opportunities and standards, but, on the whole, there is a higher standard of living and a higher standard of loving.

Thus, parents of today might consider themselves to have been deprived as children in comparison with children of their own. Some were deprived, relatively, in the sense that certain goods which are available today simply did not exist at the time of their childhood. They were therefore deprived of the enjoyment of such things as television and ice lollies! Many parents of today were deprived in an absolute sense as children, having been brought up in homes where there was financial hardship and privation during the times of industrial depression.

Many such parents have become successful through their own efforts and are amongst those responsible for raising the general standard of living.

VALUING DEPRIVATION

They may look back upon their deprivation with some affection, and think of it as the instrument which helped to form their characters. Mistakenly, they thus wish to give the benefit of that deprivation to their own children and to other children. They deplore the higher standards of consumption, and feel that the defects of character which they see in the younger generation are due to a lessened regard for money and for what money buys. Such parents may even begrudge their children the standard of living which they themselves are at present enjoying, recollecting that they were not able to have some things at the age at which they come automatically to their children.

All parents show something of this when they tell their children that they ought to be grateful for what they get in food, toys and pocket money, because they themselves did not have them as children. They expect the kind of response from their children that they themselves would have given in an epoch of general or personal privation.

LOOKING BACK IN ANGER

Other adults today who recollect the distress of their families look back in anger at the authority and social system which allowed their parents to suffer. Their resentment continues and remains directed at individuals who represent "the establishment" in a world which has changed in some respects but which seems to remain the same in others. They are unable to forgive those who did not seem to suffer in childhood, or who did not suffer in the same way as themselves.

GIVING TO THE IMAGE OF ONESELF

A third group of adults wish to make up for what they themselves missed by giving it to their children, and sometimes force on to the children goods that they themselves would have liked, but which may not be of special interest to their own children at some particular stage. Like the parent who begrudges his child his goods, these parents too are puzzled at the unexpected lack of response from their children. Perhaps it is because they are giving not to the reality of their child but to the residue of the child within themselves.

FINDING A BALANCE: BUILDING UP FAMILY STANDARDS

All these processes may occur to a marked and predominant extent in some individuals, and they also occur at times and to a lesser extent in all of us. A large number of people, however, carry the scars of their deprivation fairly comfortably. They can look back with compassion at some of the hardships that they and their parents suffered, and remember also that these were endured because the family accepted the hardship as a necessity and not as a virtue in itself. There are those who are able to give freely what seems to be appropriate to their present standard of living and the standards of the time.

Prevalent standards can provide special problems. Material standards have risen rapidly and some parents have not acquired any certainty of the appropriateness of the amount of money and other material satisfactions for their children. Times of hardship gave them the certainty of knowing what they could not afford to give.

Where a parent feels it is wrong or over-indulgent to give money and goods at the same level as other families in the neighbourhood, it may be a perfectly reasonable viewpoint. The difficulty is to convey that viewpoint to his child as part of the standards which the family as a whole can share. It is no use saying, about some purchase of which he disapproves, that he "cannot afford it". Often, in such cases, the child has taken money for frivolous purchases like those of his schoolmates from the uncounted contents of his father's pocket. Sometimes this has gone on for months or years before accidental discovery of the theft. The point is that the father said he could not afford it, and he *did* afford it, because the money went, and he did not even know.

Children are more likely to accept individual family standards as their own when the reasons for them are shared with them, and when they have an appropriate degree of participation in the making and changing of the family standards.

THE SPOILT CHILD

We should include a word about the spoiling of children. A spoilt child is usually one who is hated by other children, by the parents of other children, and even by his own parents. A spoilt child is thought of as one who has everything he wants. It would be more correct to say that a spoilt child is one who has everything he *asks for* as a substitute for other levels of attention. He is given goods instead of love. It is not surprising, therefore, that what he asks for, and what he is given, never satisfies him. He asks for what he sees. If it is a toy, he does not play with it. If it is food, he leaves it on his plate. He is refused things at times but has only to storm and rage to alter his parents' decision. Parents feel wrong when they give, and wrong when they deny. Such a child is a deprived child. He is deprived of love, he is deprived of the appropriate level of outlets, and he is deprived of standards.

Some children are indulged out of love and not out of apathy or inability to give standards, and the results of such indulgence are less harmful if the parents do not think of it as indulgence but regard it as a pleasure to them as well as to their child.

To summarise, acceptance is consideration for the child as he is, as a living individual who is not a miniature adult but a complete person of his own age and stage. Rejection is the preference of the parents' image of what a child should be to the reality of the child. The problem is that the fantasy competes with the reality. Parents reject themselves as well

as their children because they have a fantasy of performance which they
impose upon themselves as well as the fantasy of performance which
they did impose upon their children.

AIMING AT PERFECTION

Parents may wish to make exactly the *right* provision for the children,
and the danger is that they will feel entitled to perfect children in
return. They try to give them what I have outlined above—exactly the
right kind of love, the right kind of outlets, and the right kind of standards. They try to give them the right kind of food, proteins, calories
and vitamins, and sometimes in their anxiety to give the right amount
and kind of food, it is forced down the child's throat. The child has to
read the right kind of books from the start, enjoy the right kind of
entertainment, and the standards imposed on him include the right kind
of manners. One must confess that it is impossible for parents to do
right, and perhaps they should not try all that hard. They should be
content merely to do their best!

The anxiety to achieve perfection can be part of a general wish of
parents to be approved themselves, and, if they derive their approval
from their cultural activities, they will seek confirmation of their status
from their children's activities and achievements.

A newspaper account of a Christmas pantomime included a description of audience reaction, and quoted a conversation overheard between
two families with children on their way out of the theatre. One mother
said to the child of her neighbour "What part of it did you like best?"
and before the child could reply, her mother said "*We* liked the ballet
best." It would have been a lowering of status to have enjoyed the
vulgarity of the clowns.

This anxiety about perfection is played upon by advertisers of
children's food preparations, clothing, and detergents. Goods are adver-
tised as those used for children by "mothers who care". A beautiful
example of this kind of advertising appeared some time ago in *The New
Yorker*. The picture showed a child of perhaps 6 or 7 years old standing
in a circle of his toys. He is carrying a space helmet, is holding a space
gun, a rifle and a machine gun. His belt contained a dagger and a sword.
The toys around him included a train, wagons, cars, toy boat, armoured

cars. His mother is sitting and his father kneeling at the boy's feet, the mother holding a toy aeroplane. Yet there is an anxious look on these parents' faces and above is the caption "What do you mean—we are neglecting the child?" Below are the words "Neglect? This child of ours? Why, he has everything—everything we can give him for his health and happiness! But has he? Without realising it you may be neglecting one of the most precious, most meaningful events of your child's growth—his appreciation of great music. He ought to have had a Child's Library of Musical Masterpieces."

This was *The New Yorker*, but are we sure that in this country, too, we do not have the same anxieties about our failure to give exactly the right thing? The most important thing about acceptance is the acceptance of human limitations and the preparedness to do our ordinary best.

MAKING UP FOR DEFICIENCIES

Degrees of deprivation are a factor in disturbances of the thoughts, feelings and behaviour of children. Sometimes such a disturbance is considered to be due to some damaging experience, but more frequently a long-standing deprivation is responsible. Consequently one can prescribe the supply of the missing provision as the cure. It is surprising how frequently popular remedies, which are recommended for behaviour disturbances or delinquency, can fit into one of the three levels of provision that have been described. Some people say as their regular prescription "Give them love", others say "Give them outlets and opportunities—Youth Clubs, hobbies, special classes", others say "Give them discipline—punish them hard." None of these remedies is effective when given alone. Love is not enough; it needs a background of outlets and a discipline which is appropriate. The best classes and clubs are useless without the love that is the respect for the individual and a framework within which the young person can recognise the community to which he belongs. Punishment is ineffective except against a background which accepts with affection the individual's personality and which gives him a recognition of his need to develop and express himself.

Personality is a living organic whole, and the needs must be recognised in their entirety.

CHAPTER 10

Deprivation and Provision:
Separation and Union*

WE SPEAK of normal development and depict a series of stages in which the child, with his inherent capacities and potentialities, receives provisions that are necessary to take him on to each succeeding stage. The word "normal" can mean the average which is observed, or it may imply ideal standards by which we judge the imperfect actualities of the lives of each individual. To some extent normality is relative, as the standards by which health is judged have a tendency to rise.

In every community, and in some communities more than others, there are many individuals for whom the provisions are far below the standards which are called normal under any criteria. The lack of the necessary provisions is *deprivation*, and deprivation is looked for as a factor in the developmental history of those individuals who suffer some disturbance or disorder of personality.

DEPRIVATION OF MATERNAL CARE: SEPARATION

Physical deprivation is recognised in malnutrition or in the results of neglect of the material needs. The *emotional* needs have been discussed earlier in terms of relationships with other individuals, particularly the mother. The most important emotional deprivation is any interference with the child/parent relationship. The importance of the mothering relationship in the development of the child was emphasised by Bowlby in his monograph *Maternal Care and Mental Health* published in 1951

* Much of the material in this chapter was included in a paper which was presented at the Inter-Clinic Conference of the National Association for Mental Health, April 1963.

by the World Health Organisation, which had the declared aim of calling attention to the part played by deprivation of maternal care in the aetiology of mental and social disorders. The word deprivation has now become firmly associated with the idea of separation from the mother. The word arouses strong feelings : some think of separation as the basis of all psycho- and socio-pathology, others seem to be at pains to prove that maternal care is an unnecessary process in the upbringing of a child. Some seem even to go so far as to think of mothering in the first place as a pathogenic process, and readily resort to enforced separation of the child from his family as a favourite therapeutic procedure !

The acceptance of Bowlby's thesis was widespread but not universal. Some observers rightly called attention to the nurturing process in which a father also has a role; to the extended family with multiple mothering; to the professionalised mothering in a variety of organisations, such as the Kibbutzim in Israel; supplementary mothering by a succession of adults in private homes where, in addition to the natural mother, there are nurses or au-pair girls; and the day nurseries and child minders and grandmothers for another social class. Inferences have been drawn from all these processes to show that upbringing in the absence of the mother does not inevitably lead to pathological development or, if it does, that the results are not irreversible.

The world of child-caring professions became divided into "supporters" and "opponents" of maternal care. The supporters said that the baby must never be separated from the mother. The opponents said "Prove to us that the effects really are bad, or, if they are bad, that the results are permanent." "Why," the opponents also asked, "does it have to be the *natural* mother?" "Can't someone else do what is necessary, the father perhaps, a relative, a nurse, a trained member of the staff of some institution, or just some goodhearted woman? Why, this 'mystique' of mothering?" They added "Prove what you say *scientifically*." The word "scientifically" is a powerful word in any argument. The supporters had to go on the defensive, and deprivation of maternal care has since been defined more precisely.

DEGREE OF INTERACTION WITH MOTHER FIGURE

A re-assessment* of the position lays down that it is not the physical presence of the mother that counts, but the amount and quality of the interaction that takes place between mother and baby. It also summarises three major sorts of condition in which deprivation may occur :

1. Insufficient care or interaction with a mother figure when the child is separated from his mother and placed in an institution or hospital.
2. Insufficient care or interaction when in the care of the mother or mother substitute (due to her illness or inadequacy).
3. Inability of the child to react with a mother figure even when one is present and willing—a condition which is due to previous breaches or interactions.

This is an important and comprehensive statement, and takes into account the deprivation that can take place within an apparently normal home as well as in foster homes. But note that we no longer say just "mother" but "mother figure"—or, if we do use the word "mother" we add, almost automatically, "or mother substitute". . . . It suggests that we have reached the point where we can't tell the stork from mother !

PREGNANCY : THE BEGINNING OF MOTHER/CHILD RELATIONSHIP

Could not the challenge for scientific proof be met by the assumption, in accordance with the principle of cause and effect, that a mother and child, who have already had experience of one another during the months of pregnancy, will have a different relationship with each other from the relationships of people brought together in other ways? Then we could try to discover what those differences might be.

The effects of separation need not be assumed to operate in precise categories of symptoms—which are themselves not representative of uniform processes. Delinquency, for example, is a *social* category which includes an agglomeration of many different kinds of behaviour. If we

* M. D. Ainsworth, *The Effects of Maternal Deprivation*. Public Health Papers No. 14, W.H.O., Geneva, 1962.

submit any hypotheses to statistical study, we must first make sure that the nature of the study is one to which the method is appropriate. Perhaps the subject is one where the shortage is not one of statistical studies but of hypotheses. It is true that there is a call for the kind of scientific examination that is communicated by measurement, but this call is not met satisfactorily by using precise mathematical criteria in the arrangement of imprecise clinical impressions about patients, who are referred fortuitously, against equally imprecise observations on "controls", who are assumed, as a matter of course, to be "normal".

Dennis, writing on "Scientific Methods for the Investigation of Child Development" in *Psychopathology of Childhood* by Hoch and Zubin,* stated : "While statisticians have made great progress in determining how to test for the presence of relationships, they have no special way of determining which of the millions of possible relationships should be examined. This is the field of theory. . . . A particular relationship should not be examined to establish an isolated fact, but to find a fact that plays a key role."

The restatement of the concept of deprivation is given point by a casual contribution made by Bowlby to a discussion reported in *The Determinants of Infant Behaviour†*—"The moral of all this is that we should never just say 'deprived' about a baby, but 'deprived of what, at what time and in what conditions'."

New Postulations I

COMPLEMENTARITY OF SEPARATION AND UNION

It is therefore proposed to make some postulations with regard to the necessary provisions of maternal or parental relationships, the general environmental and social requirements and, in addition, to make some further comments on the interactions within the family. It is a fallacy to look upon separation as a single and once-for-all process, and likewise to seek its effects in the child alone. Separation is merely one part of a double process and is an essential element of every human relationship. To unite with another and yet to seek to become a separate identity is the two-sided process of living together. Everyone begins in physical

* Published by Grune & Stratton, New York, 1955.
† Methuen, London, 1951.

union with a mother. The capacity to separate increases, and, in the development of each individual, it is necessary for the capacity for separation to have appropriate expression—appropriate to each stage. Complete separation never occurs. We seek reunions and new unions. It is a disorder of development if we fail to emerge as separate individuals, but it is equally abnormal to separate too completely. Thus, in studying the basic theme of separation and union, we must not attach value judgements to the processes themselves. We must not say that separation and dependence are good or bad in themselves. It is a question of how much, and when. *We must learn to recognise the complementarity of separation and union in normal family relationships before we can proceed to define those relationships which are disordered and in need of help.*

THE FAMILY AS A FUNCTIONAL UNIT

We must also postulate the functions of the family as the promoter of the mental health of its members. We can do this under three headings :

1. The procreation and the care of the young.
2. The transmission of the culture.
3. The satisfaction of adult male and female sexual needs.

The three functions are interconnected, and each participant shares in transactions and interactions, giving and receiving, belonging together and moving apart.

The family itself has no point of beginning. A child is born to parents who have pre-existing complicated family involvements to which is added the new relationship with each other and with the child that they are going to have. The child is a fantasy—welcome or unwelcome—before it is a reality. Even in their own childhood, the parents had pictured themselves somehow in their own parents' role. Both mother and father of a child have some kind of image of the child that they are going to have, and of the part that they will play in his life. The image may have no relation to the real child, and the tragedy for some children—and some parents—is that it is hard to give up the image for the reality. Sometimes a real child moves more quickly towards a separate identity than the imaginary child, but, in the case of a handicapped child, the dependent state may be retained at levels beyond those which the resources of the parents can support.

New Postulations II

DEFINITION OF DEPRIVATION IN TERMS OF PROVISION WHICH IS LACKING

The provisions made within the family or the community setting can be expressed as (see Chapters 1 and 7) *environmental*—referring to material provisions—*personal*—referring to the organic or mental aspects of the individual—or *inter-personal* with reference to relationships with significant individuals. These three categories of description of needs and provisions are not mutually exclusive. Any problem or disorder can be described in terms of any or all of them. Moreover, provision can never be complete, and deprivation of some degree is universal. Deprivation is only of value as a diagnosis when there is some awareness of lack of fulfilment of need, and where that awareness leads to some abnormal feeling or behaviour.

Discussion of the definition of the deprivation is a form of diagnosis, and should be the basis of a decision for treatment or intervention. Help can only be given if a problem can be presented within, or translated into, the terms which are relevant to the techniques and resources of the agency which has been consulted. Help is sought from medical, social and educational services for the effects of deprivation, and sometimes it is a matter of chance rather than of abstract principles as to which particular service is consulted.

ILLUSTRATIVE CASES

The problems set out below, which were referred to child guidance clinics, are quoted as examples where there was the possibility of different viewpoints, and where satisfactory consultations needed action and co-operation of different agencies. Some conclusions are drawn from these cases but, more important still, fresh questions have to be posed regarding the basic principles of professional help.

First case. Michael was referred at the age of 5 for a behaviour problem at home and at school. The family doctor's letter stated : "Only one teacher is capable of handling him, and, as a result of this, she has spent two weeks recovering from an attack of asthma." Michael was not allowed to stay at school for school dinners, and the mother complained that *she* hadn't time to go backwards and forwards for him at mid-day. When she took him out shopping with her, he kicked and screamed or wandered away, and was then picked up at a distance by the police. A brief account of the history and conclusions is given in a section of the report* to the family doctor.

> Both parents were born abroad. The mother had a disturbed childhood and came to England at the age of 15. She met her husband on a return visit to her home and they married and settled in England. When Michael was *3 weeks* old they went back to her home country; he was ill on the journey and was admitted to hospital. A series of hospital admissions followed. For a while he was in the care of the maternal grandmother, and for part of this time the mother was again in England. There were still a number of journeys backwards and forwards, and the second child was born at the grandmother's home. Michael's most serious illness was an infection with cerebral symptoms and paralysis. He was given penicillin and streptomycin and recovered completely. . . .
>
> In my view the behaviour problem is that of a child with an unorganised personality. He has had no consistently present parent figure, and he has been exposed to different standards, and sometimes he has had a complete absence of standards. It seems probable that conditions have been more stable during the last year than previously, and I feel that he is beginning to show some degree of integration.
>
> Having missed parental contact when in hospital, there are some stages in his development in which he is lacking, and he needs, for the time being, the kind of attention from the parents that would normally be given to a much younger child.

Perhaps that report was a shade optimistic. He was admitted to an observation class consisting of five or six children, under an individual teacher, in which the children present problems of educational or clinical diagnosis. Several months later I made the following note :

"The problem of precise diagnosis remains undecided but the possibilities include :

First, brain damage following the cerebral infection.
Secondly, subnormality.
Thirdly, emotional maladjustment associated with the repeated separations from the parents.

* Some details of reports are omitted or deliberately altered.

Fourthly, deficiency in the incorporation of social controls due to the instability and inconsistency of parental attitudes."

I added that these diagnoses were not mutually exclusive, and that the educational problem was more a behavioural one than a cognitive one. His behaviour continued to be difficult even within the small observation class. Arrangements were made through his family doctor for him to be admitted to hospital for physical observation. An X-ray of the skull, electroencephelogram and air encephelogram were all carried out and were all normal. A combined report from the neurologist and psychiatrist attached to the hospital stated that "He gives the impression of being a brain-damaged child even apart from the history being in favour of this." He was transferred to a psychiatric bed but his behaviour in the ward led to his rapid discharge! After his return home he was found to be uncontrollable in the observation class, except for short periods, and the suggestion was made that he should attend for mornings only. The mother commented "Of what use is that to *me*?"

A psychological assessment of his ability gave him an I.Q. of 73 on the Stanford Binet scale, and the psychologist found him to be amenable enough in an individual setting during the limited time of the test. In another interview he showed imaginative constructive ability with building bricks, making complicated symmetrical structures in each of which he introduced all the bricks that were at his disposal.

What would be the diagnosis here? Deprivation of mothering? Inappropriate mothering? Inherent defect? Brain damage due to infective processes? And, speaking of the diagnosis, sometimes I think that we diagnose by association of words. We say "over-active", and translate that into "hyperkinesis". We treat the word "hyperkinesis" as a precise diagnosis, and equate it with brain damage. This "diagnosis" is sometimes made on the evidence of a history of some injury or infection even if there are no objective signs of actual damage. If there is neither evidence nor history of any damage to brain tissue, we say "*minimal* brain damage"!

What would be the appropriate treatment process in this case? Should the boy be admitted to a psychiatric in-patient unit, and, if so, how long should he remain there? Was his need more that of primary experiences of which he had been deprived? This problem had (1) social and education, (2) individual and clinical, (3) inter-personal and familial aspects.

The suggested solution was the transfer to a residential school for educationally subnormal pupils, where, it was hoped, home and school in one process would have some of the maturational effects which we would seek from therapy. He would return home during school holidays, but it would have to recognised that the parents would continue to be unable to contribute to the developmental or therapeutic processes —although they are well able to organise their own lives in a manner which appeared satisfactory to themselves and their acquaintances.

Second case. Maureen also was referred to a child guidance clinic at the age of 5 years—she was the third child and only girl in a family of five children. It was stated that she was undersized and not talking.

At the age of 3 years she had been admitted into the paediatric ward of a general hospital in a stage of extreme emaciation. She gained weight on an ordinary diet and without treatment, and it was inferred that the emaciation was due to neglect of feeding. On her discharge she was referred by the paediatrician to a specialised clinic for psychiatric investigation, and the report included the following paragraph :

> My first interest was trying to find out the nature of the relationship between the mother and the child which could lead to the child reaching such a desperate physical state without the mother kicking up more fuss about having the child seen; that is, I got the impression of an unusual lack of concern on the mother's part.

After the diagnostic interview two years later at the child guidance clinic the report included the following passages :

> There are many anomalous features in this case. Maureen is undersized, looking more like a 3-year-old child than her chronological age of 5 years. She is the middle one of five children and the only girl, and, from the descriptions given by the mother, the others are all normal.
>
> Maureen is described by the mother as "backward" and having no initiative. She is "well behaved", never runs about and never shows affection.
>
> During her interview with me, Maureen played silently with toys and, although she made no open response to my participation, she followed some of my movements later.
>
> The mother stated that at home Maureen mostly plays with toy cars and has a wheel-barrow and a doll's pram. She places the cars on top of one another as if they were bricks. She uses the doll's pram as a general purpose vehicle and not for her dolls, and, although she has dolls, she never plays with them and she never cuddles a soft toy. Her play is mostly with the toys of the two younger children, whom she follows around.

She has only a few words with which to communicate with her parents, saying "Mum", "Dad" and "sweets" and she recognises the bell of the ice-cream van. She probably speaks to her brothers more than to her mother and father.

At one stage in the history, it had been implied that her feeding was neglected to such an extent that she became emaciated, but, according to the history given by the mother today, it seemed that the mother fed her with a great deal of perseverence in the face of refusal to accept food. The mother states that Maureen now eats very well but still has to be fed. There remains, however, as has been previously noted, a strange lack of contact between Maureen and her mother. This may centre on the fact that Maureen, although born at home, was taken straight into hospital because she only weighed 4 lb 4 oz. She remained there for six weeks until her weight was 5 or 6 lb.

I should be inclined to explain the present state of affairs on the assumption that the mother has herself a low level of capacity for the mothering process and for the responses that develop successively at critical periods during the early stages of the infant-mother relationship. It may be that the child also has some inherent defects which have affected her capacity to respond in a way that normally reinforces the mothering reaction.

This girl, too, was admitted to the observation class and some progress was made, albeit slowly. The child acquired a small vocabulary and made contacts with the teacher and with other children.

During further interviews, the mother seemed to be on the defensive against possible criticism, and her comments all implied that if there was any blame, it was on the child—"She never stops eating, yet she *refuses* to grow."

Growing was, indeed, so slow that the possibility of some endocrine abnormality which might lead to dwarfism began to be considered. A conference, with the family doctor, school medical officer, the teacher at the observation class, along with the clinic staff, reached the conclusion that further physical examination was necessary. Investigations included tests for ACTH assimilation, anterior pituitary function, and an air encephalogram was carried out to reveal the presence of any structural defects within the skull. All proved negative. Hard objective facts to explain this child's condition were absent, but some explanatory assumptions could be made with regard to the possible aetiology and pathology.

This child had certainly suffered nutritional deprivation. Was she deficient in supplies or in her utilisation of them? Was it possible that the mother was an individual with a less than average capacity for mothering, and that special circumstances created a different relationship between her and the child from that with other members of the family?

Could we assume that mothering in general has three components? The *first* is the general potential of care and concern that every individual has for the young and helpless. This is present in men as well as in women, and in children with regard to younger children. The *second* component is the cluster of sign-release phenomena studied by ethologists as part of the tie between the young and the mother in animals and human beings. Were these processes missing in this case, at first because of Maureen's prematurity and stay in hospital, and later because of physical retardation? The other four children received a degree of mothering, but Maureen seemed to be excluded almost as if she had never been accepted as her mother's child.

The *third* component in mothering is the learned technique which can be picked up by observation of others and which can be professionalised by planned teaching.

In this particular case, where the mother's capacity for mothering seemed to be low, it might be limited to the primitive built-in responses which did not receive the signals for their release.

What should the next step be?

Third case. This is one where the complaint came entirely from the school. Robin was seven years of age and of above average intelligence. Complaints had been made about him when he was 6 years old, and more recently the Headmaster stated "Robin is quite beyond control in the classroom; when he is criticised at all, he resents this so much that he lashes out and kicks his desk. He puts up his fists as though to attack the teacher, and puts out his tongue at him and generally disturbs the class. There is no alternative but to exclude this boy from school."

His mother thought that this was a storm in a teacup. He is no trouble at home except that he is enuretic. At the age of 4 years he was in hospital for three months "to have his legs straightened" and afterwards had to wear splints. The mother feels that he may have been indulged at home afterwards because of this.

The phrase "indulgence" had been used elsewhere about this boy, implying that he got a higher level of provision than the average child. This might be true if we take into account only the interaction in which a parent responds to the child's demands for some gift, for some privilege, or to be excused from some duty. We have, however, considered in an earlier chapter provisions as including *standards* which provide a required framework of essential behaviour. Indulgence in this sense is deprivation of that framework.

Robin was never subjected to social controls within his family; and school with its rules, was a new and strange experience. His aggressive response suggested an attempt on his part to enter into an interaction with the teacher at an adult level—a fantasy life in which he inflated himself to adult size. This is the essence of the oedipal situation which, when it occurs at an earlier stage, and is resolved, leaves behind the foundations of the superego.

Here, the *social diagnosis* was behaviour problem; the *individual diagnosis*, unresolved oedipal situation; the *inter-personal diagnosis*, uncertainty of role.

But what of the teachers' participation?

Life in school involves acceptance of an ideology in which there are reciprocal roles of child and teacher. The acceptance of each others' roles makes it possible for one teacher to control forty pupils. Transference is at first to the impersonal role of the teacher rather than to his own person, and the transference is based upon expectation, or an image, of the teacher, which has already become elaborated as part of the superego structure.

If the child is deficient in these images the teacher has to fall back on the resources of his own personality. It becomes necessary for him to contain the immediate situation and to become the source of the first introjection of controls. This is a slow process and is part of the growth of personality which should have taken place in earlier years of infancy. But the teacher, and any other adult concerned, may at times respond with the immature part of his own personality. An adult may fear his own unresolved oedipal features. Every adult feels at times to be a small inadequate child, who has to blow himself up to grown-up size to do an adult job. The teacher, therefore, like the parent, needs support and reassurance. He should not be made to feel more inadequate by criticism of his failure or mismanagement. He needs help with the problem of the child and support for his own role.

The child's therapeutic needs in this case could not be supplied by the procedure frequently described as "free play". It was necessary to provide a kind of freedom which is contained within a framework of control that is possible of acceptance. The solution offered was part-time attendance at a remedial class with a teacher who was able to give individual attention along with freedom of activity that was legitimised within a framework of a special kind of school life. Here the therapy remained within the educational system. There was no further need of the services of the clinic and the boy continued to attend the ordinary school for the major part of each week.

Comment might be made on the fact that although enuresis was mentioned by the mother, no attempt was made to treat that condition. It had not been presented by the parent as a problem, and it is doubtful whether psychotherapy would have been effective in the absence of concern about this aspect of the problem. The enuresis could be re-garded as just another indication of the immature part of the boy's personality which was being fostered by his mother in an attempt to make up for what they had *both* missed when he was in hospital.

ESSENTIAL PROVISIONS: THE DEPRIVED CHILD AND DEPRIVED PARENT

We are now ready to make some general statements on deprivation of the provisions which are essential for the development of personality.

1. Mothering depends upon the three factors or components—(i) the general potential for care, (ii) the ethologically studied processes, and (iii) professionalisation or learned techniques.

2. A child will suffer deprivation of some of these factors if physically separated from the mother (or mother substitute!).

3. There can be defects in the mothering *process* even in the presence of mother, or mother figure, if there is some barrier to the mothering process.

A mother may be inadequate as a result of a temporary depressive illness after the confinement, or through physical illness or more perma-nent mental or social subnormality. There are mothers who can manage to cope with two or three, or perhaps four children, but whose capacity gives out with the birth of another child. A woman who is a mother has other roles as well. She has the care of other children in the family, she is the wife of her husband, she may have a role in her extended family, social obligations and occupational responsibilities. She is a person in her own right, and has her physical illnesses and mental disturbances, and her day-to-day problems. There are times when something has to give way. Dr. Hoffmeyer of the Mothers' Aid Centre in Copenhagen* uses the phrase "mothering insufficiency" which is an operational rather than a clinical diagnosis.

4. The family process does not depend upon the mother alone. There are the interactions directly with the father or the indirect effects of his support of the mother, or his competing demands upon her. There is the equally complex interaction with brothers and sisters.

5. Barriers in the child may prevent him from receiving a mothering process which is available. Physical, sensory or mental handicaps can lead to a failure of the child to perceive or to respond to the care.

6. Deprivation in the child causes deprivation in the parents. The parenting process is one in which the parent undergoes development of personality as well as the child. If the child is separated from the parent, even if sufficient care is given elsewhere for the child's developmental needs, the parent is deprived of the processes which are normally set going by the changing responses of the child. The parent/child relationship is undeveloped. Some responses from the child *initiate* processes in the parent, and some responses *reinforce* them and maintain them; and the further responses which come from the child, as the child grows, can *inhibit* some aspects of the tie and therefore allow separation to occur when dependency is no longer appropriate. A retarded child does not give the first initiating signals, and he may be "rejected" because those responses are not present. He does not give the latter signals and is "over-protected" then because these later inhibiting signals are delayed.

Deprivations, separations and physical, sensory or mental handicaps are not static conditions. They may multiply their own ill effects. For example, a mentally handicapped child starts with a lower potential for development. His handicap prevents him from receiving some of the personal interchange that is offered him, and he may not therefore develop even up to the level of his own potential. Next, his failure to

* H. HOFFMEYER, *The Feminine Role and Motherhood*, W.H.O. Seminar, Athens, 1962. Mimeographed working paper EURO.206 2/WP6.

reach the expected normal stages at appropriate times robs the mother of the rewards that come in the ordinary way from a child who benefits from her attention. We can recall that Maureen's mother felt that her child *refused* to grow.

7. Separation can be a deprivation, but it is also a deprivation to deny the child levels of independence and individuality that are appropriate to each age or stage of development.

8. A further level of deprivation could be called *cultural deprivation*. Intellectual development depends upon experience of the surroundings and of the various objects encountered. A child needs to learn the textures of materials and the names of things. Words become a means of communication and the tools of thought. Bernstein* has shown how poverty in the vocabulary which is available in the home can starve a child there of the material for intellectual development, and that this can also affect emotional growth. Vocabulary differences in different social classes can be associated with differences in personality structure.

It has been suggested above that the experience of deprivation is relative to the general standards which are available, and which become the norm in a particular epoch or country. It has been mentioned earlier, too, that parents can feel deprivation in comparison with their own children who are experiencing a higher standard of living than a previous generation.

THE DEPRIVED CLINICIAN

The recollection of a personal deprivation can affect others as well as parents. We can speak of the deprived clinician who, with the recollection of his own unsatisfied needs, identifies with the child and becomes hostile to the parents, to other professional workers, and to the community as a whole.

We can apply ethological findings to professional motivation, as well as to the tie between mother and child.

It has been observed when studying the behaviour of the female rat and her young that there is a "retrieving" phenomenon. The mother brings back any of her progeny which stray from the shelter of her body. When, experimentally, an adult mouse is substituted for an infant rat,

* B. BERNSTEIN, Aspects of Language and Learning in the Genesis of Social Process, *J. Child. Psychol. and Psychiat.* **1** (1961).

the mother spends so much of her time and energy retrieving the actively mobile mouse that her own offspring may die.

The hedge sparrow feeds the cuckoo that ousts the natural offspring from the nest. Once, on a visit to friends, my hostess described how she had been the witness of the whole course of the upbringing of a cuckoo in a nest in her garden. She described how busily the hedge sparrow brought food to the cuckoo which eventually grew bigger than the foster mother. There seemed to be something in the cuckoo's cry that drove the hedge sparrow to work at a frantic rate. At one point other hedge sparrows gathered around the nest. One of the other guests present asked "What were the other hedge sparrows doing?" I intervened with the facetiousness over which sometimes I have no control, and said "Those were the social workers!" But perhaps my facetiousness revealed a truth. We are sometimes driven by the cry of distress to give even beyond our resources.

RELATIVITY OF DEPRIVATION

Let us return to the concept of the relativity of deprivation.

We adults of the present generation were all deprived in comparison with the children of today. There is a higher standard of living and a higher standard of loving which is demanded now as the minimum. Some adults of today were deprived even by the standards of their own generation during the unequal hardships of the industrial depression.

Deprivation of material needs is not inevitably pathogenic. In some homes a loving and united family surmounts the difficulties.

The unity of a loving family is not a simple or static process. Provision has to be made for the achievement of separate identity. Satisfactory families are the ones from which it is easiest to separate and re-unite. The simultaneous nature of the drive towards union and separation means that at times one aspect is hidden. There is no need to look for hidden processes when everything goes satisfactorily. When there are disturbances in family relationships we need to study the family interaction as well as what goes on in the single individuals.

Professional work advances into the areas where discontents are becoming apparent. For some disturbances it is enough to deal with the individual; for others we need to know more about the structure of the family in health and illness.

When we come to consider the prevention of disturbance, we need to know more about the structure of society itself, and the transactions between the individual, his family and society as a whole.

The growing areas of medical, social and nursing work are areas of uncertainty. Scientific knowledge is always limited and relative at one time and one place.

Without the feeling that somewhere there exists some permanent lines of reference to contain and guide us we lose sense of purpose and of direction. Uncertainty becomes the basis of growth when it proceeds from a central core of faith, and when acknowledgement of our doubts leads to the search for more knowledge.

Care-taking professions owe their existence to a belief that human progress is possible and that people can help one another through their interaction.

The feelings that lead to our caring for the young can extend to the caring for mankind in general. The energy expressed in conflict within an individual, and which also exists between individuals and between groups, can also be the source of adventure and creativity. We can recognise good and bad in their expression, but the underlying process is neither good nor bad. We cannot improve our nature by seeking to eradicate from ourselves that which might *become* bad.

We must recognise the inevitability and the universality of the conflicts that exist in ourselves and our organisations, knowing that we have, at the same time, the urge to find harmony within ourselves, with our neighbours, and with as much of the universe as we can comprehend.

CHAPTER 11

The Importance of Play

REFERENCE has been made to the stages of psycho-sexual development and to some aspects of the relationship of the child and parents. The physical and intellectual growth needs to be taken into account simultaneously.

THE PHYSICAL MATRIX OF LIVING ACTIVITY

The physical and intellectual aspects of development have their stages with lines of demarcation between them. The toddler is a different being from the child who is, as yet, unable to walk. The growth of intellect has its stages, which have been described, notably by Piaget. He studied mental processes as a representation of the inborn capacity for motor responses, growth taking place by assimilation of the perceptions of the environment and with the subsequent accommodation of the experience. Piaget's stages represent the increasingly complex organisation of perception and performance. The description of the separate stages becomes possible by the revelation of new dimensions of action and thought.*

The physical appearance of a child changes in the second and third year, and the relatively large-headed baby or infant is succeeded by a well-proportioned little person with a more recognisable individual personality. The human infant is born at an immature stage in the active life of the individual as compared with the young of other animals and, therefore, there is a longer period of infantile dependence to be spent outside the womb.

* J. PIAGET and B. INHELDER, *The Psychology of the Child*, Routledge & Kegan Paul, 1969.

I recall that once on a visit to a farm I was shown a litter of young pigs which had been born the day before. The farmer proudly told me about their accomplishments, how each piglet immediately after birth found its own way to a nipple of the sow, and how that particular nipple became the personal property of that particular piglet for the whole of the feeding time at the sow. He also commented on the fact that the piglets were all lively and independent, and he compared them favourably with human babies who are unable to make such active movements. I was able to point out that in the case of the pig we would not see much difference in the later development except for size, but the human baby starts in a more dependent stage and yet is able later to reach heights of thought and understanding that seem unparalleled in the animal kingdom. The most significant difference between the human being and other animals is the size of the brain relative to other tissues.

Of all the body organs, the brain of the human infant is nearest at birth to its full size and, therefore, the head is larger in proportion. Perhaps birth can be delayed no further as otherwise the head would be too large to pass through the pelvis of the mother. Birth thus takes place at a stage where the body is immature and where capacity for physical activity and movement is low. Although the human infant compares poorly in this respect with the young of other mammals, the dependence in infancy, prolonged to some extent into childhood and adolescence, allows for the personal transmission of the skills and knowledge of the immediate family and of the culture of the race and, at the same time, allows for the individual response of each new personality to that culture.

Physical growth is rapid, and co-ordinated movements increase in complexity with the growing mastery of the self and the environment. Intellectual growth is represented by the mastery of language and, with a rapidly growing vocabulary, language becomes a factor in the child's growth. During the emotional development there is a conflict between acceptance of the imposed role and the search by the child for his own identity. The child imitates members of his family as a token of his identification with them, and shows negativism in emphasis of his own individuality.

For the landmarks and chronological steps in a wide variety of accomplishments the reader is referred to Chapter 3. It is my purpose, however, to discuss the process through which these developmental stages are reached. Play is an activity which serves as a medium through which the individual develops.

THE NATURE OF PLAY

Play occurs throughout life from infancy to old age, but it is associated particularly with childhood. Play is the opposite of work for the adult, and of lessons for the child. In the industrial north of England a man is said to play (or laik) when he is away from work, even if this is due to unemployment or an industrial dispute. In the austere times of a previous generation, men and children could "play" but the womenfolk always had the responsibility of carrying on the serious business of life.

Play as a leisure activity is difficult to define, as some individuals choose as their relaxation (so called!) the work that others carry out for a living. The wealthy business or professional man may be a weekend farmer and perhaps carry out heavy work, or he may be a yachtsman and master the technicalities of seamanship almost as competently as the regular sailor. In more everyday life the householder, after a week's work in a factory or office, may spend long hours working in his garden or making equipment for his home. Some may find relaxation in inactivity, but in this case there must be a readiness to face the thoughts which come unbidden when the attention is not directed on to some specific focus. Perhaps some people choose deliberately not to "play" in their so-called leisure hours for fear that these thoughts might be unwelcome; and some people occupy their leisure from their primary occupation in activities that are, in effect, alternative occupations.

There are certain factors of all play activity which have been expressed as *theories or descriptive statements regarding play*:

1. Play is *non-adaptive behaviour* and is not directly aimed at essential tasks. Perhaps it is for that reason that many people are intolerant of play because the activity is without an approved end-product.

Non-adaptive behaviour can be an elaboration of essential activities which have a biological or cultural value. This starts with the infant at the breast when the infant loses the nipple and finds it again, by accident. He may continue to let it go and seek it again deliberately, and build this activity up into a game which he enjoys. He may get a reminder from the mother when the game goes on too long, to get on with the serious business of feeding. The conflict of interest between play and work begins early in life !

2. Play has been looked upon as a *recapitulation of the history of the activities of the race*. Children's games have been noted from time to time to have a similarity to primitive man's adult activity. As a general theory this is discredited, but it is a fact that some children's games contain set rituals which resemble primitive religious rites.

3. *Symbolisation* is a feature of play when an object is allowed to represent ideas or other objects. Children develop their imagination in their play with simple objects, allowing them to serve for a variety of purposes. The manufactured toy has a clearer purpose, and the meanings are predetermined by the manufacturer. The simple empty cotton reel on a string trailed behind a child can represent a car, a train or a person. *Symbolisation* allows for ambiguity. In this sense it resembles wit or humour which is the artificial bringing together of incongruous meanings, and which permits the revelation or release of meanings which usually have to be hidden. The obsessional child or adult cannot tolerate the existence of more than one meaning at a time. Such an individual wishes to know the right meaning or use of each object, and that is his way of avoiding the possibility of co-existing ideas which are in conflict with one another.

It is the symbolic quality of play that is used by therapists who look for the representations (in symbolic form) of unconscious thoughts and wishes. In this sense play allows for the revelation of the aspect of mental life which is not ordinarily accessible to consciousness.

THE FUNCTIONS OF PLAY

The purpose served in the personal life of the individual can be

1. *An activity in its own right*. Play has enjoyments and satisfactions that need no other justification.

2. *Recapitulatory*. Children often repeat, in play, activities or events of the previous day whether these have been satisfactory or unsatisfactory. Perhaps this is the way children are able to absorb these activities into their minds. The play becomes an external representation

of the recollections of the activity, and serves as a focus for the integration of the ideas into the personality. In this sense, play has the same functions as some of our dreams, our art products, or our personal efforts to commit thoughts with pen to paper. When we have given body to our thoughts in movements or language, we can deal with them as if they were fresh objects of mental stimulation or inspiration; and we can not only re-absorb them but also use them as starting points for the development of fresh ideas.

3. *Anticipatory.* People practise activities in games, and play at what is in store for them in the future. Pre-school children play at going to school, or at adult occupations or recreations. A child plays at and lives the life of a milkman, a bus conductor, a housewife or a handyman. At an early stage children separate the role of the two sexes with regard to different occupations, but there is some overlap. A boy may want to help mother to cook or to clean, and a girl may help a father with his carpenter's tools. This play at the adult occupation is very little help to the parent who has to carry out the real activities, but, if the fantasy role of the child is rejected, the parent may have the immediate gain of freedom from the help that is a hindrance, but, at a later stage of the child's life, he may have to rebuke him for having no wish to take responsibility for his share of the household chores.

4. *Reparative.* Anxiety-inducing activities may be deliberately reproduced in the safer setting of play, in order that the child might be able to come to terms with them. During the war children played at being bombed; today children who have been inoculated or immunised against infectious illnesses may play with imaginary needles at giving pricks to themselves and others.

5. *Communication.* Although play can be solitary, it more often needs another individual and becomes part of the medium of communication with other children or with adults.

Play thus serves an activity which permits the development of personality through use of the child's mental and physical capacity in learning and in socialisation.

Some of the aspects are *integrative* in a natural and spontaneous way. All these aspects may serve as a medium for therapy. Margaret Loewenfeld* describes play in general terms as "the expression of the child's

* *Play in Childhood*, Gollancz, 1935. Reprinted 1965.

relation to the whole of life. No theory of play is possible which does not cover the whole of the child's relationship to life. Play is therefore taken as applying to all activities in children which are spontaneous and self-generated, that are ends in themselves and that are unrelated to lessons or to the normal physiological needs."

APPROPRIATE LEVELS OF PLAY

There is a need for adults to accept the child's play at the level which is appropriate to the stage of the child, and not to force upon him the adult image of what his activities should be. In the early stages words are inadequate and the child needs materials of play in order to express his mental intake and output. The touch, the smell, the taste and manipulation of materials are all part of his search for realisation (making real as against fantasy) of himself and the outside world. His first objects of play are the products of his own body or the objects introduced into his body through his mouth. He plays with the nipple, or the teat on the bottle, and with the regurgitation of his food. He plays with his saliva long before he learns to play with soap bubbles. Through play he learns first the similarities and then the differences between body products and external objects. Sometimes he attaches a special importance to particular objects which serve as a borderland between himself and the external world. A bit of blanket or paper or some small article or specially selected toy can be preserved by a child for a considerable time. Winnicott* gives the name "transitional object" to articles used by the child which are kept as close personal property and used by the child as intermediate between his idea of what is his body and his idea of what is outside it.

There is a gradual moulding of perceptions of external objects and external events into the idea of space and time. Play serves to organise this into the mind, or psyche, and the new facts are assimilated into existing "schemata" or patterns of thought. It is said that nobody can benefit by the presentation of facts or statements that are completely unrelated to ideas which are already present. Play serves to provide these schemata and forms a bridge between family experience and the outside world. In that sense it is related to education.

* Transitional Objects and Transitional Phenomena, *Int. J. Psycho-Anal.* **35** (1953).

Nevertheless, there is some resistance to the idea of gaining of experience through anything as pleasant as play. It is true that children as well as needing to be free, need to be directed at least part of the time. Even though the child first plays with his food and enjoys the play, and his mother enjoys his enjoyment, she brings him back into the formal and necessary activity in a way which he accepts. At each stage the child needs his framework and also needs his freedom to explore within and a little beyond that framework.

STRUCTURING OF CHILDREN'S PLAY FOR ADULT NEEDS

Manufactured toys are part of the adult framework which is supplied for children. Adult imagination sometimes helps and sometimes imprisons the expression of the child's imagination. Sometimes toys are bought for children's enjoyment and sometimes as an expression of the parent's needs for the child that he imagines, or the child that still exists within himself.

A journalist noticed during the period shortly before Christmas a large number of advertisements in a local paper, of train sets and dolls prams for sale by private individuals. Most of them were described as "in new condition". He wondered whether this was just salesmanship and decided to investigate by making application as a purchaser. He found that these articles really were "as new" and he asked about them. He was told that the child had played with them for a few weeks and then seemed to lose interest. Further enquiries showed that the cost of these articles represented a significant part of the parents' income, and were treasured as important possessions by the parents. The child was only permitted to play with them under the parents' supervision. These articles had never become possessions of the child.

Occasionally when speaking to parents at Parent-Teacher Associations in schools, I am asked by parents, "How do you encourage a child to share his best toys with visitors?" The implication is that the child should treasure the toy and at the same time show the virtue of offering his valued possession as part of the hospitality. If I ask what constitutes "best toys", it turns out that these are the ones that cost the most money and which are not available for the child except on request from the parent. Toys used in this way would appear to have only one purpose, and that would be to transmit to the child the parents' sense of economic values and to become linked with a competitive kind of consumption. This is a teaching of sorts, but a teaching which is unrelated to anything which has been within the range of the child's capacity for fulfilling his own needs. There is no existing framework into which the child can absorb such ideas into his personality.

We can summarise by saying that play is the activity which gives stimulus to the child's mastery of physical skills, his developing intellect, and his emotional relationships. It precedes the kind of formal learning that we call education, and it is a method of absorbing total experience in the period of life before a child is able to deal with the more formal abstractions that become the tools of later intellectual development.

FANTASY, IMAGINATION AND CREATIVITY

We should add a little about the games and make-believe which are a feature of the young child's life, and which leave a residue in the fantasy of older children and adults. There is a link between the game of pretending and dreaming, but children learn to make distinctions between reality and pretence, and in this sense the process is different from dreams.

Sometimes the child's illusions seem to be adopted deliberately in an effort to keep the world of his own free from intrusion by adults. We are familiar with the child's imaginary companion, a fantasy child or animal, and through this companion the child is able to retain some life space around himself into which no adult dare intrude. It is exasperating to the parent, and many parents are greatly disturbed by the child's fantasies of strange events and scenes which are described in great detail. The parents are concerned about this virtue of truthfulness and the vice of falsehood, and perhaps they are also concerned about the existence of a private world in the child's mind which they cannot really share.

Is it surprising that the child should have this private world when parents have their own world and talk to each other about affairs which are not supposed to be understandable by the child? They may even continue to talk in voices that he can hear but in words that he cannot understand.

Some fantasies the child accepts ready-made from the adult, and the parent is more tolerant and may even cherish the childlike illusions which are traditional, such as the existence of Father Christmas. For the most part we relinquish our fantasies voluntarily and the child learns to maintain an equilibrium between his private world and what he learns to perceive as reality. Perhaps we learn to recognise reality in the image of our parents' perceptions as they are presented to us. We learn about ourselves from the way that adults treat us. Our identity becomes secure when we are treated with respect, and in this we can agree with George Bernard Shaw who allowed it to be said in the play *Pygmalion* that the definition of a lady is one who is treated as a lady.

Unhealthy development of personality could be the product of a child's perception of himself with the eyes of the adult who does not value the life of childhood, and who judges the child's behaviour on the model of a scaled-down adult.

L. K. Frank emphasised the creative quality of the ever-changing roles of masculine and feminine that the child could adopt and abandon because he is not yet finally committed.* Play is tentative, a child through play can relate himself to his past and then reorientate himself into the present. He recapitulates experiences, assimilates them into new perceptions and advances into the future. Perhaps this is what Winnicott meant when he stated that part of the mother's job is to help the child "to catch hold of time".

---

* L. K. FRANK, Therapeutic Play Techniques, *Amer. J. Orthopsychiat.* (1945).

CHAPTER 12

Social Problems of Education

COMPULSION

Universal and compulsory education in Great Britain began with the 1870 Education Act. Previously, education had been organised on a voluntary basis. Many important grammar schools existed, and, in addition, the churches and various charity schools provided a wider range of education for poor children. There remained at that time a considerable section of the population which was illiterate because of the lack of opportunity to learn.

The impetus for the comprehensive educational system for the nation came from the attempt to deal with poverty and disease, which had become linked in the mind of reformers with ignorance. The 1870 Act created School Boards which were given the power to levy rates, provide buildings and employ teachers. The subsequent Acts of 1876 and 1880 made elementary education compulsory up to the age of 11 years. By 1918 school attendance had become compulsory up to the age of 14, and the 1944 Education Act made provision for the school-leaving age of 16, but allowed school leaving at the age of 15 for the time being. Also in this Act, arrangements were made for the separation of secondary education (after the age of 11) from primary education which consists of infant and junior school life.

INCREASED PROVISION FOR SECONDARY EDUCATION

Secondary education on the pattern of the independent grammar schools had become available in the early part of the century to a wider range of pupils without fees, as a result of selection by examination. An increasing number of Local Education Authorities provided secondary schools where the criterion was the possession of a certain intelligence level and not the ability to pay fees.

The 1944 Education Act contained some provisions which had been foreshadowed by the Hadow Report of 1926 and the Spens Report of 1938, and a new level of secondary education of different categories was to be made available for all. Selection was to be made on intelligence level and, to some extent, on attainment, but there was the aim of providing equality of esteem in the different kinds of secondary school.

Independent grammar schools and privately organised boarding and public schools remain a small but important part of the educational provision of the country; and educational categories become clearly marked out as the curriculum of different schools becomes more exclusively the pathway to different kinds of careers.

The types of secondary education will be discussed later, but the existence of these differences in educational provision casts a shadow on the infant and junior school, and many parents begin their anxieties about the prospect of their children's academic training in particular careers at the moment when the child enters school. Even in local authority areas where comprehensive education has made the secondary selection examination (the Eleven plus) superfluous, there is still an awareness that early streaming in junior schools can influence the internal selection procedure which will take place within the comprehensive system of secondary schools. Some parents and some teachers favour formal teaching in reading, writing and arithmetic during the infant school stage in anticipation of the placing of children into categories, according to performance, in the junior school—ignoring the ways in which the capacities for these activities vary from child to child in their rate of development.

AGE, ABILITY AND TYPE OF SCHOOL

Some parents are content for the infant school to be the place where the child learns to play with other children and at the same time, gain experience of the manipulation of materials and of ideas in a way that is enjoyable. The place of the infant school in the child's education will be discussed later.

At the age of 7 the child passes on to another department of the same school or to another school, and makes a new beginning in what is called the junior school. Here it is expected that there should be a greater degree of direction of attention to formal learning. At this stage, too, there is direction of attention to the differing abilities of children. Some children are recognised for the first time as having an ability which is significantly below the average, and these are separated from ordinary classes. These are called "educationally subnormal" children (E.S.N.), and their education may continue either in a special class in an ordinary school or in a special school. Intelligence level is not the only criterion, and the child may come to the notice of the teacher of an ordinary school in the first place because of abnormalities in his total reaction to the educational setting. Educational subnormality is thus an educational concept and relates to a level of performance in school, and it is not the equivalent of a clinical diagnosis. There is a certain amount of formality in the procedure for the ascertainment of educational subnormality, and this includes an intelligence assessment carried out by the educational psychologist and/or one of the school medical officers. The latter also carries out a medical examination. The observations from these examinations, together with the details of the personal and family history, are usually discussed at a conference between representatives of the Child Health Service and of the Education Department.

Purely on the level of I.Q., the E.S.N. group of children are often considered to be those in the range between 50 and 70. In practice, a large number of children with I.Q.s down to 60, and sometimes a little below, are able to remain profitably in the ordinary school; and some with an I.Q. over 70 need the special facilities of the E.S.N. school.

SEVERE MENTAL HANDICAP: HETEROGENEOUS GROUP

Amongst the children with an I.Q. of under 50, there are a number who differ from the majority in no other respect than the low intelligence level. They represent the lower end of the normal distribution curve. In addition to these, however, there are children whose low intellectual ability and performance is the result of congenital physical abnormalities, or chromosome anomalies—such as mongolism—and there is a further group in which the mental handicap is the result of irreversible damage to the central nervous system as a result of complications of pregnancy and the peri-natal period. Some of these complications are themselves resultant of factors associated with social class groupings.* Severe pre-eclamptic toxaemia, low birth weight, form a complex which is related to the stresses which impinge more heavily on mothers with a starting point of lower than average physical state of health and who receive less than optimum standard of obstetric care.

Thus children who are called severely subnormal, in the terms of the 1959 Mental Health Act, do not form a homogeneous category. Up to the present, however, without much discrimination between them, such children were excluded from the educational system, either because they could not benefit from schooling or because their presence was disturbing to other children. Many health departments of local authorities made provision for the day-care of these children. At first the units were called Occupational Centres because the idea was to relieve the burden which the child's handicap placed upon the parent, and at the same time, to find some activity for the children. The idea of occupation gave way to the idea of social training—hence the name "Training Centres"—but in some localities emphasis was placed not on the incapacity which the child suffered from his mental defect but on the capacities which remained and could be developed. It became an assumption that some intellectual growth was possible along with the physical growth, even though this would be at a slower rate than that in the average child. It was also recognised that there would be emotional distress in the child and in the family because of the strain of expectations which were either too high or too low for the child's capacity.

Some modern purpose-built training centres incorporated, in the architectural structure, provision for intellectual growth by means of teaching of the nursery school type, increasing slowly in complexity at each age range; provision for emotional growth through play, creative activities, and psychotherapy; in addition, those who needed it were given physiotherapy, speech therapy, and general medical care. The basic concept was not that of formal "educability" but of "developability".

* H. G. BIRCH et al., *Mental Subnormality in the Community*, Williams & Wilkins, Baltimore, U.S.A., 1970.

EDUCATION OF THE HANDICAPPED: THE NEED FOR MULTI-DISCIPLINARY SERVICES

Experience of the progress which has become possible in these training centres under the organisation of Health Departments has given the Education Department the confidence to take back into its system the responsibility for the education of the entire group of mentally handicapped children, whether educationally subnormal E.S.N. or severely subnormal S.S.N. The transfer of responsibility from Health Departments to Education Departments formally took place on 1st April, 1971.

This transfer will have important social consequences in the uniting of the whole child population as requiring educational provision. It is to be hoped, however, that there will be no illusion that teaching alone will give every child the resources for optimum development. Some forms of mental handicap are the result of social deprivation, some of physical abnormality, and in all of them there is the need to consider the interaction of the physical environment, the social and family background, and the child's individual constitutional and developmental history.* Even within the educational system there is the need for specialised and multi-disciplinary assessment and reassessment. The same considerations apply in the E.S.N. school and in the special schools for sensory and physical handicap.

SPECIAL CLASSES OR SCHOOLS AS OPTIMUM PLACEMENT

Parents are often distressed when their children are transferred from an ordinary school to a special school for E.S.N. pupils, and sometimes they make formal representations to resist the change of status. Sometimes it is suggested that earlier placement would be an advantage whenever it is possible to recognise the limited level of ability, and this would require infant or nursery departments in the E.S.N. school and also in the training centres. This actually does occur in some areas. It is argued by others that children ought to have what is called a "fair chance" in the ordinary school. This would be valid if the education in the special school should be inferior to that in the ordinary school. If,

* J. H. KAHN and J. REDMAN in *Social Work*, Jan. 1969.

however, the education in the special schools (or special classes) is more appropriate to a particular child than ordinary school life, it could not be considered that it gives a child a fair chance if he is denied the appropriate kind of treatment, and instead is put into a setting where he feels inadequate, and where he receives nothing in the way of education that he is capable of absorbing. This situation is frequently made even worse by the fact that the process of ascertainment might be set going after an incident in which the child has misbehaved. It would appear to the parent that subsequent placement is more concerned with excluding the child from the original setting than with finding something more appropriate for him.

The kind of specialisation of teaching which can benefit these children has not been reached without considerable doubt as to the value or otherwise of segregation of pupils. Many people are loath to admit such wide variations in the ability of children, and argue either that it is bad for children to realise they have a lower ability than the average, by being separated, or, alternatively, that it is good for children of higher intelligence to have the children of lower grade intelligence with them, as part of the building of their characters.

The same problem arises with children who are handicapped by sensory defects—children who have partial sight, i.e. with various degrees of blindness, or the children who have defective hearing, i.e. children with various degrees of deafness. There are also physically handicapped children, and, since the 1944 Education Act, there has been recognition of the need for special educational provision for children who are emotionally maladjusted.

The various categories of handicapped children may be educated in special schools—day schools or residential schools—or sometimes in special classes in ordinary schools. The same conflict of view exists as with difference of intelligence as to whether children with various kinds of handicap should be educated apart from the ordinary range of school children, or whether some attempt should be made to educate them within the ordinary school system.

The division of children into different categories according to intelligence level or type of handicap at this stage is as controversial a one as the division into further categories after the age of 11. It is as if the kind of school gives a label to, and determines the future of, any particular child. Often there is concern to get a child into the highest ranking school (educationally) as possible. It is believed that it is the type of school that determines the child's ability rather than ability of a child which determines the kind of school in which he should be placed.

It is a fact, too, that schools of the same category differ in their reputation. Sometimes a reputation in producing high academic results is self-continuing. Ambitious parents, who themselves have reached their higher ranking occupational levels, are likely to be drawn, to a proportionately greater extent than the population generally, from the higher intelligence levels; and amongst their children will be a likelihood of a higher than average proportion of individuals of high intelligence.

When there is pressure from these people for places for their children in a particular school, there would be a tendency to raise the average intelligence level within that school. Schools in districts where there is a distinctive distribution of social classes are likely to have an unusual distribution of intelligence level of the children attending.

SOCIAL INTERACTION OF SCHOOL AND HOME

Schools differ also in the social interaction between the families and the schools in different areas. In predominantly middle-class areas the educational aims of the school are fully accepted by the parents, sometimes even to the extent of reproducing at home the same kind of educational pressure as exists within the school.

Even in the private sector of education there are preparatory schools and grammar schools where selection becomes more and more geared to the measurement of intelligence. Many middle-class parents begin to fear that social mobility can be downwards as well as upwards, and that unless the child can be groomed for academic education from an early stage, he will be subsequently barred from entry into the channels that lead to professional training. Some middle-class children are subjected to homework after school, and special coaching, from the very moment of school entry. School ceases to be a social experience because the childdren are competitors and not playmates. Even children of high intelligence are subjected to these pressures in order to keep level with the advantages given to other children, and the result often is lower rather than higher performance because of the strain imposed when the reward of success is to have even higher standards of success demanded.

There is a special problem in metropolitan and large urban areas where there is a uniform concentration of working-class occupation over an extensive area. The ideology of the teacher (whatever his original class) is middle class. His approval goes to the attitudes and types of performance which are acceptable in middle-class areas, and he is frequently hostile to the working-class culture. A child may learn to adapt to the two cultures of home and school, or may become hostile to one or the other. This division becomes more marked at the secondary school stage, but it exists even within the primary school.

The different categories of education have been devised to fit differing ranges of cognitive or intellectual abilities of children, but social factors and social consequences are inescapable.

Intelligence has been stated to have a large genetic component, and yet the growth of intelligence, as against the initial potentiality, depends upon the total range of experiences which are post-natal. Among children of highly intelligent parents there is likely to be, as stated above, a higher than average proportion of individuals of high intelligence. Those parents of average and less than average intelligence will have a smaller proportion of children of high intelligence. Numerically, however, a small proportion of a large section of the community can be as great as a large proportion of a small section of the community!

NEW PROBLEMS REVEALED BY INCREASED
EDUCATIONAL PROVISION

The attempt to democratise education has revealed or created new problems. Some children of high intelligence may be selected for advanced education and yet fail because of lack of stimulation and fulfilment within their homes (and sometimes even within their schools). Others may have advantages of wealth and culture but, in an increasingly competitive educational world, fee paying is no longer a sufficient factor in itself for entry into advanced education. Children of families who at one time could have guaranteed succession in high-ranking occupations may now find themselves barred as a result of modern selection methods. There is thus constant change in the social distribution of intelligence in different successive generations. It is not possible to guarantee to one's children the inheritance of a particular intelligence level, yet the fact remains that the kind of experience and stimulation given to the children of parents of high intelligence is likely to develop to the fullest extent whatever intellectual potentiality exists.

The lowest levels of ability create a different problem. Some levels of mental handicap have been revealed by the very education which was intended to remove illiteracy. Wherever a significant section of the population remained without *any* education, it was possible to hope that the general provision of education would bring *all* up to the same level. When education has been provided, and some still remain beyond its reach, other explanations have to be found. It has already been stated that mental retardation is explained partly as representing the lower levels of intelligence which occur naturally in what is called the normal distribution of intelligence in the population. Others are mentally retarded as a result of injury or disease, particularly of the brain, occurring before, during or shortly after birth. The latter category is universally recognised, but there are many who refuse to believe that there is any difference in the intellectual potentiality of the normal range of children. It can be a matter of political belief that all men are equal in ability. Any differences in adult performance would then be due to the withholding of opportunities, or the differences in experiences which are dependent upon financial provisions or on social class. If it should occur that, even with equality of provision, some children still show differing responses to education, those who believe in inherent equality must also conclude that either those who fail do not avail themselves of the opportunity, and are at fault, or that they have suffered some disease which prevents them from doing so.

EDUCATION AND THE MENTALLY HANDICAPPED CHILD

Philosophy of education, and philosophy of treatment of mental retardation, depends upon the prevailing culture or political belief. We have referred to the middle-class parent who presses his child in the belief that hard work will bring any child up to the level demanded for selection for grammar school education. There are also those who believe that concentration on schoolwork will raise the mentally retarded child up to average performance. Luria, who has enlarged our perceptions on the function of speech in the development of personality, has recently written about the mentally retarded child in Russia,* and, in doing so, he gives incidentally some enlightenment on the educational aims in the schools of that country. His is an environmental philosophy, and the schoolchildren he studies are expected never "to direct their behaviour or use their knowledge to carry out some task other than the one prescribed".

Communication of language to a child is thought of as being in terms of commands and prohibitions—"Do this" and "Don't do that". This is the *regularity* function of speech.

> The child of school age finds himself in circumstances where he needs to study according to a strict programme prescribed by the teacher. This means that the child must not behave in accordance with the dictates of his personal motives and needs, but must carry out the orders of the teacher, and follow his spoken instructions all the time. He must remain within the limits set by the instructions given him, and must not allow his attention to wander on to the irrelevant things. Psychologically speaking this means that all the motives behind the activities of the child who has just attained school age must be reorganised, so that the basic motive influencing behaviour during lesson time must become "the directions of the teacher".

The child who rebels against this routine, or who fails to show ability to concentrate, becomes regarded as one who has suffered some serious brain pathology during early uterine life.

EQUALITY OR UNIQUENESS OF INDIVIDUAL

It would be easy to find fault with the underlying concepts of much of Luria's writings, and yet our own educational philosophy is far from uniform either in its presentation or acceptance.

The modern educationalist in this country is committed to a theory of uniqueness rather than equality of the individual, and to the practice of helping each child to express himself at his own particular level of ability. This involves differentials in expectations, and acceptance of variations in the routine progress. There are arrangements for different schools for children with different levels of ability or different degrees

---

* Prof. A. H. Luria, *The Mentally Retarded Child*, Pergamon Press, 1963.

of handicap. There are different educational streams within the same age range, and different rates of progress are possible in different groups even within the same class. The teacher becomes concerned with the personal life of the child, and with the social interactions of children as well as with the level of scholastic attainment. He becomes sensitive to the wider variations between children, and to the changing response of an individual child. This makes more demands on the teacher than a philosophy which assumes that the teacher gives a constant amount of information which the children absorb in various proportions according to their co-operativeness, diligence, and voluntary concentration on the work.

Where freedom is given to children to find their own level of response, new levels of creativity may be reached. Teaching can become a joint adventure between children and teacher in which, at times, both parties reach some point of understanding at the same moment. But this freedom needs a framework, and the child needs the imposition of some standards in the school in the same way that he needs them at home.

The development of *professional* concepts brings about points of change which are alternatively crisis events or stepping stones, similar to the way-stations in *personal* development. Old certainties and adjustments are destroyed before the new ones are able to give their satisfactions; and there are regrets for the advantages that came from old methods. The greatest anxiety exists when old practices are given up before the new ones have been comprehended, and disappointments are greatest when methods are changed while retaining the desire for the results which were believed to come from the former practice.

Children in present-day schools may appear more self-confident and self-assertive, and may approach the adult with a feeling of social equality. The respect for rules has to be a much more subtle process, and it is likely to break down when there is an attempt to enforce it by methods which were appropriate to a more subdued generation.

The time comes when concentration on scholastic work is possible as a voluntary effort of the child, and the attitude to work will depend upon the acceptance by the child of the ideology of the school. A framework of compulsion is necessary. It is a reassurance to the child to know that at times he has no option but to work. But compulsion itself is a process in which the child *gives* authority to the teacher and, in more abstract terms, to the community. It is rule by consent.

There is a need to build a bridge between the culture of the home and the culture of the school. In the home there should be respect for the process of education, and, in the school, respect for the separate culture of the home locality. Where the two cultures are not in contact, the child rebels in one place or the other, or in both. Sometimes a gap in the cultures exists because parents who recollect their own strict upbringing at home and in school with affection, look upon modern educational methods with suspicion.

There may be other cases where school and home together lag behind the prevailing culture of the outside world, and where the children form a rebellious group deriving an ideology from the wealth of stimulation of the mass media.

Rapid technical change and rapid change of culture produces uncertainty until new techniques and adaptations become more coherent.

CHAPTER 13

Primary Education

INFANT SCHOOL (THE CHILD FROM 5 TO 7 YEARS)

This period is marked out culturally as the age of infant school attendance. Physically it is a period of rapid growth. It is one of the "shooting-up" periods, that is, one of several stages which are marked by rapid growing followed by a "filling-out" process. There is such a period in the early toddler stage, and again in early adolescence. The years 5 to 7 also include a period where there is a maturing of some of the structures in the central nervous system, and this can be recognised by changes in recordings on an electroencephalogram. The maturation in structure is accompanied by maturation in function, and it is at about this time that there is development in the capacity of the child to adapt to external conditions, and to see the outside world more nearly as it appears to others, and less as a part of his own fantasies. The child develops a greater capacity for directed thinking.

The emotional life keeps pace with other aspects of development, and the entry into school shows recognition of the need of the average child to achieve a degree of separation from the home, and to enter into activities of the outside world.

CULTURALLY DETERMINED ACTIVITIES

School attendance begins arbitrarily in Great Britain at the age of 5 years and, although in most countries in Europe school entry comes later, the vast majority of children are ready for the break from home life at this age. Some of the developmental phases come gradually, and some follow a definite break between one phase and the next. The rate of development physically, intellectually and emotionally varies, and,

139

although a child's life should be considered as a whole, the different aspects do not always develop in step with one another.

The role of the child in society varies with the culture, and it alters along with technical changes in the background of community life. In some primitive cultures, adult activities are simple enough for the child to be able to enter into them at a comparatively early age. The sex role becomes distinct from the beginning; the boys helping the men in the search for food, hunting, fishing, trapping and sometimes helping even in their fighting; the girls helping the women with the cooking, washing, and with the caring for the younger children. With industrialisation, the child became valuable in economic terms, and children were introduced into factories at much the same age as when formerly they would have been of help in the house. During the nineteenth century the economic value of the child in poorer homes was the prime factor, and their lives were expendable. Even in homes where there was more regard to the value of the child in his own right, there was still a social distinction between children and their parents. In the middle-class home there could be three levels of provision in food, clothing, and accommodation —the best for the parents, a grade lower for the children and a still lower grade for servants. It was not merely a selection out of the food which was available in the house—three different qualities of food were deliberately purchased. This was the "adult-centred" or "employer-centred" world.

The present-day home is "child-centred" rather than adult-centred, and often it is the children who receive the highest quality and more expensive items.

The physique of children today shows an improvement over that of children born a generation ago.* Children of today are taller and healthier than their grandparents were at the same age. There is an improvement in general health; better hygiene and diet lead to a greater resistance to infections in general, and there is increased immunity to specific diseases as a result of inoculation for diphtheria, whooping cough, tetanus and, sometimes, tuberculosis.

---

* "Cosy myth that all is now well." In spite of the general improvement, Dr. Harriett Wilson stated that there are still some 500,000 children in Britain who live below the minimum standards laid down by the Ministry of Social Security. *The Times*, 19th Dec., 1966.

The needs of the growing intellect at this period are met by the beginnings of school life, but, at this stage in particular, education is not a matter of intellect alone. The wholeness of body and mind is reflected in the practice of the modern infant school which is a place where the child plays, eats, drinks, goes to the lavatory, washes his hands, dresses and undresses, and learns new levels of control of body processes. These activities are the learning of new skills and are also part of the child's emotional life. Infant school may be the first experience that most children can have of life away from home, although a few may have had previous attendance at a day nursery or nursery school.

The emotional aspect of the change to school implies the capacity to separate from the mother. There have been progressive stages in the child's life; the exclusiveness of the tie between the mother and child is broken into when relationships develop with the father and with brothers and sisters. Family life has begun. The child now extends his range of contacts and relationships to include other individuals in his neighbourhood and more remote family. School is more definitely a life in the outside world.

Some children may not be ready for the separation, and sometimes the parents may not be ready. The parents have had control of the child's environment, and the child has had a close relationship with both parents. Even his relationships with his siblings is closely bound up with his relationship to the parents—every child thinks of his brothers and sisters in relation to the part that they play in his life with his parents. The normal resolution of the oedipal situation permits the child to accept a life with children of his own age as equals.

TRANSFERENCE TO THE TEACHER

Some part of the child's fantasy relationships with his parents remains, and some of it becomes transferred to the teacher when the child begins school life. The teacher inherits the role that the child has formerly attributed to his parents. The magical qualities which the child believes are possessed by the parents, and which can be used sometimes for his benefit, and sometimes against him, disappear when the child begins to see his parents more realistically as fallible human beings where goodness and badness can exist in the same person. The child also relinquishes his own wishes for magical powers, and he is grateful that his parents survive his bad thoughts as well as responding to his good ones. The teacher at this stage succeeds to some traces of the child's primitive image of the parents. The teacher knows everything and seems to be able to see right into the child's mind.

The teacher is also a figure in his own right who allows the child to develop new levels of relationships with an adult, and from whom the child absorbs qualities which he adds to his own personality. Some of these qualities are taken in unconsciously by the process which has been called introjection, and there is also the process of a more conscious identification by a child with the qualities of a teacher whom he admires and maybe loves.

RULES AND RESTRICTIONS

At the time of school entry, the parents and the child alike need to be ready to allow some transfer of the relationships which had previously been confined to the home setting. School entry implies a life with a large number of other children, as equals, whose rights have to be respected. It is therefore a limitation of the child's demand for undivided adult attention. It includes a certain amount of observance of rules, and children need some preparation in advance for the acceptance of restrictions on their demands for immediate personal gratification. Normally this preparation has been provided within the home in doses that the child has been able to tolerate.

Children who have never had a reasonable restriction of activity may find school intolerable. Others are unable to make the transfer from relationship with a parent to relationship with the teacher because child and parent are so closely dependent upon one another that separation would cause distress to both parties.

Separation from the mother at some stages of the child's life has been discussed from the point of view of the damage caused to the child's emotional development, but there are stages where the capacity to separate is the indication of progress. Some children make such rapid progress that they are ready to separate from the mother to the school at an earlier stage that 5 years of age. Separation could be a part of further progress from a home which has been a good home. Other children need placement at some kind of nursery school or day nursery as a substitute for a home which is unsatisfactory and where progress has *not* been made, either because the mother is not there, or because her capacity to supply the child's needs is too limited.

These two different kinds of needs and purposes may be served in a single nursery school or day nursery, and it is necessary to distinguish between the two purposes. In one case, the school or nursery is an extension of the home; in the other, it is a substitute for it.

Infant school is a transitional process between a life representing a home and the more directed educational type of establishment represented by the schools which the child will attend later. The infant school introduces limitations of behaviour in a form which is acceptable and which is within the capacity of the child to tolerate. It legitimatises some of the natural outlets of expression of the child's physical, intellectual and emotional life, and sharpens his interests in his surroundings.

SOCIAL LEARNING IN GROUPS

Part of the purpose of the infant school is to bring the child into social relationships with other children. This aim affects even the arrangement of the furniture in the school. At times the children sit at small tables where a group of four, around the table, can share a task or work independently. At other times, children may form a half-circle facing the teacher, and on many occasions there is a going to and fro around the room with complex and changing participation of different groupings. In these arrangements it is assumed that when children are talking to each other they are being good. The more traditional placement of children in parallel rows, all facing the teacher, was for the purpose of maintaining a relationship of each separate child directly with the teacher and not of the children with one another. The children who are side to side or front to back have difficulty in communication with one another, except by interrupting the allotted task. Talking to one another is bad. It was assumed that the main purpose of the school was the absorption of knowledge and no thought was given during school time to the idea of setting patterns for the formation of social relationships with equals. The formal pattern imposed some strain on the teacher in keeping order, but the aim was clear. The informal arrangement demands flexibility from the teacher in order to be able to accept and utilise unexpected responses in both work and play activity. It also brings unexpected pleasures.

Formal learning has its place, and there are developmental steps in the child when he is ready to read, to make abstractions of ideas, and to form concepts. The stage of readiness has been linked with the structural maturities referred to above, and which are recognised physiologically by electrical changes in the activities of the central nervous system. These steps can also be recognised by psychologists who work on the lines of Piaget.* They occur at different ages in different children, and we cannot force these new areas of comprehension before the child is ready.

WORDS, SYMBOLS AND MENTAL CONCEPTS

Language is an instrument of mental progress.†‡§ Words are the tools of communication, and they are also the material which permit our mental processes to grow. The power to keep in mind a mental representation of objects which are not within the range of vision depends upon words. Words stand as *symbols* for objects, and later as symbols for more complex ideas. We build up concepts with words and numbers, and even the simplest mathematical concepts are more complex than they at first appear. We can say that one and one make two, but this is a complicated process of abstraction! One pint of milk can be added to another pint of milk and that makes two pints. The addition actually has taken place. We have one apple, and another apple, and then we have two apples, but the apples have not been added to one another. The addition has been done in our minds. If we have an apple and a pear and say we have two pieces of fruit we have first to abstract the quality of the unity of each piece, and also to abstract the quality that they have in common of both being a fruit. It is some considerable time before children reach the step when these mental manipulations have any real meaning, and these steps cannot be hurried.

* J. PIAGET, *The Child's Conception of Number*, 1952; *The Child's Construction of Reality*, 1955. Routledge & Kegan Paul.

† B. BERNSTEIN, Aspects of language and learning in the genesis of the social process, *J. of Child Psychol. and Psychiat.* (1961).

‡ F. D. FLOWER, *Language and Education*, Longmans, London, 1966.

§ A. T. RAVENETTE, *Dimensions of Reading Difficulties*, Pergamon Press, 1968.

At the proper time these complex processes are taken for granted and the means by which we reach them are forgotten.

Children with a poor verbal background may become retarded in their development, and there are some children who are unable to speak even at the time of school entry. A child may have a poor vocabulary because the verbal background of his parents is impoverished, but some children with highly intellectual and articulate parents may be delayed in the beginning of speech. This is sometimes thought to be due to the fact that the child doesn't *have* to speak, as he gets what he wants without having to ask for it. The suggestion is then made that he should not be given anything (meaning his food) unless he asks for it. The suggestion that he gets what he wants without speech is a partial truth. He gets what he wants in actual fact without being spoken *to*. Some parents feel unable to give the child a running commentary at a childish level as an accompaniment to his material necessities. The conversation that exists in the home is between mother and father at an adult level, and it almost appears as if they are waiting for the child to join in at this level. Eventually he does!

It is necessary to recognise that a child differs from an adult and that he is not a small edition of an adult. Children should be judged by standards that apply to childhood, and just as the standards of adult life cannot be scaled down to form a measure for the child's performance, it would be equally inappropriate to scale up the mental life of a child and expect it to represent the mental life of an adult. The normal mental life of a small child contains such a high proportion of fantasy that it would be diagnostic of insanity if it occurred in an adult, and yet this level of fantasy is normal for the child!

We must also remember to consider the child not only as having a different kind of existence from the adult, but also a personality which is in the process of formation and change, and with its own special vulnerabilities. Our picture of the child's personality needs to be considered not in isolation, but in relationship to other children of the same age at the same stage of development, and also in relationship to his environment.

SENSE OF IDENTITY

The child needs to develop a sense of identity, to know his name and to feel a sense of separateness as well as of belonging, to have possessions, to have a sense of being which is gained by the communication to him of the image that other people have of him. He begins to respect himself when adults show respect and concern for his separateness. Then and then only does he learn to respect the separate identity, the personality, the possessions and the rights of other children.

A conscious sense of morality is gained gradually as distinct from the irrational prohibitions that form part of the superego. He begins to observe the rules because the rules now appear to be rational and capable of being observed.

There is a problem at home and at school of children who defy and ignore rules. At home the children who have these problems usually have parents who are either very strict or who have no rules at all. Some parents make a line of demarcation around the child's permitted conduct, and the circle is so small that it is inevitable that the child's *normal* activities should pass beyond the permitted area. Having, in his *normal* activities, gone beyond the boundary set by his parents, there is then no further boundary to prevent him from passing into areas of conduct which are considered abnormal by general agreement. Thus the child of overstrict parents shows *no discrimination in his misbehaviour*!

Parents who offer their children no rules at all cannot expect obedience or that the child's behaviour can depend upon his own inner controls. Peace can be bought from time to time by giving in to whatever the child feels he ought to demand. This is sometimes thought of as giving the child what he wants, but such a child has no means of knowing what he wants. He can only guess at what he is expected to demand and does his best to demand it.

EXPECTATIONS AND IMAGES OF SCHOOL AND TEACHER

The majority of children have some image of school life and of the teacher's role before attending school. They learn about it from their brothers and sisters or from the children of their neighbours, and they play at school before they actually attend. The "only" child who has little contact with other children does not get a coherent picture of school in advance and is rather less prepared. Most children, however, have a picture of what to expect. The image of the teacher and of school life helps the teacher to maintain his own role. A large class if kept under control by a single teacher partly because of the child's adaptation to his expected role; the school becomes part of the child's culture. If the child has not included the school in the culture that he has so far absorbed, the teacher has to deal with him without the help of the normal child's ready acceptance to school life. The teacher then has to depend upon his own personality and gets no assistance from his professional role. Granted variations in individual capacity, it is not surprising that some teachers find it more difficult than others in dealing with the exceptionally unruly child.

The child who has not yet absorbed inner restrictions, and the child with inappropriate ones, are equally outside the normal range. The child with unresolved oedipal anxieties, who still inflates himself in his fantasies, and attempts to deal with adults at an equal level of rivalry, threatens the teacher who himself might have residues of childish anxieties. Most people at times feel that they are still small children acting the part of grown-ups, and they are afraid of being found out. Most adults have feelings of inadequacy which make them vulnerable, at times, to threats. The adult is partly protected by the general acceptance of his adult status, and the professional person has the additional safeguard of the recognition of his professional standing. It is very disturbing when an adult's professional status is challenged even by a small child. The danger of relying too exclusively on the status of the role is that there is nothing that remains but exclusion for those children who challenge that role.

Parents sometimes wish for a school to have complete success in restricting a child who has been over-active at home; yet if the permitted range has been too narrow, and the child's normal activity has become abnormal by definition, then in time it becomes abnormal in reality. Such children fear the different framework within the school as much as they defy it. School represents the authority of the community and he excludes himself from identification with the community. He has now become anti-social.

FREEDOM WITHIN A FRAMEWORK

The teacher who can accept such problems has to rely more on his personal resources, and needs a wide concept of the educational process. He becomes able to think of education as serving intellectual, emotional and social needs in one combination, and he is able to allow the child to achieve satisfaction in a wider and changing range of activities. Art, music and poetry have long been recognised as giving access to the child's *feelings* rather than to his intellect, and thus help the child's emotional development. The ability of a teacher to change the nature of the activity of a class from moment to moment can help to legitimatise the activity of some children in cases where it would become an open challenge to the teacher if he were to attempt to enforce the continuance of a set programme.

Challenges which do occur may be dealt with at times by force of character or physical force, but such challenges also lead to division between those who conform and those who do not. Sometimes, those who do not conform are merely excluded. Some teachers and other professional workers interpret the contemporary change from completely repressive control as meaning that discipline is no longer necessary or advisable. They offer freedom from discipline and hope that order will spontaneously emerge! They find chaos instead. A framework is necessary even if it is a less restrictive one than was formerly applied. There is a level of freedom which allows the child to develop creatively in the realms of movement, learning, and joining in social activities, and every stage is a new adventure. Children develop more quickly if each one can go at the pace which he is ready for at each stage of maturation of body and mind. A class of small children are all at different stages of development and, although they can have many joint activities, uniformity should never be looked for.

Freedom needs restriction at the point where the child asks for restraint. It is as if a bargain is made. "I will let go if you will keep me safe." The teacher needs to be able to anticipate the point of danger and to be able to bring the child back within acceptable boundaries before he has gone too far.

A time comes when concentration on formal learning and conscious thought are within the range of the child's mental structure but, even then, the child needs permission at times a regress to earlier patterns.

THE CHILD FROM 7 TO 11 (JUNIOR SCHOOL)

At the age of 7 years, school life begins to take a greater importance in the total experience of the child. He is more ready for formal aspects of learning, but the newer concepts of education look upon the learning process as an aspect of total experience in which the emotional life is as important as the purely intellectual.

The period is one where physical growth continues but not as rapidly as at the earlier stages. Physical skills increase and these derive as much from the informal activity of children playing together as from formal physical education.

THE SECRET LIFE OF CHILDHOOD

The emotional life, too, becomes more bound up with brothers and sisters and with classmates than with adults, and the social life of children of this age begins to develop as something apart. Perhaps there is less information about the mental life of children of this age than of any other age. They have become partly released from the boundaries of home, and they are beginning to have their secret games. There is a folklore that appears to be transmitted from one generation of children to another, yet leaving little recollection in the minds of the adults whom they eventually become.

Examination has been made of the verses* that children repeat and the games that they play, and interesting facts about the rapid spread of these activities over widely scattered areas of the country have been discovered. Work has also been done on the child's creativity in poetry† and other art forms‡ and on the part played by these creations on the development of the child's personality.

The school life becomes representative of all aspects of personality. The School Health Service is concerned with the physical and mental

* Opie, *Lore and Language of Schoolchildren*, Clarendon Press, 1959.
† Marjorie L. Hourd, *Coming into Their Own*, Heinemann, 1959.
‡ Herbert Read, *Education through Art*, Faber & Faber, 1943.

health of children and the making sure of provision for any treatment which is found to be necessary. Hearing and sight are checked; meals and clothing can be provided free on the grounds that children need to be in good health and well fed and clothed in order to benefit from education.

VARIATIONS IN ABILITY

The learning process begins to reveal variations in ability, and junior school life is often the beginning of segregation. The problem of "streaming" children according to ability is a controversial one. When schools are small, with a single class for each calendar year of the children's age range, there may be children of vastly differing ability in one class. In larger schools there can be several classes for each year, and it becomes possible to separate the class according to the intelligence rating of the children. There may be A, B and C streams or even more in each form.

It is recognised that the children of higher intelligence make rapid progress when working together, but it is sometimes implied that the teachers are separated according to ability at the same time as the children! If that is so, then children of low intelligence may make less than optimal progress merely by being downgraded educationally. An even greater danger occurs when the selection into classes is made on criteria that are uncertain.

It is necessary, nevertheless, to recognise differences of ability, and to accept that there is no educational process than can bring all children up to the same level. It is also necessary to realise that a child not only does not benefit from attempts to education at a higher level than he is capable of—it does him positive harm.

LEVELS AND GROWTH OF INTELLIGENCE

The distribution of intelligence in a large population follows a regular pattern which is observed when taking measurements of any quality which has a chance distribution.

Diagram 1 is an idealised reproduction of the distribution in a population, and the pattern which it follows is that of the "Normal" or "Gaussian" curve. This broadly describes the spread of intelligence of a large and selective group. According to Burt,* however, there is a variation from the pattern of the normal curve at the extremities of the distribution, there being more than the expected number well above and well below the average range.

Diagram 1 includes a "bump" at the lower end which is intended to indicate the effect of an increase in the number of children in the severely subnormal range, and this is due to organic abnormalities. This is in addition to the increase in the expected numbers at both extremities of the curve which is referred to by Burt.

Approximately two-thirds of the population to which this curve would refer would have intelligence quotients in the area between 85 and 115, one-sixth above 115, and one-sixth below 85. Psychologists divide the categories into broad groups, calling those between 90 and 110 "average", those between 100 and 110 "high average", and those between 90 and 100 "low average". Then there are those "above average" and those of even higher intelligence are labelled "superior". There are those also "below average" and "inferior or limited". It seems that even scientific examination of intelligence is not able to escape value judgements !

Education is one of the factors in the growth of intelligence, and although the original potential is an inherited quality, the growth of that capacity depends upon the total experiences of the child, and, in this, the quality of education is an important factor.

H. Mayman, R. Schafer and D. Rapaport† offer the following propositions concerning intelligence :

(1) It is necessary to abandon the idea that a person is born with a fixed "intelligence" that remains constant throughout life.

(2) Every individual is born with a potentiality for intellectual development that may be referred to as his natural endowment. This potentiality unfolds through a process of maturation within the limits set by this endowment.

(3) This maturation process is fostered or restricted by the wealth or

* *Brit. J. of Statistical Psychology*, **16** (2) (1963).

† *An Introduction to Projective Techniques*, edited by H. ANDERSON and G. ANDERSON, New York, Prentice-Hall, 1951, pp. xxiv–72 and p. 547. *Interpretation of the Wechsler-Bellevue Intelligence Scale in Personality Appraisal*, Chapter 19, pp. 541–80.

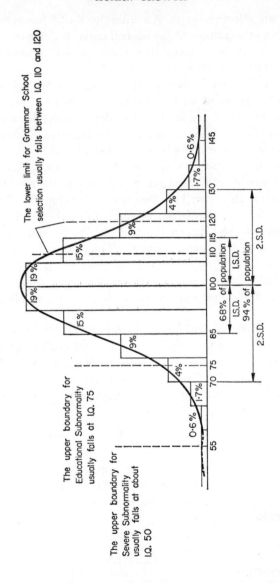

DIAGRAM 1. Theoretical distribution of intelligence in the population.

poverty of intellectual stimulation in that environment during the formative years.

(4) This maturation process is one aspect of personality development and is fostered or restricted by the timing, intensity and variety of emotional stimulation, and by the resulting course of emotional development.

(5) In the course of development, natural endowment differentiates into various functions that can be tapped by intelligence tests in which these functions underlie achievement.

(6) Formal education that provides the individual with systematically presented ideas plays a role in helping to enlarge the individual's repertoire of facts and relationships to be organised into a frame of reference for the assimiliation of new experiences and moulding of creative experiences within the limits of his emotional receptivity and endowment.

There are many other topics regarding the part played by education in the development of personality. There is the question of the value of the relationship of the child with the teacher, apart from the mechanics of learning the kind of information usually associated with education. In the junior school the child, as a rule, has one class teacher and, although there may be an occasional specialist teacher for physical education or some other subject, most of the child's time in school is spent with his class teacher. In many cases where children have unsatisfactory home or family life, the teacher is the one consistent and stable influence. It seems a pity that in the localities where the deficiencies in family life are likely to be greatest, the attractiveness of the area to teachers is so low that the teachers, too, are a constantly changing factor. Other children may miss a consistency of relationship with a teacher by reason of the social mobility of their parents—parents who move from district to district with promotion in the occupational life of the father. Some children have a disturbed educational life because the teacher moves and some because they themselves move.

The teacher's consistency may be something that the child values, but school at this stage becomes a place where rules exist, and the child who comes from a home where all rules are changeable on appeal may resent and fear the representative of a more inflexible system. Some children thus fear their teacher who represents obligations for which they have not been prepared. Others may seek the attention and the love of the teacher as a continuation of that of their parents, or as a replacement of something which they have not yet had.

School is larger than a family and is a miniature community. Symptoms of emotional disturbance may be considered to be related to school life simply because that is the area where new and important activities of the child are taking place. The emotional life becomes more concerned with siblings and with class mates rather than with adults. Although parents and teachers remain important figures within a child's mental life, his main interaction, however, often is with others around his own age. Life has become less bound up with his early fantasies about adults, and by this time the oedipal situation has become resolved.

In some circumstances the infantile involvement with fantasy representations of the parents remains at a fairly high level, and this is more likely to occur when the parents themselves find a value in the involvement of their child in their conflicts. There are special cases where there is no opportunity for the resolution of the conflict. Where parents become separated and the child remains with one, or where one dies or is absent for long periods, a high intensity of relationship with the child can be sought by the remaining parent as a substitute for the missing partner. The child is expected both to supply the emotional needs of one parent at an adult level and, at the same time, to remain a small child and be protected from undesired influences outside the home.

Some families have a self-enclosed life either by choice or force of circumstances. Parents who are socially mobile, having to move from town to town as a result of promotion in the occupational life of the father, may find it difficult to form satisfying relationships with neighbours and friends; and so do their children. If the roots of emotional involvement are torn up several times, no fresh ones will be laid down. The child may develop easy but superficial relationships at school, and even with friends in the neighbourhood; but the deeper emotional ties remain exclusively within the immediate family.

The danger of such close-knit family life is that the hostile component of the developing feelings is restricted to home consumption along with the affectionate component. Emotional life is lived at too intense a rate, and parents and children sometimes find themselves damaging to one another.

Other families build up a life which is centred on their material possessions, and this applies particularly to families where the parents are deriving satisfaction from the acquisition of the furniture and equipment as a result of their own efforts, and at a higher level than that which existed in their home of origin. It is a natural wish that their children should enjoy these possessions as much as they themselves do. Evenings are spent around the television set, and the weekends in outings in the newly acquired family car. In such homes the mental life seems to be entirely restricted to preoccupation with objects and with ideas, and there is an undervaluation of emotional fulfilment at a normal childish level.

It is difficult for parents who feel that they are making such rich provision for their children to realise that they may be impoverishing them, at the same time, with regard to emotional and social relationships.

The same kind of problem exists when families live in a social setting which is not in accordance with the family standard. The child whose parents live on the premises of a corner shop in a slum district, suffers from the expectation that his parents have of a higher standard of behaviour from him than is expected from the children around. The habits of thrift which are necessary to maintain the small business may seem less desirable to the child than the extravagance of the feckless people who live near.

The tripartite nature of the child's life—home, school and community —becomes important, and the personality becomes best integrated when there is some coherence in these factors. Many children make their adaptation to differences or conflicts between these cultures. Sometimes emotional disturbance seems to be based on the child's confusion as to his identity or to his choice of a particular identity that receives active disapproval from home or school or the neighbourhood.

CHAPTER 14

The Secondary School Child

ANTHROPOLOGISTS who study primitive societies in the belief that those cultures are less complex and more rigidly uniform than our own are sometimes impressed by the precise role which individuals in those cultures have at each stage in their lives. It has been thought that the expectation of a particular status at each stage of life gives the individuals an advantage in that they know clearly the boundaries of each stage. It would seem, however, that the life of children in this country has been divided in a like fashion by the different stages of school life.

BIOLOGICAL AND CULTURAL BOUNDARIES IN LIFE OF CHILD

The phases of personality development include many that are biologically determined, and the boundary lines recognised by psycho-analysts and described in Chapter 3 include early stages in infancy where there is dominance of sensations in successively different areas of the body. The oedipal situation follows that in which the genital sensations predominate, and then comes a latency period.

The next stage is that of puberty. Puberty, however, begins at different ages in different children, and there is also variation in the average age of commencement in children of different countries and in different epochs in the same country. In the last 60 years in Great Britain the average age of the first menstruation in girls has been lowered from approximately 15 years to under 13 years.* The figure of 13 years is the average of wide variations ranging from 10 years and

* J. M. TANNER, *Growth at Adolescence*, Blackwell Scientific Publications, 1962.

under, to instances where the onset is delayed beyond the age of 15 years.

Reference has already been made to the nature of secondary school education. Since the 1944 Education Act there has been an almost complete separation between the primary education (infants and junior schools) and the secondary schools. The primary schools are frequently "streamed" but in general are unspecialised. Secondary schools, however, may be of entirely different types. The most frequent pattern in the immediate post-World War II phase was of three types : secondary grammar, technical high, and secondary modern school. The aim was to have schools in which the special curriculum could be adapted to the graded ability of the child population. The intention was to provide an education that would be suitable for each level of ability. The different schools would earn equality of esteem—the esteem deriving from the ability of the teachers to give the correct educational stimulus.

Equality of esteem, however, has never been attained and there is never any doubt about the high prestige given to those children who fit most effectively into an academic programme. The secondary grammar schools were intended to carry the educational heritage of foundation grammar schools, which at one time in Britain were the only representatives of secondary education. This kind of education was the entry into many occupations with middle-class social implications or it was the preparation for the entry into university education and training courses for the professions. In providing secondary grammar schools on a wider scale, the intention was to give these opportunities to children of all social classes but on the proviso that the intelligence level of the child made it possible for the child to be receptive to that type of education.

The secondary technical school (or technical high schools) are a special case, and they are intended for children of the same general level of intelligence as those of the secondary grammar schools, but the children selected for them are those whose capabilities are in the direction of studies which can be applied to industry and commerce. The secondary grammar schools are predominantly academic. There is a tendency in some areas to use the technical high school as a kind of intermediate educational category, perhaps in the belief that technical sciences need less intelligence than subjects such as the arts, languages, and pure mathematics, which are uncontaminated by possible usefulness! Technical subjects as taught in the technical high schools require, however, the capacity to absorb theoretical concepts which need verbal ability, and the educational process is different from that of the old industrial apprenticeship where young boys learnt a craft in a factory or workshop.

ANOMALIES IN SELECTION PROCEDURES

In so far as the selection procedure has been geared to the level of I.Q., the cut-off point for selection for secondary grammar schools and technical high schools was around 115. In different localities selection criteria could vary according to quite irrelevant factors, such as the extent of provision for specialised secondary education existing before the 1944 Act came into operation. As regards secondary modern education, although this, too, was intended to have its own selection criteria, in practice it meant that those not selected for the grammar or technical type of school, i.e. what was usually the remaining five-sixths of the school population, had to be fitted in. It was selection by exclusion of those thought to be unfitted for another kind of school. The intelligence level within a secondary modern school could be anything between an I.Q. of 60 to 120 according to variations in the cut off for E.S.N. education or selective secondary school. Many secondary schools of all kinds have been eminently successful. Against all the odds, many secondary modern schools have achieved a high reputation and embody a high morale in staff and pupils. In some cases, however, there has been dissatisfaction, either with the local experience of secondary education or as a result of challenge of the basic principles. Some people consider that selection for different kinds of secondary education is, in itself, a bad thing and others challenge the validity and reliability of the selection procedures. If the allocation of a type of secondary school determines the future career, then any error in the allocation could do an injustice to the whole future of individual children. Many educationalists look upon the selection itself in terms of a prediction as to the type of educational response that a child is capable of. Others who might agree with this say at the same time that it is a prediction which is self-fulfilling. It is considered that the practice of streaming, i.e. putting children into graded classes, according to educational ability, in the *primary school*, becomes a judgement which has an irreversible effect, this type of teaching determining the educational progress. It is also believed that the self-image deriving from membership of a class with a low- or high-graded label either confirms a child's low esteem which is linked with low performance or gives an encouragement to the high performance associated with a favourable self-image. A suggested remedy has, therefore, been comprehensive schools at secondary school level and the abandonment of the practice of streaming in the junior school.

COMPREHENSIVE SCHOOLS: NEW IDEAS OR IDEOLOGY

Comprehensive schooling has become partly a political issue, but this should not obscure the educational factors, and there are dangers that these latter factors can be diverted by giving the label of "comprehensive school" to a grouping of different secondary schools in separate buildings with separate educational policy. Even if comprehensive schools are created within a single large building, or in a group of buildings on the same campus, it would still have to be decided whether, within the same school, divisions of different types of education would exist for children of different abilities. There are some experimental comprehensive schools in which the classes are unstreamed and these are most successful when the change from streaming is accompanied by a change from the set lesson within a set syllabus. Children of different ability could benefit from co-operative contact with one another if they are freed from the 45-minute working period with each child attempting to follow identical instructions from the teacher, and where this is substituted by joint tasks and projects with teams of teachers, and where work space spills over from classroom to classroom and to central hall and to specialised workshops.

It cannot be emphasised too strongly that there is no virtue in a change of name of type of school if there is not simultaneously a change in the educational policy and practice. At the same time it should also be recognised that in many schools a great deal of progress has been made within traditional lines of educational activities.

NEW BEGINNINGS, NEW PROBLEMS

There are problems in the transfer from junior to secondary school, whatever category the secondary school might be, and these problems are similar to those of school entry. The child who enters the infant school leaves the confines of the home, and goes into a wider world. The new area of living, which occupies so much of his waking life, is frightening to some children, and some of them show their distress for a day or two, or a week or two, before settling down to school life. Others have a longer period of distress. By and large the child's personality grows to the school and the school shrinks in size as he becomes familiar with it. His class-mates become identifiable, and each year he has a class teacher who is responsible for the greater part of his teaching and the supervision of his behaviour. There may be one or two specialist teachers in the primary school, but each class has one teacher whom a child looks upon as his own.

The modern secondary school of any type is likely to be larger than the primary school in order to justify the expensive equipment and spacious playing fields of the newly built schools by a spread of the cost over a large number of children. Pupils are drawn from several primary schools, and, to the newcomers, the older children look to be as tall and as powerful as the teachers.

The large yearly intake means that there are a larger number of classes for each year group. There are more specialist teachers taking each class for one subject only and, therefore, the rules which formerly were carried to the child in the person of the class master are now no longer attached to any particular individual. Rules are known to exist, and the consequence of breaking them seems to be dire, but the child is less clear as to what the rules are about. No wonder that many children entering secondary school have a recurrence of the anxiety that they first felt at the time of entry into the infant or junior school. They are now leaving the school which had become as familiar as their home, and pass on to something frightening and unknown.

For most children, settling down in the new school can be as easy and as brief a process as if the first school entry. For other children, however, the transfer becomes one of the factors in school phobia.*

* J. H. KAHN and J. P. NURSTEN, *Am. J. Orthopsychiatry* **32**, 708 (1962).

The segregation of children into different secondary schools carries a social problem. Children become separated from their friends by going to different schools or widely different sections of the same school.

DIVERSITY IN STAGES OF GROWTH

Even when attempts are made to minimise the differing experience allotted within the educational system to different children by the secondary school stage, nature has provided a new and widening range of inequalities. For some the entry into the secondary school is the beginning of puberty. Other children have not achieved this biological stage until the school-leaving age of 15 or 16 years. There is the inequality between girls and boys in which, at the beginning, girls have an advantage of almost 2 years. For many it is a period of rapid physical growth, the secondary school period enclosing the "adolescent spurt". Girls have their peak rate of growth between 12 and 13 and have achieved maximum height (plus or minus 13 months) at $16\frac{1}{4}$ years. Boys, whose peak rate of growth is later and occurs between 14 and 15 years, are able to overtake girls as regards height and do not achieve mature stature until $17\frac{3}{4}$ years (plus or minus 10 months).*

The social class differences are likely to affect the general response to education and the time of school leaving, and there are a variety of factors related to home neighbourhood, family circumstances and attendance at particular schools, which can increase expectation of becoming delinquent.†

GRAMMAR SCHOOL EDUCATION: BURDEN OF FULFILMENT

At all stages, too, the burden of grammar school type of education on the way of life of a child becomes heavy. The secondary modern school child usually looks forward to school leaving at the age of 15, although some may stay on till 16 years. The secondary grammar school boy is expected to remain at least until the age of 16, and often to the age of 18, and may even have his sights directed to some kind of

* See Tables 1 and 2, pp. 172–173.
† M. POWER (1969), Younghusband Lecture to the National Institute for Social Work Training (to be published).

further education. It is a long-term prospect. There are examinations ahead, and a good deal more is expected in the way of homework. The teaching is even more specialised than in the secondary modern school, and the process of teaching leaves more to the individual child than before. There is an expectation that the child has his own motivation for school work.

The secondary modern school pupil is less likely to have homework. He may at an early stage take a part-time job helping a milk delivery man, or he may have a newspaper round of his own. He thus has more money to spend and more leisure in which to spend it. The secondary grammar school pupil needs the kind of support from home which comes from a high valuation of this special kind of education; otherwise he is at a disadvantage compared with his former friend who is in a secondary modern school. This kind of support and valuation of education is taken for granted in the middle-class sections of the community. The family as a whole is identified with the educational process. In large working-class areas, the child of high intelligence who is selected for the grammar school type of secondary education may come from a family which is actively opposed to his education or merely indifferent to it. In many cases it is not part of their ideology. Likewise, the ideology of the school may be hostile to that of the boy's background. Thus there is a schism between his life at home and his life at school, and the child suffers either by failing in his performance at school, or by drifting away from the family.*

Grammar school education involves a good deal of self-denial of immediate pleasures and, therefore, it needs the capacity for a long view on the part of the child and his parents.

PROBLEMS OF DISCIPLINE

The later years of secondary modern school life bring problems of discipline. The teacher controls his class by the consent and acceptance by the pupils of his role and status, and, to a large extent, this is given to him. At all stages of school life, however, there are some children who had derived no sense of identification with school life. These children, who have no reason to accept the general standards of the school, place

* *Education and the Working Class*, Jackson & Marsden, 1962.

themselves outside the ordinary observance of the teacher's instructions. In dealing with them, the teacher is deprived of the support which originally comes from the child's deference to the impersonal role of the teacher. He has to fall back upon the resources of his own personality, and, in this case, he either has to help the child to incorporate something entirely new into his personality, or to exclude him from his class.

This problem becomes intensified in the last years of the secondary modern school if the education should seem to be irrelevant to the child's life. It becomes almost an impossibility for a teacher to control a class of unwilling pupils when they are equal in size to him. Where adolescent boys and girls would accept discipline in a factory from someone who is teaching them a job which they want to learn, the remedy for the problem might seem at first sight to be a return to earlier school leaving. A better remedy would be to modify the educational process in such a way that the children of average, and lower than average, intellectual capacity can be accepted at their own level, and be provided with educational aims that are not formulated for another category of children.

Mutual rejection of standards as regards school and home is less likely to happen when the teacher can take a part in community activities of the locality where he teaches, and where he has not separated his own self from the ideology of his home of origin in the process of his own education. Respect for different ideologies is more possible when there is contact and continuity. The problem of division of culture between home and school becomes even more complicated at this stage when, with the beginning of adolescence, the young people develop a culture of their own.

The secondary grammar school child has similar problems, but there is, in general, a higher degree of acceptance of the culture of the school by the child, and of acceptance of the child by the teacher. The danger here sometimes seems to be not the rejection of the school, but the rejection of the standards of the home. The child from a middle-class home has no problem, because home and school have identical standards. The child from a working-class home also may have parents who appreciate and understand the education that their child is having at a grammar school, and give him ample support, and this is particularly likely to happen when the teacher can take part in the local community activities, and is not a stranger coming into the district each day. It seems a tragedy, nevertheless, that in some cases the high intellectual ability of the child may lead him to have to choose between failing at school or cutting himself off from communication with his parents; and it is a tragedy for parents when they have the alternative of discouraging a child from benefiting from his ability or losing his membership of their family.

The Newsom Report on Secondary Education, and the Robbins Report on University Education, H.M.S.O., 1963, both open up fresh social considerations with regard to provision for advanced education for still wider ranges of intellectual and social categories of the population.

I have not thought it appropriate to deal with further education for school leavers on day release, in evening classes, and through youth clubs. These are subjects which need more detailed study from experts in that field.* Education has been thought of as serving the needs of the individual and of society, and the process of education is itself becoming a subject of study at a time when society is in the process of change.

NEED FOR NEW CURRICULA

One wonders how far progress has been made in the provision of appropriate curricula for the needs of young people at different ages, different levels of intelligence, and in different social settings, and to what extent the educational process can be created anew as a joint adventure during every contact between teacher and pupil.

Before long the secondary modern school leaving age will be sixteen years. No child then will be able to leave school before the age of 16. We should recognise at this point that it will not be simply a matter of providing a new syllabus for an extra year. The whole syllabus of the secondary modern school (or its appropriate class in a comprehensive school) will need recasting. New problems will be created or revealed. There were problems which did not exist in the past because secondary school education was restricted to those who choose it or were selected for it. Those who had no wish to remain at school left at the age of 13 or 14 years. This was an evasion of the problem because the experience

---

* JOHN LELLO, *The Official View on Education*, Pergamon Press, 1964.

of comprehensive schools has already been sufficient to show that the comprehensive secondary school can provide an environment which raises the level of attainment of a much larger proportion of children than was formerly selected for the longer education of the specialised secondary school.

Margaret Miles states :* "It is now apparent that the smallness of the proportion of boys and girls formerly considered capable of advanced work was due not to lack of talent but the lack of opportunity." She adds, however, that there are disturbing aspects which have already become evident, and that in this case :

> When all young people of 11 to 15 or 16 are together in the same sort of school they are expected to conform to a code which formerly applied only to about one-fifth of them. The pupils at the pre-1944 secondary schools were, as we have seen, all "willing" pupils, but the pupils in the post-1944 secondary schools are there for the most part because they have got to be. The majority are glad of the opportunity, but there is bound to be a minority of boys and girls who reject the school uniform and all it stands for, are longing to leave, refuse to do homework and so on. A very small percentage of these unwilling secondary school pupils make demands and cause anxiety out of all proportion to their numbers . . . (Furthermore) the fact that all the boys and girls up to 15 are now in school confronts the teachers with behaviour problems which simply do not yield to the kind of treatment which in the past seemed adequate.

We cannot escape the obligation to provide the best education for all children of all levels of intelligence and all kinds of social background. To do this means that the teachers will be facing demands of an unprecedented nature. The educational provision which they have been trained to give becomes inappropriate, and the type of education that must replace it has yet to be created. The teacher needs to have some renewal from his own professional training sources and, in addition, he will need support, for the problems that are inevitable, from the professional staff of the School Psychological Service and Child Guidance Clinic.

CRISES

School entry, change of school, and school leaving are episodes which mark the transition between developmental stages or levels of function-

* *Bulletin of the British Psychological Society*, July, 1963.

ing. They may appear as crises events. When the outcome is favourable the episodes mark the attainment of new levels of capacity. Adverse effects, however, may appear as regression to earlier levels.

Failures of school attendance are discussed elsewhere under the heading "School Phobia" or "School Refusal".*

The lengthening of school life for the whole population is likely to create new problems which are related to the issue of compulsion. From the earliest years of universal education it was considered necessary to enforce participation in a service provided for the benefit of the child population. Although, in most cases, school attendance is now a willing acceptance of provision offered by the community for its individual members, there are many instances when the whole force of the law has had to be brought to bear upon those who would otherwise refuse participation. If children truant, or if the parents withdraw them from school attendance, prosecution can take place; and in the last resort the child can be taken from its parents into the care of the local authority which will then ensure school attendance. Illness is an excuse, and some forms of school refusal fit into a medical or psychiatric framework which allows for treatment to be offered. Thus, a child not attending school must either be ill or breaking the law. The few exceptions were those where the parent was making some adequate alternative arrangements for the child's education.

LIMITS TO POWER OF COMPULSION

The extension of universal education into adolescent years was intended to give the total population the benefits that some of the more favoured sections of the community had been able to obtain privately or through willing and joint participation with the local education authority. Those who continued their education into the later teenage years were a volunteer minority. The school could create a framework of its own choice for those pupils, and any who did not fit into that framework could remove themselves or be removed. When this kind of educational provision is made generally available, it will be necessary to recognise that there are practical limits to compulsion. If a boy or

* J. H. KAHN and J. P. NURSTEN, *Unwillingly to School*, 2nd ed., Pergamon Press, 1968.

girl of 15, 16 or 17 years rebels against school life, and does not attend, there should be more alternatives than to be categorised either as delinquent or ill. The dilemma of those representing the community is real, because it may be felt that those who are most in need of opportunities to mature in an educational setting may be the very ones who would wish to withdraw early into an external world of work and pleasure in circumstances where they could become exploited or join the exploiters.

CHAPTER 15

Adolescence

ADOLESCENCE is the interval between childhood and adult life. There are biological, social and cultural boundaries between the two stages. Puberty is the biological division; cultural and social aspects of adolescence refer to the status and role of the young person in society.

TRANSITIONAL STAGE: SOCIAL IMPLICATIONS

In countries or cultures where the technical aspects of living are comparatively simple, adolescence is an abrupt division between childhood and adult life. The transition may be marked by some initiation ceremony of varying degrees of importance, and in this case there is no in-between period. After the ceremony, the young person has the full privileges and obligations of manhood or womanhood. In some other cultures there are a succession of in-between stages, each with a well-defined role. It can be an advantage for an individual to know exactly what is expected of him at each stage, but the deviant, whose progress either has been retarded or has taken a different direction, is unable to fill the expectations of him. He may find no place at all in his community.

LENGTHENING OF PREPARATORY STAGES FOR ADULT ROLE

In cultures characterised by more complicated technical processes of living, there is a need for longer preparation for adult life. With each advance of available knowledge, occupations become more specialised and need longer training. There is therefore a tendency towards a lengthening of the period between the stage when the child has reached adult capacities and the ability or permission to put those capacities into operation.

Puberty comes at a definite point in the life of each individual, although the time varies from one individual to another. It is the stage when the sexual organs in the male and female begin to carry fertile cells, one of which can unite with a corresponding cell from the reproductive organs of a member of the opposite sex.

The period of adolescence includes the various social and cultural changes, and the boundaries are uncertain because the different functions of adult life require different qualities. The laws and customs which regulate the various aspects of living activities have developed independently of one another. It is not permissible to marry in Great Britain before the age of 16, whatever the age might be when procreation can begin. Marriage has obligations over and above the procreation of children. We recognise that children need a family, and the parents of children need to have sufficient maturity to take on family responsibility.

Recent legislation* has brought the age of majority down from 21 to 18 years. Young people now have the vote at 18 years, the capacity to enter into agreements involving financial obligations and the freedom to marry without having to seek parental consent.

With regard to the criminal law, there have been considerable alterations in the age at which young people are answerable to the courts for their offences. The changes were foreshadowed in the White Paper *Children in Trouble* (Command 3601) and are embodied in the Children and Young Persons Act, 1969. The age of criminal responsibility remains at the age of 10 and in this respect there is no change from the Children and Young Persons Act, 1963, notwithstanding that the Ingleby Report, on which this Act was based, had recommended the raising of the age of criminal liability to 12 years. There is, however, a change to the effect that children between the age of 10 and 14 will not be subject to prosecution but at the time of writing this section has not been brought into operation. Up to the age of 14 children can be brought before the court under "Care Proceedings" and, over the age of 14, under "Criminal Proceedings". Further details of the current

* Family Law Reform Act, 1969.

legislation are to be found in the Home Office *Guide to the Children and Young Persons Act, 1969,* and more detailed interpretation of the present position is given in Watson's book on the Juvenile Court.*

The most radical change is that in the future no person may be charged with an offence except homicide, "by reason of having done or omitted while he was a child", i.e. under the age of 14 years. At intervals the age at which the child will be excluded from criminal jurisdiction will be raised to the twelfth birthday and then successively to the thirteenth and fourteenth birthdays. In effect, a good deal of the responsibility of children who formerly would have been regarded as offenders will be transferred to the newly created Social Work Departments of local authorities, either through supervision orders or care orders. It will have to be seen whether committal to care with placing in "Community Homes" will be regarded by the public as being different from former placement in remand homes or approved schools.

Adult status in occupational life depends upon the degree of training required. Many industries have apprenticeship schemes which terminate at the age of 21, after which the individual ranks as a skilled worker. In some technical and professional occupations, qualification comes even later, but in many unskilled trades maximum salary and status do not seem to depend on age or length of service.

MARKS OF MATURITY

The uncertainty of the functional boundaries of adolescence is matched by an alteration of the custom of marking out periods of life by the assumption of different styles of clothing. Earlier in this century a young girl would "put up" her hair at about the age of 18 years to signify that her girlhood or adolescence was over, and that womanhood had begun. A young boy indicated his manhood by wearing long trousers for the first time. In the present time women's hairstyles bridge the decades, but there may be some styles which teenage girls may adopt collectively to assert a coherence in the social life of adolescents as a special group : more than children, and consciously separate from the adult population.

Boys may begin to wear long trousers at the age of 11 or even earlier.

* JOHN WATSON, *The Juvenile Court, 1970,* Shaw & Sons Ltd.

Both sexes may wear clothes in the fashion of their own creation, but nevertheless, the changes previously accepted as the mark of maturity begin earlier, and the lower limit of adolescence seems to be coming earlier. Yet the granting of full adult status becomes more and more delayed. The gap between the child and the adult which the adolescent occupies seems to be becoming wider and wider, and a new social group has come into existence.

PHYSICAL GROWTH

Physically adolescence is a period of rapid growth which is sometimes associated with enormous appetite. Young boys and girls "shoot up" in the early part of adolescence, and may "fill out" a little later. Some girls, however, try to curb their appetite, and "diet" because of the fear of becoming too fat. Sometimes this is because they seem to wish to delay their physical development and remain child-like. Some girls become self-conscious about the development of their breasts, and acquire a stoop which conceals them. There are others, however, for whom the mature figure cannot come too soon, and whose main concern is about the mystic curves which receive a designation in "vital statistics".

MENSTRUATION: SEMINAL EMISSIONS

Physical growth includes the maturation of primary sexual organs, which are the testicles in the boy and the ovaries in the girl. There are also changes in other organs, and these are called secondary sexual characteristics. They include the growth of hair around the genital organs and under the armpits in both sexes, and on the chest and face in young boys. There are changes in the shape of the breasts and hips in girls; in young boys the tone of the voice alters along with visible changes in the shape of the larynx.

All these changes may be welcomed by the adolescent who looks upon them as a sign of maturity, but many are unprepared for change which needs the acquisition of a new image of the self. The rapid physical growth gives a young person a body with which he or she is unfamiliar. The long limbs need a new kind of posture or balance, and, therefore,

TABLE 1

Normal Maturational Sequence in Boys

Phase	Appearance of sexual characteristics	Average ages	Age range*
Childhood through pre-adolescence	*Testes* and *Penis* have not grown since infancy; no *Pubic Hair*; growth in *Height* constant. No spurt.	—	—
A Early- D	*Testes* begin to increase in size; *Scrotum* grows, skin reddens and becomes coarser; *Penis* follows with growth in length and circumference; no true *Pubic Hair*, may have down.	12–13 years	10–15 years
O L E Mid- S C E	*Pubic Hair*—pigmented, coarse and straight at base of penis becoming progressively more curled and profuse, forming at first an inverse triangle and subsequently extends up to umbilicas: *Axillary Hair* starts after pubic hair; *Penis* and *Testes* continue growing; *Scrotum* becomes larger, pigmented and sculptured; marked spurt of growth in *Height*, with maximum increment about time pubic hair first develops and decelerates by time fully established; *Prostate and seminal vesicles* mature, spontaneous or induced *Emissions* follow but *Spermatozoa* inadequate in number and motility (adolescent sterility); *Voice* begins to change as *Larynx* enlarges.	13–16 years	11–18 years
N Late-C E	*Facial* and *Body Hair* appear and spread; *Pubic* and *Axillary Hair* become denser; *Voice* deepens; *Testes* and *Penis* continue to grow; *Emission*—has adequate number of motile *Spermatozoa* for fertility. Growth in *Height* gradually decelerates, 98% mature stature by 17¾ yrs ± 10 mo; Indentation of frontal *Hair Line*.	16–18 years	14–20 years
Post-adolescence to adult	Mature—full development of *Primary* and *Secondary sex* characteristics; *Muscles* and *Hirsutism* may continue increasing.	onset 18–20 years	onset 16–21 years

* Normal range was accepted as (80% of cases) 1st to 9th decile.

TABLE 2

Normal Maturational Sequence in Girls

Phase	Appearance of sexual characteristics	Average ages	Age range*
Childhood through preadolescence	No *Pubic Hair*; Breasts are flat; *Growth* in height is constant, no spurt.	—	—
A Early- D	Rounding of *Hips*; *Breasts* and nipples are elevated to form *Bud* stage; no true *Pubic Hair*, may have down.	10–11 years	9–14 years
O L Mid- E S C E	*Pubic Hair*—pigmented, coarse, straight primarily along labia but progressively curled and spreads over mons and becomes profuse with an inverse triangular pattern; *Axillary Hair* starts after pubic hair; marked *Growth* spurt with maximum *Height* increment 18 months before menarche; *Menarche—Labia* becomes enlarged, *Vaginal Secretion* becomes acid; *Breast*—areola and nipple elevated to form primary breast.	11 14 years	10 16 years
N Late-C E	*Axillary Hair* in moderate quantity; *Pubic Hair* fully developed; *Breasts*, fill out forming adult type configuration; *Menstruation* well established; *Growth* in height is decelerated, ceases at $16\frac{1}{4} \pm 13$ mo.	14–16 years	13–18 years
Post-adolescence to adult	Further growth of *Axillary Hair*; *Breasts* fully developed.	onset 16–18 years	onset 15–19 years

* Normal range was accepted as (80% of cases) 1st to 9th decile.

young people often appear to be ungainly, not knowing what to do with their arms and legs. Young girls are sometimes disturbed by the growing protuberance under the nipples, and many a girl is taken to the family doctor in the belief that there is some tumour developing when one breast develops a little in advance of the other. The boy whose voice is changing may be taken by surprise by the unfamiliar noise which comes from somewhere in his body, and his voice may alternate unpredictably between high-pitched and gruff sounds.

Sexual capacity, likewise, can be a source of pride or anxiety.

When a girl reaches puberty the ovaries begin to discharge fertile egg cells. One passes each month from an ovary, which is within the abdominal cavity, through one of the channels, called Fallopian tubes, which are at either side of the uterus or womb. Meanwhile the lining of the uterus develops an increased blood supply and enlarges in preparation for the supplies that would be necessary if the egg cell should become fertilised by spermatoza from the male. When fertilisation does not take place this preparatory lining is shed, and this is menstruation.

Menstruation can occur to some girls without previous warning, and may give rise to alarm, the loss of blood causing a fear that some internal part has been damaged. A girl without sexual knowledge is not without sexual thoughts; and feelings of guilt are attached to the process of menstruation. Such a girl, who tells her mother anxiously about the flow of blood, is likely to have a mother who is still, even at that stage, unable to give her any satisfactory explanation. Quite frequently the response of the mother is in these exact words "This will happen once a month, and now you must keep away from boys." The lack of explanation increases the fears, and peculiar fantasies may be built up regarding the relationships between the two sexes. There may be a dread of the most ordinary contact in games or at dances.

Most girls, however, have been prepared well in advance, and are able to look forward to menstruation, with pride, as a badge of womanhood.

The boy has two testicles in a bag called the scrotum close to the penis. During the course of an individual's embryonic development the testicles are within the abdomen in a place comparable with that of the ovaries in the girl. During intra-uterine growth of the infant male, or sometimes later, the testicles descend from the abdominal cavity into the scrotum, but each is still connected by a tube which has accompanied the descent of the testicles through a channel (inguinal canal) in the groin, and these tubes link up at the level of the prostate gland at the base of the bladder with the urethra which is the passage carrying the urine from the bladder through the penis. Thus the passage through the penis carries urine during the emptying of the bladder, and semen which is produced by the testicles. Ejaculation occurs as a result of sexual excitation, and this is usually preceded by erection of the penis which gives the firmness that allows the penis to penetrate into the female passage (vagina) when sexual intercourse takes place. With the emission of semen the erection usually subsides.

Apart from sexual intercourse, emissions of semen can occur as a result of manual stimulation of the penis (masturbation), or as a result of fantasies. These may occur spontaneously in dreams, or sometimes they may be deliberately stimulated by the choice of erotic reading material, erotic pictures, or by recollections of previous experiences. An emission gives relief to sexual tension and is pleasurable.

Sexual activity in both sexes follows a pattern of awareness of a need which is accompanied by tension and the seeking of relief for that tension. Even in the satisfaction of the need there is, however, an overwhelming quality about the experience. Sensations that are unusually intense are often associated with anxiety. Satisfaction ordinarily relieves the anxiety, but sometimes the anxiety outlasts the physical relief. This is a pattern which has been previously noted in the intensity of hunger and its satisfaction, and in the tension of a full bowel or bladder and the release of that tension in vacuation. The release can have a pleasure of its own, but, wherever an essential biological activity has been associated with prohibitions and restrictions, it becomes linked with ideas of guilt. Satisfactions are then incomplete. There are instances where satisfaction is so bound up with guilt that an individual may be unable to search for satisfaction except in circumstances which increase guilt.

A generation is growing up which is freer from guilt than the previous one, but, at the same time, boys and girls are exposed more than in previous generations to excitation of their developing sexuality. Many young boys and girls feel called upon to discuss and to experience some forms of sexual activity before they are fully prepared, and many seem just as vulnerable as their predecessors to anxiety which is its accompaniment.

There is a good deal of inconsistency about parental and social attitudes to menstruation and seminal emissions. Some superstitions and irrational attitudes continue through the generations. There is folklore regarding menstruation which is associated with fears of contamination. In many cultures, women who are menstruating are compelled to keep themselves apart from the rest of the family, and are not allowed to touch any food that has been prepared for others. Many people in our own culture believe that it is dangerous for a menstruating woman to wash her hair or have a bath. Such prohibitions have no rational foundation, but are part of the embarrassment concerning the physical events which call attention to the sexual role.

Parents are equally embarrassed with regard to their sons if the bedclothes become contaminated with seminal emissions. Some boys and some parents regard emissions as something bad; they are unable to accept them as part of the normal process of growing up.

LIMITS OF PHYSICAL GROWTH

Generally, physical growth reaches its height in early adolescence, and the maximum seems to be reached at an earlier age than previously, perhaps because the better general standard of diet allows individuals to get their growing done earlier. Many young boys and girls approach their maximum height at the age of 14 or 15, but some do their growing at a later stage, up to 18 or 19 or even 20 years.

Much of the growing takes place in the long bones, particularly of the legs, and the growing process occurs in the cartilage which divides the shaft of the bone (diaphysis) from the two ends (epiphyses). Growth of these bones finally ceases when the last union of bone with bone takes place, replacing the cartilage; the vertebral column may continue to grow up to and sometimes after the age of 20 years by addition of bone to bone on the upper and lower surfaces of the vertebrae.

NUTRITION AND HEALTH

Some illnesses have had a special association with adolescence. Tuberculosis, which formerly had a peak incidence in the late 'teens, is now rare, and is more responsive to treatment when it does occur. A severe form of anaemia used to be prevalent in young girls, perhaps because of the general standard of nutrition which was insufficient for the replacement of blood lost during menstruation. This kind of anaemia is uncommon now, but minor degrees of haemoglobin deficiency still occur. Where diet is inadequate menstrual loss is still a significant factor in the general level of the blood count, and textbooks record a different "normal" blood count for women than for men. In many homes, a woman's diet was, traditionally, less substantial than that of the menfolk and, in addition, the loss of blood from the monthly flow and the extra demands on the body during pregnancies and lactation were not made up. At the present time, with increased care and higher living standards, men and women have similar "average" blood counts.

In some medical textbooks different norms for the two sexes are still specified. Similarly, physiology textbooks have described different types of respiration in men and women. Masculine respiration was described as "thoraco-abdominal", the muscles of the chest and abdomen moving with each breath. Feminine respiration was described as "thoracic", i.e. movements restricted to the muscles of the chest. It would appear that these physiologists had never seen a woman without her corsets!

INTELLECTUAL MATURATION

The intellectual capacity of the individual is assumed to reach a maximum level during the period of adolescence for the purpose of calculation of many intelligence tests. Measurable growth of intelligence seems to cease in some individuals at an age between fourteen and sixteen years, but in some individuals measurable growth continues up to the age of eighteen or later. Perhaps there has been a false analogy of intelligence with height, and views about the cessation of intellectual growth at adolescence may not be valid. It is recognised that some limitations which were formerly thought of as being an unalterable inherent quality are instead the product of the original potential together with the cultural experience. Growth is likely to finish early when there is cultural deprivation, and may possibly be resumed if provision is made of the intellectual experiences that previously were missing. Thus it is possible to justify the continuation of education of young people at all levels of intelligence, but this would need the working out of educational principles which take into account the different needs and the different capacities of assimilation in different groups of young people. We must give a kind of education which is related to the personality of the individual and the mental framework which already exists. It is no use giving at any one time more than can be taken in at that time.

Here we can recall one of the propositions of Mayman, Schafer and Rapaport quoted in Chapter 9 which emphasises that nothing can be absorbed unless it can be organised into a frame of reference which already exists, and that the assimilation of new experience occurs within the limits of emotional receptivity and endowment.

LEAVING SCHOOL

Separation of individuals into different groups has already occurred within the educational setting. Children are either in different kinds of secondary school or different types of class within the same school. A further separation occurs when some children leave school at the age of 15 or 16 years, and begin work, while others continue to attend school. Educational differences lead to social differences.

There is a difference between the kind of life of school leavers and of those who continue their education. The young worker has more money to spend, and more leisure, and the opportunity for different kinds of pleasure. Boys and girls who attend grammar schools and continue their education have to do homework in the evenings, have little leisure, and are likely to have limited pocket money. It will therefore depend a good deal upon the ideology of the home as to whether the life of these young people is satisfactory to them or not. In the home where education is valued, it is possible for a child to forego the leisure and pleasure that other young people are enjoying. Some young people find support for their educational life in the common purpose that exists in their own immediate neighbourhood, and are scarcely aware of the other world which has a different set of values. It is more difficult where there are neighbours or even other members of the same family who are enjoying a life which has more immediate satisfactions.

LEISURE AND PLEASURE

The high earnings and leisure activities of the early school leaver may not be an undiluted satisfaction. The esteem that leaders of the community attach to intellectual ability and prolonged education, may give a feeling of unworthiness to those who intellectual level makes them unsuitable for academic work. There is continued emphasis on educational opportunities, and there is an attempt to provide more efficient selection of a larger number of young people for higher education. Even although it is recognised that innate intelligence levels differ, there is an implication that those who are not selected have failed a test, and are somehow or other responsible for the failure. We must recognise that even with an improvement in secondary school education, and with an increase in the number of university places, the majority of the population will not be able to be accepted for the highly valued experience of academic life.

If this majority continues to be impressed with its inferiority, it cannot be surprising that the seeking of any pleasure that is available sometimes has an arrogant attitude. It is possible that one of the by-products of the particular emphasis on equality of opportunity in education is having a harmful effect when it is also implied that this equality of opportunity confirms the inferiority of those who are unable to benefit by it.

FURTHER EDUCATION AND OCCUPATION

The recent increase in the number of university places, and the proposals to establish still more universities, has become a controversial topic. Some teachers in established universities with experience of selection of students for their own colleges have expressed the fear that *"more means worse"*. Others have been equally certain that when students have been accepted from a wider range of applicants than the traditional sources, the results have been entirely satisfactory. Perhaps it would be more appropriate to say *"more means different"*. We must recognise that there are social aspects of education, and that some individuals have absorbed in their home life an ideology which has been taken for granted as part of university life. Others are deficient in this. A deliberate attempt has to be made to identify and supply the factors which are necessary for a comprehensive education which harmonises the life of home and school.

We must return to the consideration of the occupational life of the school leaver. Early leavers may be helped in their choice of occupation by Youth Employment Officers.* Sometimes the choice of job has taken place long before the time for leaving school, and the choice may be either that of the child or his parents. Often this choice is entered into enthusiastically, sometimes in a docile manner, occasionally in a resentful one. Sometimes the job is a product of the parents' ambition which is accepted by the child. Sometimes it is one chosen by the child *in opposition* to something which the parents had in mind. Sometimes an occupation is chosen with very little thought at all except for the wage, and in such a case the job may be changed frequently and with very little sense of responsibility.

There has been some change in the attitude to the occupation of girls. At one time little importance was attached to the choice of career in the belief that "they will get married anyway", and their occupation was considered to be a stop-gap. There now seems to be a trend for girls of all social classes to seek and enjoy work which is appropriate to their ability.

From the young persons' point of view, the way in which they are received into a job is very important.* The change of status and of customs involved in passing from sheltered school life to the more robust life of office or factory can be very disturbing for some. Many large firms arrange for a formal introduction of new employees, and for training schemes which make the role quite clear. In others there are rivalries between old employees and a newcomer which are similar to those in a family when a new baby arrives. The old employees rag the newcomer, sometimes good-humouredly, and occasionally in a very cruel way. The newcomer who is able to "take" the ragging is readily accepted, but there are some who feel to be on the outside of the group, and who suffer very severe anxiety and distress.

* Now known as "Careers Officers".
† E. VENABLES, *Leaving School and Starting Work*, Pergamon Press, 1968.

CONFLICTS IN THE HOME

Emotionally, adolescence is a disturbing stage. There are conflicts within the individual, and between him and the adult world. At one moment he has the wish to be independent, and to establish himself as an adult, and at another time he has the wish to retain all the privileges of childhood. At some points of stress (and points of stress occur whenever there is a change of status), there is a need to go back, or regress, even further. At one moment his behaviour is mature and responsible, and at another moment he shows tantrums resembling those of his infancy.

There are similarly conflicting wishes within the parent, who may say to the child "Now you must take grown-up responsibility", and yet still wishes to protect him from the danger that comes from bad companions, sexual activity and the choice of unsuitable jobs. The wish to see the child as a responsible separate individual is incompatible with the simultaneous wish to protect and to keep control of him.

INSTABILITY DURING TRANSITION

Emotional instability in adolescence is partly due to the contradictory wishes of the individual. Many disturbances which, in an adult would be regarded as a symptom of mental illness, occur in the normal range of life of young people. At the same time, adolescents are vulnerable to criticism and sarcasm, and feel that even when being accepted, the acceptance is of no value because it is given on conditions. There is a special need during adolescence to be treated as potentially the equal of adults. There is the need for respect as individuals.

Responsibility is not something which can be forced on an individual. It is something that can be granted at the moment the child senses it and is ready for it. In some instances we find that when the adult is ready to grant it, it is already too late for the young person to receive it. A girl does not suddenly become a useful help in the house because she has reached a certain age. If later she is to live her role of wife and mother, she needs the example of a mother who is satisfied with her status as a woman and who has been able to allow her daughter to share in the enjoyment of the work when she might seem more of a nuisance than a help. A young man can take masculine responsibility if his early pretensions at manhood have not been ridiculed.

Throughout adolescence, young people feel uncertain of themselves, and seek reassurance partly by entering into a conformity of standards with others of their age group. They need, in addition, the reassurance of those in authority and of the older ones of their own family that they are valued in the roles for which they are preparing.

SOCIAL ATTITUDES TO THE ADOLESCENT

Some of the social problems of adolescence are similar to those that exist in any organisation when a newcomer enters and seeks the privileges of the established members. Existing members are jealous of the traditions which they have helped to create, and feel that some of the privileges which have been earned over a long period are going to be demanded by the newcomer who has not, as yet, established his right. They also feel that the newcomer may want to alter or destroy that which had previously been created. Clubs protect themselves by selection of membership. A living culture cannot protect itself in this way. It is not possible to stop children from becoming adolescents, and adolescents from becoming adults. Antagonisms between the generations have some justification because, as a result of technical change and changes in education (for which the adult is most responsible), the young person has been brought up with a different set of values from those which the adult himself experienced.

CONFLICTS IN THE COMMUNITY

The question of authority in the community and in the home over the young adolescent becomes a difficult one because the young person is now becoming equal in size and intelligence (but not in experience). Authority cannot now be enforced either by brute force or by illogical arguments. Authority at this stage is still necessary, but it has to be founded on previous good relationships, and reinforced where necessary by logical reasons. Rebelliousness is almost inevitable. The young person wishes to test out the strength of the authority of his parents and of the community, and sometimes finds weaknesses. He may also be reassured to find strength. He is attempting to assert his own individuality, and yet there can be uniformity within the adolescent age group, and the protests can fit in with, or be responsible for, particular fashions of the age. Young people may wear outlandish clothes—outlandish by adult standards, but conventional within their own group.

Sometimes rebelliousness goes beyond that which can be contained within the ordinary standards of society, and many young people go through a phase of delinquency, but this is usually something which they outgrow.

There appears to be a general impression that in this generation adolescence is a more turbulent phase than ever before. It would be more accurate to say that the stage of adolescence, which is the phase between the reaching of adult capacity and adult responsibility, has come to be looked upon as the entitlement of the population as a whole, instead of being restricted to that of the educated minority whose dependence and privilege is traditionally prolonged into adult life. Another factor is that the new and larger group of adolescents, who feel to be excluded from adult life, have created a new culture of their own which is separate from adult life. Yet there are divisions in adolescence that seem to correspond with the divisions of secondary school education. The grammar school adolescent may have an ideology which is familiar to the adult world, and which is acceptable. He may identify himself in advance with the culture that he will enter into his own adult life. The secondary modern school pupil and school leaver seems to be doomed to the creation of a culture of his own which is *not* acceptable. There are divisions within the culture, and the contemporary young people create their separate fashions of clothing to indicate their ideals and identifications. The enjoyment of a high level of expenditure has in this generation been extended to a wider range of the population than ever before. Young people, in particular, are able to express themselves in the creation of rapidly changing styles.

Some emphasise the quality of toughness in a stark simplicity of clothing—leather jackets and high boots which have a sexual significance. Others of both sexes wear make-up, their clothes are more fanciful, and the male clothing is feminised. Something that would be indicative of homosexuality in one individual is "fashion" when worn by thousands. The fashion reveals the *latent* homosexuality in the normal individual. Many people are disturbed by the open revelation of feminine characteristics of clothes and hairstyle in the young male, but these fashions have obvious links with those created by the "bucks" of the Regency period. In this present age, female fashions have included masculine items for a good many years, and these no longer shock. A girl may now wear clothes originally designed for the male, and, surprisingly, the result may be an enhancement of the feminity of her appearance. The newer fashion of long hair and the use of cosmetics by males may, in like manner, be not incompatible with masculinity.

PREPARATION FOR SEXUAL FULFILMENT

The young person's entry into adult sexual activity has its conflicts in youth and in the adult community. It is frequently stated that this is a permissive age and that youth receives encouragement for protest, for aggressiveness, and for the free enjoyment of sexuality. The word "permissive" may not always be appropriate because young people do not need to ask permission.

The contraceptive pill has separated the burden (and perhaps the satisfaction) of procreation from the pleasure of sexual union. Familiar addictive drugs, and some new ones, have become available to a population in which young people are prominent, and many adults are hesitant to condemn their use without undisputable proof that they produce irreversible harm. "Sex" and "drugs" are themes which stimulate social excitement and lead some of the adult world to take up an unduly repressive position, while others take up a position at the opposite extreme. Attitudes towards sexual activity and towards drug dependence are a good indicator of the position in which individuals stand in relation to ideas of authority and submission. I would maintain that extreme permissiveness is the ultimate authoritarianism. It is as if one is saying "I shall forbid you nothing; and then, whatever you do, you will not have been allowed to do anything that I have forbidden."

DRUGS, DELINQUENCY AND SOCIAL EXCITEMENT

The problem of drug addiction is confused by the attempts to define the behaviour in terms of mental or emotional illness. Delinquency provides another example of the use of a label, applied imprecisely to some kinds of behaviour, becoming regarded as the equivalent of a disease entity. Yet delinquency covers a wide variety of different acts in different circumstances, carried out by people of different family and personal background and with different kinds of motivation. There is the common characteristic that the law has been broken.

The behaviour of young people is often described in words that are intended to convey a precise meaning but which carry emotional overtones. Sometimes psychiatric and social services are called upon to deal with something that is described as a problem in young people, without having the authorisation of a body of knowledge, of valid theories on which to base investigations, and practical methods of treatment. There are even more elusive problems of communication between professional disciplines and the mass mediae which have their own criteria in the selection of what is newsworthy. The mass mediae seem, at times, to be nearer to the problems of youth than professional people. These mediae are more sensitive to areas of excitement, to themes on the fringe of existing knowledge and to the topics that arouse controversy.

TOLERANCE TO DEVIANT BEHAVIOUR

It therefore follows that newspapers, popular journals, radio and television programmes, and the entertainment industry, find interesting material in the tentative explorations by young people of activities that had previously been forbidden. The use of this material by the "communicators" can serve many purposes. It provides a vicarious satisfaction for those who want to read, or look, but not take part. It may provide a further incentive for the breaking down of yet other taboos. It may *increase* the tolerance of the community to members whose behaviour is "deviant" when the deviancy is relative to cultural factors in the epoch in which people happen to live. It should not, however, be assumed that it is always progress for the community to become more tolerant to some particular aspect of behaviour or item of consumption. Whatever the ethical justification may be, there has always been a section of the community which has presumed to try to impose general limits on habits which they believed to be injurious to those who indulge in them. At the present moment, medical organisations are engaged in the exercise of attempting to *decrease* public tolerance to the practice of smoking tobacco in the form of cigarettes.

Public opinion is not uniform, consistent, or coherent. Some generalisations have wide acceptance, and value judgements are attached to the descriptive words; and categories of young people are created, each with its own image. A stereotype may become associated with a specific hairstyle or style of dress, and the stereotype is then made to represent rebellion, delinquency, promiscuity, and the abuse of drugs. At the other pole, there can be a reversal of values in which the established organisation of society is considered bad, and where there is a romanticisation of rebellion against it.

EXPLOITATION OF THE YOUNG

These are areas in which youth can be exploited. There is financial exploitation (for example, in the use of drugs by criminal and by commercial interests). There is also emotional exploitation which can occur with the best of intentions on the part of worthy members of adult society. Many "pillars of the community" have secretly imagined that they alone in the adult world are completely in tune with the young. An inner core of a still living youthful enthusiasm and vitality tells them that the adolescent group is really the generation to which they personally have always belonged. None of us is unbiased, unemotional, or uninvolved in these themes.

REBELLION AS AN EXPLORATION OF HUMAN POTENTIAL

Consolation can be found for those who are anxious about the experimentation of the young in the fact that a large majority of young people escape from these experiences unharmed. For some it is a creative exploration of human potentialities, and they are the means by which the standards of culture are altered. Others of these same people, however, become personal casualties.

With regard to sexual activity, there is justifiable protest against some of the repressive attitudes of a previous generation. New methods of contraception have allowed more freedom for the enjoyment of sexual intercourse outside the permanent relationships such as are envisaged in marriage. Many adolescents no longer need to defer the enjoyment of their sexual potential in the fairly long interval between puberty and marriage.

A large number of young people protest against society's rules and have no compunction in breaking the law, and may be instrumental in changing the law. Some pass through a delinquent period as a temporary phase before settling down into respectable adult life.

Some young people experiment with the use of drugs, simply because drugs are available and a sensual experience is available for the taking of it. Some of them feel that it heightens their sensitivity to external perceptions and inner fantasy life.

There are, however, young people who try out the experience of freely available sexual activity and, in spite of the availability of contraceptives, some have unwanted pregnancies, some get venereal disease, and some, who begin an association which is intended to be casual, find that one partner has become more involved than the other : contraception is not a protection against a broken heart.

Many young people try out their confrontations with the law, in company with their peers, and a proportion of them acquire criminal records that affect their future.

Amongst the number who experiment with drugs there are those who become hooked and who progress from the use of one drug to the use of others.

REBELLION CARRYING RISKS OF CASUALTIES

The young people of every generation have it in them to challenge the constraints which society (represented by their elders) imposes upon them. There is one thing that the adult world should not do and that is to compel the young to make the challenge for the vicarious satisfaction of those who have already passed through their own youth. After all, it is the young who carry the casualties.

It is one of the duties of the adult to show respect for the young, but it is also the duty of the adult to be adult, and to have adult ideas. He should be sensitive to the growth potential of the immature and, at the same time, be able to recognise the value in the immature. There is an immense contribution which the young can make while they are still young, and adolescence is long enough to be a period in its own right. H. M. Maier has called it "adolescenthood";* to match "childhood" and "adulthood".

* H. W. MAIER, *Social Casework*, Jan., 1965.

EGO IDEAL AND IDEALISM

Adolescence has been described in the preceding section as a focus of conflict, but at the same time, during this period, young people are building into themselves an image of an ideal identity. The label "ego ideal" is applied to a process which is more deliberate and conscious than the infantile introjection of the irrational superego. The ego ideal can be derived by the taking in of single qualities from a number of people, sometimes making a composite whole, and sometimes containing opposites. The ego ideal can be partly derived from literature or history, and its nature can also depend upon the trends of the moment.

It seems to be a new feature in the life of young people that ideal representations are being found within their own age group. Teenage entertainment stars have an appeal for the teenage population, and also it would seem that many of them have an appeal for a wide section of the population of all ages. At least in the entertainment world the teenage culture seems to be finding acceptance.

In spite of the materialism and apparent cynicism in many young people, there is often an undercurrent of idealism, and many have much higher standards within themselves than they would be prepared to admit.

They feel under-privileged, and demand freedom and equality for themselves in comparison with adults. Sometimes they are able to direct this attitude into the seeking of freedom and justice for under-privileged members of the community in general. Many young people are willing to work for the rights of people who are oppressed, and many have gone to far-off countries to fight for the rights of others. Some find an outlet in working for charities which provide for the hungry in other lands. The same young people may occasionally seem selfish, and to view the world as if it were revolving round themselves, and yet often it is during adolescence that the outlook becomes broader, and, for the first time in an individual's life, the feelings of other people are taken into consideration.

Young people may begin to be interested in religion at this time. To some it merely means punishment for such sins as masturbation. Others become concerned with ideas of purpose in mankind and in the universe.

Cultural interests may take a new importance. Poetry, art, and music

—often of a bewilderingly modern type—maybe a kind of folk-art peculiar to a part of the young person's life. The tastes of young people may seem queer to older generations because each generation builds up its own culture. Unusual clothes and unusual art forms come together, and outlandish rhythms may be nothing more than a confirmation to older people that younger ones are now a community in themselves. They have an image of their own, and older people are just "not with it". Young people would not *like* the older ones to be "with it". It would be robbing them of their own creation. A recent cartoon in *Punch* showed a middle-aged married couple dressed in pullovers and slacks and kneeling down on the hearthrug over a record-player, and their young daughter, just opening the door, is saying "Oh Mum and Dad. Why can't you be squares like other girls' parents?"

Wider social contacts become possible in adolescence, and young people have the freedom to choose their experiences and their friends outside the family circle, and sometimes outside the circles of their own school or work. They may begin to lay the foundations of friendships with members of both sexes, and some of these remain friends for the rest of their lives.

Adolescence is still a period of development, and there are still developmental needs. There is the need for acceptance, there is the need for outlets of expression of the capacity or potential in physical, intellectual and emotional fields, and there is the need for standards with which to conform or against which to rebel.

Each generation of adolescents also provides a means of bringing out new qualities in those who represent the older generation. The young are their inheritors, supplanters, rivals, and their future. They also represent, in some sense, the present. It was the older generation who created the jet and the electronic age, but the older generation has spent most of its time in the era before the existence of instruments which have transformed the nature of human activities and human perceptions. The young people have been born into this world, which is their birthright, and therefore it is the old who are the newcomers into it. Youth and age embody in their personalities something of one another.

CHAPTER 16

Courtship and Marriage

DURING late adolescence and early adult life, new possibilities of inter-personal relationships are opened up. In childhood, the relationship of boy or girl with his parents is at an unequal level. Both child and parent may attempt to distort the inequality by accepting a "pretend" relation-ship as if they were on the same level. The parent may inflate the child up to adult level, and the child may accept the obligations of this fantasy status. It often happens in such cases that the parent becomes alarmed by the childishness of the child, and that the child feels over-whelmed by his inadequacy to meet the mature demands that he attempts to make upon himself.

During adolescence, when sexual excitement becomes possible with adult potentialities and consequences, the young person still feels im-mature compared with the adults upon whom he is dependent. Many of his early feelings are reactivated either in relation to his parents, or in relation to other adults who are objects of his admiration and sources of identification or of rivalry.

RECAPITULATIONS OF EARLY STAGES

One can understand these phases of adolescence by comparing them with some of the earlier stages of development. It is almost as if, at each new phase, we have to recapitulate some of the previous stages. The adolescent, beginning to express himself sexually in a fuller way, repeats some of the situations in childhood which were described in terms of the oedipal situation. He re-experiences some of the conflicting feelings which existed at that time between himself and his parents. Sometimes he acts out the drama with other people in their stead, idealising some individuals, condemning others outright, as if unable to see individuals

190

as complete persons with their strength and weakness, goodness and badness. He has to abstract one particular quality from each one, idealise it, and allow that one quality to represent a whole person. Most people pass through phases such as this, but some remain in this adolescent stage even after reaching adult life. All of us retain *something* of this stage, in our fantasies at least, and get enjoyment from the love stories which preserve the idea of the romantic love partner who can satisfy all our needs. The idea is that there is one particular individual in the universe who exists for each person. This individual is the "right" person, the right partner; and this partner must be met by some fortunate chance. If two people, who meet and marry, are the "right" people, then everything is all right. If, somehow or other, one meets the "wrong" person, then everything is doomed to failure. It is a simple life aim to seek the right person. It is a repetition of fantasy which we try to match in the personality of people who are important to us at all stages of our lives.

It was mentioned at an earlier stage that parents behave in this way in their expectations of their children. Parents have in mind a perfect child, a fantasy child, and their own child can never come up to this fantasy. Children later learn that their parents are not perfect. They built up, in imagination, a picture of a perfect father and mother which their own parents can never be; although some are placed in a position of illusory perfection. Every individual is disappointed by reality and feels hurt. Parent, child, friend, courtship partner or marital partner— all fail to reach the standard of a mental representation. If the other person is expected to fit the role of the fantasy which has been treasured in imagination, then the real relationship is doomed to failure. Try as we will to deceive ourselves in the perfection of those we love, human qualities break through and then we feel that someone has let us down.

In the relationship between therapist and patient during psychotherapy, the fantasy is called a "transference relationship" because in part it is brought ready-made to the situation. It is called a "positive" transference when the therapist is idealised, and a "negative" one when hostility is evident. Paradoxically we can regard a positive transference as being in some senses a negative one, because, when the therapist is endowed by the patient with ideal qualities which he does not possess, his *real* personality is being rejected as insufficient. The idealisation of one individual by another is no compliment. It is a demand that the therapist should be that perfect healer or answer for his failure. It is equally important to remember that the therapist may demand perfection in the responses of his patient, and seek the satisfaction of patients who become cured.

If a parent idealises a child, if the child idealises a parent, if a husband idealises a wife or vice versa, it is a demand that each should *remain* perfect. Therefore, it is a demand that none should ever be their own selves. It is a rejection of the reality in favour of a fantasy.

FANTASY AND ROMANTIC LOVE

The ideal of romantic love is, nevertheless, encouraged when people derive their fantasy of the person they are going to marry from literature and not from their experience of living people. Young girls may picture their ideal man from adventure stories, such as those which form a continuing series where in each one the hero meets a girl in distress, saves her, but remains free for the next episode and to represent an ideal to all. To marry one would be to deny all others access to his perfection. The hero of the "Western" never actually stays with the girl whom he rescues from the bandits or Indians. He wins her heart, and then rides off alone into the sunset. These people never can really marry. They are unattainable and they have to remain the untested ideal—never tested by the reality of flesh and blood marriage.

Infatuation is the imposition of such a fantasy on somebody who would normally appear to be unsuitable. Infatuation can be defined as an attachment to somebody one's mother doesn't approve of! This is said frivolously but is meant somewhat seriously, because infatuation is an almost deliberate choice of someone not acceptable to the family of origin. As such, it is a turning to an individual, not because of any positive qualities within that person, but because of the qualities which are different from those approved by members of one's own family. There may be a difference of social class, of age, or religion, colour, race or cultural background, or even of the intellectual level. Marriage may be *sought* because of those differences.* It is not implied that marriage is necessarily unsuccessful between people with such differences. Many very sound marriages exist between people of very different

* See Chapter 7 (Rejection).

kinds of background, but the chances are loaded against success if the differences are the *only* things that are sought; that is, if the marriage is sought for the differences themselves and not for positive qualities which could form a basis of an identity.

Choice of marital partner is influenced by many factors, conscious and unconscious, yet there is little need to examine the motives when individuals choose partners on the basis that two individuals, with something in common, are prepared to build up joint experiences. One could then think of marriage as the beginning of the relationship and not the final end; the beginning of a story where something new happens which could not have happened with either alone. The romantic ideal of perfect partners is, conversely, a static one of completely formed individuals. It is also an excuse for not doing anything personally about a marriage. One *has* found the right person, or *has not* found the right person; there is no need to do anything more oneself. The idea of two people building up something new together, in contrast to this, is an obligation which may be felt as a burden.

CONSCIOUS AND UNCONSCIOUS FACTORS IN CHOICE OF PARTNER

We have to allow not only for the deliberate and conscious choice (which must not be ignored), but also for the unconscious factors which depend upon the personal history of each partner. These owe a good deal to the personal experiences of both individuals during adolescence, their friendships and their fortuitous opportunities, and they also owe a good deal to what has been absorbed about the marital roles from the parents in infancy. The child gets his concept of male and female roles, his concept of his own role in marriage, and the concept of what would be the role of his marital partner, from the attitudes of his parents. He gets this not only from what his parents say, but also from what they do and how they behave towards each other.

There are satisfactory and unsatisfactory factors in every marriage and, sometimes, when these satisfactory and unsatisfactory factors are faced squarely, and not distorted or denied, a child can just accept them as he grows up, and be content himself to repeat some of the satisfactory aspects of their life or perhaps do a little better. There are some people who are able to derive their patterns quite satisfactorily in this way, and to link their lives with their own families with the satisfactory recollection of their own childhood in their family of origin. Sometimes there is the wish to reproduce the *perfection* of the parents' marriage, a perfection which wasn't a real one, and which depended upon denial or illusion. It can be very disturbing if the unsatisfactory features of the parents' marriage are still denied at the time when recognition of one's own unsatisfactory relationships begins to be realised. Feelings of failure arise when the *actual* marriage is compared with the *fantasy* of the perfect success of the parents' relationship.

REPETITION OF PATTERN OF PARENTS' MARRIAGE

Sometimes, what is attempted to be reproduced is not the parents' relationship with each other, but the relationship of one parent with the child. Either partner may wish to reproduce that perfect relationship which is remembered as having been enjoyed in childhood with the mother or with the father. The man seeks another mother, or a woman seeks another father. Sometimes both want a relationship as with a parent rather than a relationship of marital partners, and neither can receive satisfaction. If an immature woman seeks a repetition of fathering from her husband, and manages to get it, the marriage may work satisfactorily at that level. It can also work when a man marries someone who is glad to be a mother rather than a wife. The choice, however, is not wholehearted and, sooner or later, one partner may protest against domination even though it was exactly that which had been sought. There is a resemblance at this stage to some of the features of adolescent rebellion. While seeking a mothering relationship, a young man can, at the same time, protest against it. He complains, as time goes on, of having a domineering wife, even if he had chosen her for this very quality and groomed her in the part in which he had cast her.

Sometimes in these marital dramas, the marriage has been undertaken in order to re-enact conflicts which have existed between the parents, almost as if it were to re-live the parents' life on their behalf and give *them* a second chance to do better by proxy. Sometimes, a child who has been aware of conflicts between father and mother will almost demand to repeat them in order to prove that he or she could have managed better. A girl who has been brought up in a family where a father and mother quarrel, and where father has seemed to be in the wrong, may have a feeling that if *she* had been mother the marriage would have been more satisfactory. She feels that although father behaved badly, this would not have occurred if he had received the level of love from mother that she herself would have been prepared to give him. She will repeat the situation through the choice of a man who is doomed to recapitulate the unsatisfactory behaviour of her father.

Sometimes, the attempt is to re-enact conflicts which have existed between the parents and child; not the perfection of the mother/child relationship but the imperfection of it. Not being able to relinquish the ancient struggle, a man with a nagging mother may marry a nagging wife, as if he could not be comfortable without the relationship.

Sometimes, there may be an attempt to alter the type of conflict, or to solve it, by choosing somebody opposite to the parent. A man who has been brought up in a very efficient, thrifty and austere home might seek a glamorous, provocative, vivacious wife and then, from the moment of marriage, try to convert her into a replica of his mother almost as if to prove that mother was right after all. Thus he marries somebody and then attempts to break the very qualities and spirit for which he had chosen her. The same thing can happen with a woman who has had a very worthy father, who seemed dull in his respectability. She may marry a reckless young man, and then regret the instability of the marriage and try to reform her irresponsible husband. Likewise, a girl whose father has been drunken and unreliable may marry a very steady young man and continue to regret the gay and frivolous life that she might have been able to lead with another individual.

Sometimes there is a tendency to solve the problem by alternating the person to whom the person is attached. This can occur before marriage or even after marriage. In some levels of society it is an accepted practice to have one type of person as a wife and another type as a mistress. Men may think of girls as being of two types; the good type such as one's sister or mother who would not have sexual intercourse, and bad ones who do. Some attempt to combine the two in some way. There are men who attempt to rescue a prostitute and make her into a *good* woman. At first they have freedom to have sexual relationships because she is bad, and then have the moral satisfaction of trying to make her good. The attempt fails, as the recollection of previous promiscuity continues to haunt and torment the individual who feels that sexual relations are a contamination.

UNITY OF PERSONALITY

In general, we are faced with problems when people refuse to accept the unity of personality and are unable to look upon sexual activity as inseparable from the self. Thus when a marriage is in difficulties, people give advice as to the "cause" of the difficulty and the "cure" of the difficulty The married partners themselves, while seeking help, try to pinpoint the problem on to some one thing. "Everything will be all right if only . . .", e.g. "If only the sexual side of married life were satisfactory". The person giving advice would then recommend "techniques" for sexual relationships, or, if there is a fear of pregnancy, would recommend contraceptives as a means of relieving the fear.

When the personality is considered in fragments, as if everything would be all right if "that" and "that only" were to be put right, there would seem to be no need to discuss the whole of the background and life experiences of each partner. One aspect only of a problem is presented to a therapist of some kind (a social worker, marriage guidance counsellor, psychiatrist, family doctor) saying "Just cure that, don't bother about anything else; everything else is all right".

SEXUAL PROBLEMS IN MARRIAGE

In marital problems, it is often some aspects of sexual relationship which is described as being the "cause" of the difficulties. In such cases, there is strong resistance to any request for description of life as a whole. There is resentment if questions are asked about life aims and past history. There is merely a search for a particular technique which will make everything all right. This is a way of denying the wholeness of marital life and of personal responsibility.

The marital partners of individuals seeking psychiatric help have a higher incidence of psychiatric disorders than that of the general population. This has been explained alternatively as the result of "assortive mating" or as the "interaction" on one another. Kreitman*

* *Brit. J. of Psychiat.* **110** (1964).

studied the presumably normal partners of patients at a clinic, and compared the results of replies to a questionnaire with those from "normal" couples.

His conclusions were that pairs in the "normal" group seemed to have similarities which were the result of mutual selection rather than inter-action. In the group of patients and spouses, both interaction and selection were factors. Interaction was more important when there was social isolation, and wives were more likely than husbands to reflect the illness of their spouses.

There are some overt sexual problems or patterns of behaviour which are sometimes presented as "the problem". A woman can be described as frigid, a man as impotent. There can be a preference for mastur-bation even within marriage. Some people can complain of, or be complained about, as being over-sexed, or for lack of interest in sexual activity, and some for the practice of perversions.

Some of these will be discussed briefly. FRIGIDITY is not infrequent. A refusal of acceptance of sexual activity could be said to have many "causes", but it would be better to say that it can be *associated with* a number of other types of behaviour rather than to say it is *caused by* some activity. It can occur in a woman who appears sexually attractive, and whose behaviour is, in fact, provocative—a person who, almost deliberately, arouses sexual excitement and then refuses final satisfac-tion. As such, one can think of it as an aggressive reaction to the male. Although she may look exceedingly feminine, she might be a person who resents and envies the role of the male as compared with that of the female. Such a woman may have latent homosexual tendencies. There is, however, in this field a continuum between what is abnormal and what is within normal limits. It is normal for a young girl, as she becomes aware of her feminity, to rehearse her sexual role and to see how attractive she can be without committing herself. When, however, this is continued right through life as an unchanging pattern, it is an expression of a very disturbed personality.

Sometimes, the explanation of refusal or of lack of satisfaction in intercourse is a clear, straightforward consequence of a breakdown of the marital relationship while the marriage still remains in existence. Where one partner has continually humiliated and destroyed the love of the other, it may not be the one who refuses sexual advances who needs psychiatric treatment, although sometimes the problem is presented as if all that was required was some treatment to make one partner respond to the sexual advances of the other.

There can be other aspects of frigidity. There are those who fear losing control of themselves in sexual activity at the moment of the orgasm. This is the same kind of fear of losing control as that which finds expression as fear of death, or the fear of falling asleep, fear of insanity, fear of the violence within oneself. This fear of "letting go" is, in fact, not very different from the fear of letting go of the contents of the bowel and bladder. The fear of final "letting go" can inhibit sexual activity in either the male or female, and it can also inhibit any other form of expression of human activity.

Occasionally, repudiation of sexuality is complete. There is an exclusion of sexual expression that seems to be due to some deficiency in personality structure.

IMPOTENCE in the male can have a similar kind of background. A man might be impotent with one female and not another. A man may feel it is improper in every sense to have a sexual relationship with somebody whom he admires—with somebody who is good. There are men who can be potent only with somebody whom they feel is already accustomed to sexual intercourse.

In some cases, a man may be impotent because of the fear of his own aggressiveness and the thought of his own violence in the act of penetration. He might look upon sexual activity as an attack. Early adolescent sexual fantasies frequently include some kind of violence as the essential part.

Impotence can also be due to the overvaluation of the sexual act as an index of a person's worth. This occurs when a man wishes to have sexual intercourse not for his own satisfactions, but because he wishes to prove that this is possible for him.

Topics which are the subject of anxiety are also the subject of popular humour. There is the story of a man who went to his doctor and said "Doctor, I can only manage to have sexual relationships once a month." The doctor asked how old he was. The man said that he was 65, and the doctor said "Well, that is all right." The man then said "But doctor, a man at my club, who is the same age as I am, says that he does it twice a week." The doctor replied "Well, *you* say you do it twice a week."

In this story the act was valued for its occurrence rather than the satisfaction of a need. This type of valuation is often attributed to old men, but it can occur in a young man who is not quite sure of his manhood and who is seeking sexual satisfaction, not for himself, but the satisfaction of the ability to "act like a man".

Impotence and frigidity can be associated with marital infidelity. There are persons who have homosexual qualities which are repressed and who do not seek sexual activities with others of the same sex. They seek heterosexual contact through a succession of partners without ever attaining full satisfaction. They may marry, become divorced, and remarry. Satisfaction still eludes such people because they are searching for something in someone else to make up for a feeling of deficiency in themselves. They may try to gain satisfaction by forcing satisfaction on to their partner. The partner's orgasm is their proof that satisfaction exists.

Another type of disturbance in marriage is where masturbation continues as the main satisfaction, sometimes accompanying actual sexual intercourse, sometimes as a substitute for it. Such an individual retains his dependence upon fantasy and refuses complete involvement with another individual.

The disturbances of relationships are thus seen as immaturities. At each stepping stone or crises point there are some who try desperately to retain earlier childish or immature satisfactions. Others pass imperceptibly and happily into the next stage. The majority of people pass towards maturity with no more survival of the infantile patterns than a recollection which seems, by comparison, to enhance the enjoyment of the newer levels of experience.

"Wife swapping" is a phrase, at present in vogue, and which is used to describe a practice of changing partners in order to enhance sexual excitement. Equality of the sexes has not yet reached the point when it could be called husband swapping.

CHAPTER 17

Adult Life

ONE of the purposes for undertaking the study of personality is to provide a picture of normality as a background for comparison for that which is thought to be abnormal. The traditional way is to think of disorder in terms of *disease entities*, each one complete in itself, distinguishable by characteristic symptoms and signs, and each with its own pathology and aetiology. A second way is to consider disease as a *process* in which there is a regular pattern of disturbed function involving a number of factors which include inherited constitution, previous provision and deprivation, beneficial and harmful experiences, and the immediate circumstances connected with the onset of the disorder. A third way is to consider disease as *deviation* from the norm, and in this case the abnormality is merely one of degree of intensity of a phenomenon common to us all.

The *normal* activities of adult life are hardly an appropriate subject of psychiatric investigation. Yet the psychiatrist and social worker needs some knowledge of social, occupational and domestic activities of people with whose disturbances he is called upon to deal. There are, in fact, possible dissatisfactions in every aspect of living activity, and a host of professional workers are called upon almost indiscriminately to deal with the marital, occupational, recreational, financial, sexual and behavioral details—normal and abnormal—in the lives of people who consult them.

MAXIMUM RESPONSIBILITY

Adult life is the stage when the individual is expected to be able to take responsibility for his own care. During infancy and childhood, and, to a lesser extent, in adolescence, the individual is dependent upon others. In later life, physical capacity deteriorates, and, although provision may be made for old age by the individual himself in anticipation of lessened capacity, some support is needed. In the adult stage of life, people take responsibility for their own selves, for their children, for their own old age which is yet to come, and perhaps for the care of older people who are part of their present family. This responsibility and this care of others may be accepted as an obligation which is purely personal, as an obligation within a larger family framework, or it may be delegated to the community in general through the contribution in taxation which the adult is called upon to make for the provision for social services organised by the state.

In addition to these responsibilities for the young and the old, there are also the burdens of those who are temporarily ill or injured, or for those who are permanently disabled, defective, or merely inadequate, who also receive care which can be a personal, family or a community service. The adult phase of life is the one which carries the burden of the family and the community.

Up to the adult stage we have spoken of the *development* of personality. In this stage now we may speak of the *use* or the *purpose* to which this development can be applied. Burdens can be privileges or even pleasures. The adult, in becoming responsible for his own life, may be able to direct it into paths which satisfy him.

In adult life there is some degree of fixation of role, and the individual's concept of his own role may receive its valuation within him from some particular aspect of his activities. He has his domestic, his occupational and his recreational activities which may give him different kinds of satisfaction. Individuals may get their concept of their status as adults at different stages of their biological and social development.

In some species of living organisms, the phases of youth and maturity are more clearly marked out than in the human being. In the insect, the grub, which hatches from the egg, seems to have no function other than to eat and lay down tissues for a future stage which has no relation to its present life. The resting stage of the chrysallis shows no activity that we are aware of, and the final stage of the complete insect seems to have its main function in making provision for the next generation.

Human maturation is uneven. There are legal and social divisions of function as well as the biological ones, and an individual becomes regarded as adult at different stages for different purposes.

SOURCES OF SATISFACTION

The physical, intellectual and emotional aspects of personality all receive their fulfilment in the domestic, occupational and recreational life of the adult. Marital life, with the beginning of a new family, is the most important part of living for many people. Occupation is then looked upon as something to earn the means to maintain the home; and any recreational and social life is centred on the home. Others fulfil themselves in their job, and look upon the home merely as a place in which to recuperate for the next day's work. There are, again, others who seek a social life outside their job and their home, and who make that their most important goal.

Domestic life can be thought of in terms of the new family which is being created, and also it is necessary to take into account the links with the family of origin of each partner. A new family cycle is initiated, and the inter-relationships and the emotional interchanges within the family depend upon the ideas that each married partner has of his or her role. The reader is referred to sociological and anthropological studies.*

A good deal of what is satisfactory is never studied, simply because there is no need to question it. Some facets of family life and participation are studied because we are aware of the changing nature of marital roles and of attitudes to different members of the immediate and wider family. There are changes in the attitudes to the wider network of grandparents, aunts, and uncles when the move to other districts separates families, and there are additional changes where differing education and economic progress give young parents different cultural or material values from those of their own parents. Attitudes to children have changed in the last two generations along with the general diminution in family size. Children, being numerically fewer, become individually more important. Moreover, the smaller modern family is frequently the product of the first few years of married life, and child-

---

* E. Bott, *Family and Social Network*, Tavistock Publications, 1957.
  Young and Wilmot, *Family and Kinship in East London*, Routledge & Kegan Paul, 1957.

bearing has become largely restricted to a period of five or six years in the early part of a young couple's married life. The children then grow up, together with their still youthful parents, in a family life in which no more planned children are born. It is not necessary for us to say whether this is good or bad. It is sufficient to recall that conception can be largely controlled, and that sexual relationships can be enjoyed without reproduction. Wherever it becomes technically possible to control some biological function, people will use that possibility.

Similarly, feeding processes exist which allow the upbringing of infants without the necessity for breast feeding, and some proportion of mothers will feed their babies artificially whether they might have been able to feed them at the breast or not. Mothers, therefore, now have a freedom from some of the restrictions that used to be associated with the child-bearing function. A wife can be a mother for a limited period, and then still have an active social and recreational life that is almost as free as that of her husband. She may even continue or resume her pre-marital occupational activities. The concept of any role of husband and wife, and the image of role that each has of the other, changes with different activities, and the pattern of family life must present a different picture to the children of each generation.

CHANGES IN FEMININE ROLE

Sometimes the change of role of the woman brings about fresh problems. The wife and mother who goes out to work is still expected to maintain the major responsibility for the running of the home. She still expects herself, and is expected, to take the main interest in the physical care and in the emotional ramifications of the lives of her growing children; and it is to her that all the family turn for nursing in times of illness. Sometimes it would seem that new-found freedom savours more of exploitation than emancipation.

OCCUPATIONAL FULFILMENT

The *occupation* of the male or female adult is something which can represent predominantly the physical, intellectual or the emotional aspect of life. Physically, the individual has reached the peak of height but not of weight. In the early twenties or sometimes in the late 'teens he has his maximum strength. The maximum can be maintained only for a short time. If an individual chooses physical activities as his ideal representation of his personality, and is able to develop these gifts in an athletic occupation, then the time of his "prime of life" is going to be very limited. When a particular sport depends upon peak performance for a long period, athletes are "finished" at the age of 25; less strenuous activities may enable success and fame to be continued for another ten years, and there are some activities like golf which can be maintained into later life.

There are some industries in which men do extremely heavy work for high wages and where no provision is made for the period of life when that physical level of output can no longer be maintained. This leads to industrial casualties. There are other occupations which also still depend upon physical activity, but where an individual can maintain his skill and usefulness for much longer periods so long as the rhythm of activity is maintained. Interruption caused by illness, accident or unemployment leads to loss of that rhythm, and it is sometimes impossible for him to return to that work. Perhaps the idea of fixity of role, occupational or otherwise, in adult life is one that needs to be revised, and we ought to be able to think of development of personality as something which can continue in fresh ways even when some capacities have declined from the peak which occurs in the early twenties.

Some individuals find occupations in which their intellectual attributes are their chief asset. Perhaps, in this case, physical activity becomes expressed in leisure pursuits, but there are people for whom physical activity appears unimportant and merely incidental to other interests. Intellectual activity also has its peak (or plateau) between the ages, perhaps, of 18 and 25, and those whose unusual gifts are stretched to the fullest extent, such as in advanced mathematics, usually do their most original creative work in their early twenties. It is said that the work in later adult life of many brilliant and creative scientists and artists is merely an elaboration of the originalities of their early career. However, in intellectual as well as in physical activity, there is much work than can be originated or developed with the experience of maturity as well as with the freshness of unfettered youth. It has been suggested that the level of creativity is more likely to be maintained if there is a change of style of work, or change of direction of career, as there are limits to the possibilities of development in any one approach. Platt* quoted an idea that people should change their careers every twelve years in order to prevent the loss of originality which results from the diminishing returns when the same ideas or methods are followed for too long a period. Technical progress in industry may enforce such radical changes of occupation when a traditional process is made obsolete.

The *emotional* aspects of personality can also be the material of the working life. Some occupations depend upon the professionalisation of the use of relationships. Social work, in general, has origins in the desire to make provision for the care of people who are temporarily or permanently unable to make provision for themselves or to find help entirely within their own family. The community as a whole represents the collective wishes of individuals, and shows concern for the helpless with the same ambivalence as parents do for their children. In both there is rejection and acceptance, but whereas children can be expected to grow up and become responsible for themselves, the disabled and inadequate may remain disabled and inadequate, and the rejecting processes may become more evident.

SOCIAL CLASS AND MOBILITY

There are many factors in the recognition of different social classes, but for statistical purposes the Registrar General's categories are based on occupation. The highest grading in social class seems now to be based upon occupations which depend largely on intellectual activity. Physical activity and skill may carry considerable esteem as in the achievements of the notable athletes or the endurance and initiative shown by the explorer and pioneer, yet it is largely assumed that those who have both high intellectual and physical capacity will choose their main occupation for its intellectual opportunities. Social grading of occupations seems to depend upon the assumption that people always choose the occupation with the highest proportion of intellectual content. On this basis the most strenuous and most unpleasant jobs therefore have traditionally been the most poorly paid! Extension of the opportunities for education, however, has increased the number of candidates

* Reflections on Ageing and Death, *Lancet*, 1–6 (1963).

H.G.D.P.—H

for the jobs that are based on intellectual activities, and the wage structure is being altered by the relative scarcity of candidates for the unpleasant jobs which are necessary to keep a civilised community working. Alterations in wage structure bring dissatisfaction, and a person who has a job which he enjoys, and which calls for a high mental ability, is discontented upon hearing that an unpleasant job (which he would not think of undertaking himself) carries a salary that is the equal of his own.

The study of rewards for occupations is complicated, and at present we are left with the fact that many people are dissatisfied with their earnings, not because of the *amount* of their earnings but because of a comparison with the earnings of another class of individual. Satisfaction appears to be relative, and, although choice of occupation may be partly voluntary, there are people whose choice of occupation was dictated by economic processes and industrial developments over which they had no control.

There is the problem of the relationship of occupation to community organisation, and to family life. Individuals and families can no longer be self-supporting, and the building up of communities became necessary because of the need for specialisation in work. Technical changes, which have more recently been introduced, involve the use of complicated machinery; and occupational organisations of increasing size are being built up. Some such organisations have their own network of communications between their different branches and they form a social unit of their own within the larger community. A man may enter such an organisation, and, in his various stages of advancement, may move from one town to another but still be employed in the same industry or even in the same firm.

We thus have the problem of simultaneous geographical and social mobility as a man receives promotion within his occupation. The difficulties and dangers of such processes were described by Whyte in *The Organisation Man** where it was pointed out that individuals working for large combines are expected to find their *social life* within their organisation. They feel unable to join social groups in the local communities where they live, and are unable to throw down roots which help people to establish themselves and their families in local life. Family

* Jonathan Cape, 1957.

and social life become subservient to occupational life, and the children may suffer in their development, as a child will find it difficult to form emotional bonds with other children if these are likely to be destroyed by frequent moves to other areas. There is a tendency for any emotional relationships which are formed to become shallow.

There are problems of social mobility even when moves take place within the same locality. A husband and wife may have an unequal capacity for adaptation to the customs of different social classes, and in any case the transitional period is a difficult one. To remain in a former area with friends who may envy the social ascenders can be as difficult as moving to a new area where they may feel insecure. There are parallel difficulties with people who have declined socially or financially. If they remain in a district where they are unable to keep up their previous standards, the children are at a disadvantage as compared with the children of neighbouring households. If they move to another neighbourhood, they are told by their parents that they are superior to the children of the district, but find themselves treated as if they were inferior.

LIMITATIONS IN REALISATION OF FANTASIES

We must return to a feature of all the problems which have been referred to—that of the image which we have of ourselves, and which we use as a standard with which to compare the reality as we perceive it. In the adult phase of life we have reached the point which has been looked upon as a fulfilment of all the previous preparation, and yet many people still preserve the image of themselves which they had during adolescence. This was the stage when our fantasy had no limits, and the realities of adult life may not compare favourably with adolescent dreams.

We preserve the idea of progress throughout adult life, and may go some little way towards realisation of our fantasies, but there is an understandable tendency to preserve the ideal of the youthful stage when the future had no limits. The adult finds it hard to give up the personal picture of him or herself as a young man or a young woman. Some are able to accept their failures or the limitations of their success, and transfer the dreams and the problems to the lives of their children.

Complete satisfaction eludes the majority of people who pursue it, and yet the belief in its existence seems to be one of the necessary illusions in our lives.

It was stated at the outset that one of the reasons for the study of human development was the wish to make provision for human needs in sickness and in health. In adult life, use can be made of the qualities that have developed. Perhaps mental health is a balance of aspects of personality in the outlets that are available. Physical, intellectual and emotional qualities find fulfilment in the domestic, occupational and recreational life of each individual. The balance is not static in one individual, and in different individuals it can be attained in different proportions of involvement in each area of life.

When dealing with provisions for the needs of children (Chapter 8) reference was made to the necessity for appropriate opportunities for expression of the child's potentialities and capacities. In adult life, we judge more by the performance than the potentiality, but even here there is the need for intake as well as output. The adult, like the child, needs love that is the acceptance of his separate individuality, and standards which, when their rules are observed, give recognition of his identification with a community. The triple needs, over and above material needs, are love, outlets, and a framework within which he can be approved.

THE SINGLE, WIDOWED, SEPARATED AND DIVORCED

It is usually assumed that, for adults, the normal state is expressed in married life, which allows for the satisfaction of mature sexual needs and which provides a matrix for the upbringing of children. There are, however, a significant proportion of people who do not marry, and, of those who marry, some are separated, some divorced, and some suffer bereavement in the loss of the partner. In addition to those who marry and have no sexual fulfilment there are those who enjoy their sexual life and do not marry. There is marriage without children and there are children born outside marriage. Even if membership of a family is looked upon as being a criterion of statistical normality and a desirable state, the minority not in that state constitutes such a large number of individuals that we should hesitate to label them as abnormal. Most of them do not seek help and do not need help.

Of the single who never marry, in some cases it is by choice and in some cases there is a problem of availability of suitable partners at the time when a particular individual is mature enough for marriage. The different aspects of personality, referred to earlier as requiring outlets for fulfilment, grow at different rates; and the intellectual aspect may be finding rich fulfilment in occupational and social life, even to the exclusion of preoccupation with sexual activity. Some people, in times of social and occupational mobility, suffer the penalty of being in the van of progress. Rapid personal progress takes them away from the company of their former peers who could make close relationships with members of their family of origin. The need for close personal relationship of the kind found in marriage may make its appearance at a stage when it becomes a momentous individual decision, rather than one taken in the company of a group of young people developing together.

There is, however, a bi-sexuality in mankind which promotes some degree of satisfaction in sharing in imagination the experiences recorded in literature and available in some degree in various companionships.

The balance of satisfactions is never complete for anyone, and a large proportion of people build the structure of their personality as a complete whole out of the bricks that are available.

There are similar problems for those whose marriages break down, and who suffer; yet here again the large number of marital failures (one in four marriages in the U.S.A. and approximately one in ten in the United Kingdom) makes one wonder whether the permanence of the marital state is something that can be insisted upon as the norm. There is even separation within marriage : separation of interests, the wife's life fixed on the children and the husband's on his work. There are men who work late, and even those who have two jobs. There are husbands who work in the daytime, and wives who work in the evenings. There are those who fall asleep in each others company in the evenings, and there are families who silently watch television together, each member being more closely united with the scene on the screen than with one another.

Loss of the marital partner brings helplessness and social embarrassment to many males. Widowhood and divorce may make a woman sexually vulnerable. A large proportion of men and women who lose their partners are, however, able to re-marry. A large number of adults, married or single, find a measure of fulfilment in the sharing of adult interests with working colleagues; and, with the lengthening of life beyond the reproductive stage, this capacity for corporate adult enjoyment becomes increasingly important.

CHAPTER 18

Middle Age

MIDDLE age has biological and cultural boundaries. At one time, each period of life was marked out by special clothing, and stages were distinct. The middle-aged man and woman each wore an altered style of dress in accordance with the dignity of the new status of middle age. The period of middle age probably extended from the middle forties to the age of 60, when old age began. The change of status and change of clothing corresponded with alteration in physical capacity. It was recognised that peak performance was over, and yet the individual who accepted the status of middle age could feel that he was entitled to respect that did not depend upon physical competition with the young adult.

The intellectual and emotional aspects of personality undergo a simultaneous change. Reproductive capacity begins to decline and may cease in the female in the late forties but continue for quite a while longer in the male.

At the present time there is a blunting of the cultural divisions between early and later adult life. Men in middle age may dress in some of the casual styles of the sporting young man; and it may need a close look at a woman's face to guess her age—it is not always possible to guess it from her clothes. Nevertheless, changes continue in body activity, and problems might arise from the refusal of an individual to accept a new image of himself which will correspond with the changes which take place within him.

PHYSICAL WEAR AND TEAR

As regards the physical attributes, tissues begin noticeably to show signs of degeneration. Body tissues wear out unevenly. There is some "wear and tear" at every stage of life. Tissues degenerate and become

211

damaged, and, although some become repaired by natural processes, there is always a certain amount of permanent effect of the wearing out process which accompanies the process of growth. In that sense it has been said that the process of degeneration begins the moment we are born!

People who work in heavy industry or who do heavy manual work may wear out selectively and begin to show signs of degeneration in the cardio-vascular system, and become unable to continue in their occupation.

In some instances this problem is circumvented by promotion to supervisory posts where appointments are made by seniority. Although this practice may often have successful results, there are many individuals who are unable to teach or control those who have been previously their equals. Some workers may, in any case, have to continue in a heavy job with diminishing physical capacities, and increasing anxieties. The result may be a loss of confidence and self-esteem even if employment is maintained. This applies particularly to a person who continually works close to the limits of his capabilities and resources. As a rule, any individual can increase his output to a surprising degree for a limited time if he has sufficient motivation for it, but that is because there usually is something in reserve. Those who work nearer to the limits of their capacity find themselves living on their reserves in order to maintain the balance of energy exchange in daily life. When there is a reduction in their total capacity, the reserves become exhausted and there is nothing left but to break down.

ALTERATION IN IMAGE OF SELF

As an individual's physical capacity becomes reduced there should be a corresponding alteration in his image of the self, which would allow him to reduce his expectation in performance. Perhaps for that reason the custom of changing the fashion of clothing for different periods of life was a good thing.

If a person dresses young, feels young and sometimes acts young, he may get a sudden reminder that his fantasy of himself is different from the reality. For example, a man may have been accustomed to playing a game such as tennis; he may give it up and then, at a later stage, decide to take up the pastime again. He may attempt a stroke with a movement based on the recollection of the kind of movement that he would have made ten years before. His muscles are unable to respond to the call, having in the meantime lost their elasticity or range of movement. He may rupture one of the tendons, or there may be more serious consequences of over-exertion if an individual is out of practice and out of condition. The effects of any undue strain on the circulation to the muscles of the heart could be severe at a moment when there is more call upon the general circulation than he is accustomed to. A person who gives up physical exercise for a while, and then takes it up again, is more vulnerable than the one who keeps up a continuous and reasonable degree of activity; and there are many leisure activities which allow for adaptation of the manner or rate of movement, in accordance with the physical condition of the participant.

In addition to illnesses which are associated with selective degeneration of tissues, there are illnesses such as cancer which seem more prevalent now because, with a longer span of life, people are living long enough to suffer from them. This applies in general to illnesses where the incidence is greater in later years of life.

Intelligence begins to suffer decline, but there are compensations in the contribution that experience can make to the use to which intellectual capacity is put. The young person may grasp problems much more quickly, but the middle-aged person, especially if originally of high intelligence, can bring recollections of previous experience which might help him to reach a more balanced judgement than was possible in his earlier years. Some middle-aged men have a spirit of competition with young men in the intellectual field, just as others are reluctant to admit that a young man is better equipped than they are for physical work; and in either case they lose the special value of their present qualities when trying to retain the qualities of their own past.

In many professions, middle age is the time when some workers have risen to administrative posts because of their good fortune in having entered the profession at a time when it was expanding. Such men, often exceptional in personality, may not have had the training which is provided as a matter of course for the new recruits who become their subordinates. Sometimes they credit the newly trained worker with a knowledge that nobody really could have, and expect the training to provide a skill which exists only in people's imagination. This is a process with which we are familiar in the relationship between clients and the professional worker. The clients attribute to the professional worker powers which they feel *ought* to exist but which they cannot quite believe in. They wish the worker to have that power but at the same time try to prove that it does not exist. The same processes also exist in the relationships between parent and child, child and parent. The parent has an image of the perfect child, and the child also attributes perfection to the parent; both are disappointed at the failures. There are the same reciprocal processes between colleagues of different ages, and sometimes this becomes expressed in disputes about the value, or otherwise, of new concepts of professional work. The young new recruit, with the latest training, may feel at first that he is being held back by old-fashioned traditions, but, at the same time, he might have a hidden and perhaps exaggerated veneration for the wisdom of the older official in charge.

The emotional life of the individual is bound up with the physical and intellectual qualities, as the image that is entertained of the personality as a whole depends upon every aspect of personality. The emotional life finds expression chiefly in relationships within the family. The children may now be grown up, and a new kind of relationship has to be established between husband and wife. There is the question of the importance of sexual activity at this stage. Menstruation ceases in the woman some time in the late forties or early fifties. The presence of menstruation is often thought of as an indication of the continued fertility of the woman, but although menstruation may continue past her fiftieth birthday fairly frequently, it is extremely rare for pregnancy to take place even in the late forties.

There is no male equivalent of the female climateric, although there are gradual involutional changes in the reproductive organs of the male. Potency and fertility, however, may be retained in males into the sixties and beyond, and it seems possible that some of the anomalies in sexual interests and activities of older men, whether these be of reduction in potency or heightened interest in sexuality, are a psychological phenomenon. There are some cases where there is a physical stimulus to sexuality due to the pressure of an enlarged prostate gland on the ducts leading from the testicles.

INVOLUTIONAL CHANGES IN SEXUAL ORGANS

To some people the changes of involution, which is a degenerative change in the organs of reproduction, makes a difference to marital relationships. In some cases the wife feels that she will not be attractive if she is no longer able to have children; but, in actual fact, the capacity to enjoy sexual relationships continues in both sexes after fertility has ceased. To some there can be a renewal of affection and of the wish for sexual contact when the sexual relationship is no longer linked with the having of children. Some women feel a sense of relief that one episode of life is over and that new status and new potentials are opening out. A woman may feel that the children of the family now no longer need close support. She no longer experiences the constant responsibility for the family which she felt before, although some may try to maintain the dependence of the children on them, cherishing the burden long after it is appropriate. In some cases the menopause is treated as being the end of a sexual life which had never really been fully realised. Some men and some women make what seem to be irresponsible attempts to get the satisfaction which had so far eluded them in the past, in what they feel to be the little time left to them, or to try to store up experiences to last them for the barren years ahead.

For many, a new phase of life begins in relation to the children—sometimes at this stage the children have married and have left home. If there are grandchildren a new level of relationships emerges which is different from that between children and their parents. The grandchildren can receive from the grandparents that part of parentage which is accepting and free, without the part of parentage which is restricting. Sometimes this causes friction between the grandparents and the actual parents of the children, the parents remembering the strictness of their own upbringing in contrast with the indulgence to the new generation. The attitude of grandparents to a grandchild may be doubly in conflict with the parents' standards for their children. There is a difference between the basic ideas of the grandparents' generation as compared with those of parents of today with regard to child rearing, and, at the same time, the grandparents' present standards differs from the one which they held in their original role of parents a generation ago. This difference of standards with regard to the upbringing of children can become the source of conflict between the generations; but many families are content with the frequent but temporary appearance of benevolent grandparents who ask to share an enjoyment of the changing and developing activities of a child who has been brought up more permissively than would have been possible in the general culture at the time that the grandparents were having their own children. They may offer a welcome relief to parents when they are prepared to baby-sit.

CONFLICTS, ANXIETIES AND NEW LEVELS OF FULFILMENT

The contrast and conflict between the generations may be partly the result of social and economic changes that have taken place. Many of the parents of today were brought up as children in times of financial hardship and restriction, and the grandparents may feel that they can now give to the grandchildren what they would have liked to have given to their own children but were unable to do. Pleasures sought in that way may be pleasures that are enjoyed by all concerned.

The emotional aspects of middle life are, therefore, complex, and should not be considered from the point of view of any one individual but an interaction between members of a family which may extend to three generations.

Sometimes emphasis is placed on the aspects of middle age which are seen as sources of disturbance and anxiety. It is just as frequent, however, to see changes which become the basis of new levels of satisfaction and of fulfilment. Each change of status in life can be a crisis point or a stepping stone. At the point of change there may be anxiety. Anxiety could be felt in relation to loss of previous status and also in relation to the imagined happenings which face an individual in the next stage of his life. There are values that can be found in each new status and these values come from the acceptance of the differing quality of an individual's capacity at each phase of life. Each new status can be experienced as a personal discovery which adds to the contentment of life. It becomes a new level of maturity.

Some of the emotional changes in middle age are linked with the reality of death. There is a gradually increasing mortality rate as people get older and, therefore, those who survive become more aware of the loss by death of others closely connected with them. It is a time when the middle-aged person becomes likely to suffer from the loss of his parents, or his other elderly associates, and he also may lose colleagues who succumb to one or other of the disturbances and diseases which can come in middle life. The mortality of middle age has to be considered then, not only for itself, but also for the effect on others.

DEPRESSION IN MIDDLE AGE

The characteristic mental or emotional disturbance in middle age and later middle age is depression; and depression is described as occurring in two categories. There is the *endogenous* type of depression which is associated with changes which occur within the body, i.e. metabolic changes or chemical changes of various kinds, and there is the *exogenous* or *reactive* depression which is associated with external events. It is possible to link these two kinds of change with each other and consider all depression, in some way at least, as being associated with loss. There is the loss of closely related individuals through death, loss of possessions and, sometimes, loss of one's own esteem, which can be associated with a good many conditions, including the fear of loss of potency. If we think of depression as being associated with loss, we can bring together *endogenous* depression, where there is internal loss in the form of loss of the image of the body as a vigorous and sexually fertile individual, and *reactive* depression where the losses are external.

THE NEED TO MOURN

Depression was associated by Freud with mourning. He compared depression, which is pathological, with grief, which is normal; and the difference is one of degree. With the death of a member of the family or a close associate, the loss means losing some part of one's own self. People need a period of mourning to accommodate that loss. People need a period of mourning in order to redistribute their own feelings within themselves. In fact, mourning is a healing process; it is a necessary process in which people adjust to their feelings about the situation.

Mourning begins to take place early in life. There is a link between the mourning which takes place with regard to the death of people who are close to us and the losses which occur in the changes from one status to another in childhood and onwards. A child who is weaned loses the close association with the nipple and has to accommodate to a new type of feeding experience. Here, as mentioned before, there are some advantages in the new status. All loss is a stage towards personal independence, and even our mourning can be a process which helps us, not only to accommodate the loss, but also to re-establish, within our personality, a representation of the person to whom we have been closely attached.

Individuals are sometimes robbed of their mourning processes by being "jollied" out of the state, by being consoled at inappropriate times, or even by having some stages hurried along at a faster rate than they can accommodate. There is a saying in the Talmud : "Don't console the mourner in the presence of his dead."

REGRESSION AT POINTS OF CHANGE

When people appear to pass from one stage of development to the next stage too quickly, they sometimes have to go back again to stages that seem more infantile than the one from which they had just passed. We call this "regression".

Developmental stages all take time. It takes time to recover from the severance of ties to people and places when we move house. Even journeys take time. I have heard it said by people who travel by air that it takes some time after they arrive before they really "catch up with themselves". It is almost as if they have left themselves behind, and they have to wait at their destination until they arrive !

The attitude to illnesses, to operations, to childbirth, has become more and more mechanistic. It is for very good reasons that people are discharged from hospitals two or three days after an operation or after a confinement, and for very good reasons that they are got up out of bed at early stages after operations. There is a tendency for clotting to take place in deep veins when a patient is kept rigidly at rest. Early movement helps the circulatory system. But, because of this new trend towards early activity, people generally make too little of their illnesses and their operations, and women of their confinements. They no longer allow for the time which is necessary to accommodate themselves to the changes involved, or, in the case of operations, for the insult to the body. They do not allow themselves the time to make adjustments to the alteration necessary in the body image. People are cheated out of some necessary regression, and of the gradual nursing back to levels of adult responsibility, if they are expected to take their illnesses in their stride.

DEFERRING SATISFACTIONS

Financial affairs can be a factor in the emotional stages of middle age. Some people at the beginning of adult life incur obligations which help them to live at a particular rate. They buy houses with mortgages which permit the cost to be paid off over a period of (say) twenty years, and in the course of paying off these mortgages they have accumulated a certain amount of capital. They may also make arrangements to save money at the same time, by taking out insurance policies, and they may be able, in addition, to add to their household possessions. Some people try to save money for unexpected expenses. This habit of putting something aside for the future becomes a habit of deferring enjoyment and deferring satisfactions. It contrasts with hire purchase, which is a way of getting immediate enjoyment in the present at the cost of the future. Saving becomes a way of not having something in the present for the sake of what is going to be had in the future, and this, to some extent, can be a necessary process in the arrangement of the lives of many people in the middle classes.

Some people accept the need to save for the future, and then begin to find satisfaction in the process of saving and planning for the future, and not in the enjoyment of the present. A time comes when some of the aims have been realised; the mortgage has been paid off, an insurance has matured, or a particular post has been reached, and yet in the end there seems to be no satisfaction in it. All the satisfactions have been chanelled into the process of preparation, and none for the arrival of the actual benefits. Sometimes, then, the cause of depression is not a loss, but a gain. It may be that it is not what a person *does not get* but something that he *gets* which seems to initiate a period of depression. A person can become depressed at attaining a very long-deferred ambition or aim because he has pictured that happiness awaited him when financial security had been reached; and yet, when he has attained the material success that he dreamed of happiness seems to be no nearer.

ATTAINMENT OF AIMS AND DEPRESSION

Life is unsatisfactory for everybody to some extent. There is always a feeling that it is going to be satisfactory at a particular stage in the future. If that stage arrives, and the individual still finds that life is more or less the same, it is devastating. If the aim still remains some distance ahead, there can still be the feeling that perfect happiness, to which we feel that we are entitled, is there, if only we could reach it. Thus there is depression which follows the *attainment* of a particular kind of ambition.

LOSSES AND DEPRESSION

But there are actual losses. There are financial losses, and there are failures in one's occupation or ambition. Some people not only save, but speculate. Some gain and some lose. If people gain, they may feel that they have some kind of special worth which has entitled them to that gain, and yet they are not quite convinced. If they lose, they may become angry. Sometimes they are angry with the universe, sometimes with other people, and sometimes with themselves. They feel that they have lost a sense of worth within their own selves. Sometimes a financial loss sets up a train of events which leads to depression, and that loss can be a comparatively small one. Some people worry unduly about a particular small financial transaction or an unfortunate purchase—a purchase which promised to be a bargain but wasn't. Often it is a purchase where the article itself carries some value to the individual. Many people link their status with external objects such as motor-cars, and on more than one occasion I have come across a person who has been much more depressed and concerned about an unfortunate transaction concerning the exchange of a motor-car than might have been expected from the dimensions of the transaction itself. The conclusion is that the loss which causes depression (as against transitory regret) is *the loss that we cannot afford*. The loss that we cannot afford is the loss which makes a difference to our estimate of ourselves.

Thus the concept of loss comes into the picture of depression in every aspect discussed so far.

DEPRESSION AND PHYSICAL FACTORS

Pollitt divides depressive illnesses into two main groups, psychological or physiological.* He calls the former type 'J' (justified) and the latter type 'S' (somatic). The emphasis in the type 'S' is on symptoms and signs of characteristic bodily changes dependent on persisting altered function in the central nervous system. These changes have been referred to by Pollitt as "the depressive functional shift". This refers to symptoms such as early morning waking, loss of appetite, loss of weight, and loss of sexual desire—irrespective of the severity of the depressive mood accompanying the changing functions. Attempts have been made to find characteristic metabolic features, such as alterations in the rate of water excretion, the carbohydrate metabolism, or disturbances in the balance of sodium potassium and cholesterol levels. It is suggested that a co-ordinating role for all these different physiological functions is to be found within the hypothalamus, which is one of the vital centres situated deep in the brain. These observations at a physical level are the justification for the search for forms of physical and chemical intervention in the treatment of depression and these efforts have been eminently successful, within a narrow clinical field. The process is still empirical as the action of the drugs is not in any way rationally related to discoverable alterations in body processes. Moreover, the use of these drugs should not divert attention from the search for disturbances of inter-personal and intra-personal conflicts.

There is no justification whatever for giving these drugs in a routine way for the frustrations, discomforts and conflicts that come within the broad range of ordinary satisfactory and unsatisfactory human experiences. Neither is the use of drugs a justifiable alternative to the attempt to explore the possibility of gaining access to better material resources or to the better use of the personal internal resources.

Other physical treatments are dependent upon producing profound but temporary changes in the central nervous system. One example is treatment by artificially induced convulsions. In the first form of this kind of treatment, convulsions were produced by the intravenous administration of powerful drugs in small doses. Later, convulsions were produced by electrical methods. An electrode was placed over each side of the area of the skull corresponding with the frontal lobes of the brain,

* J. POLLITT, *Depression and its Treatment*, Heinemann, 1965.

and an electric current was passed. This was known as ECT or electro-convulsive therapy, and in this treatment a convulsion is followed by a brief loss of consciousness.

The convulsions involved contractions of the muscles of various parts of the body which were so powerful as occasionally to cause fracture of the bones. The modern modified treatment is given under a general anaesthetic. A drug which temporarily paralyses the muscles is also used, and this prevents the contractions, but the neurological equivalent of the convulsion remains.

The physical treatment methods are remarkably successful in shortening the course of severe depression and may avert a danger of suicide.

Physical methods of treatment are empirical, i.e. there is no clear explanation of the way in which the successful results are obtained. One suggestion with regard to ECT is that there is a temporary blocking of the pathways between the forepart of the brain (which carries the higher mental processes, including sensitivity to anxiety) and the centres in the deeper parts of the brain, or basal ganglia (which are the areas of the brain linked with primitive drives and emotions). This temporary blockage of pathways during ECT has been compared with the per-manent and deliberate cutting of nervous pathways in the operation known as pre-frontal leucotomy.

Another type of explanation of the benefits of ECT on dynamic lines is that the treatment is a symbolic death, which is what a depressed person is looking for. It is noteworthy that, where an individual has made a determined attempt at suicide and is rescued by medical or other treatment, the depression seems to clear up along with the re-covery from whatever injury has been inflicted.

The use of ECT (or electroplexy) has now been largely superseded by drugs such as the Imipramine Group (e.g. Tofranil) or Monoamine Oxidase Inhibitors (MAOI). These drugs act in a powerful way and need to be given under close psychiatric supervision. They cut short some of the severest depressive illnesses, which previously carried high risk of suicide. Even in cases where the depression can be related to psychological causes, it may be necessary to administer suitable drugs before the patient can become an active participator in a psycho-therapeutic process.

One further point is that the danger of suicide is sometimes greatest at the stage when a patient is beginning to recover from the deepest phases of depression. There is a degree of apathy which makes it impossible to carry out any effective purpose, and a patient may improve just enough to be able to put his self-destructive drives into action.

TAKING CHARGE OF THE PATIENT

The problem of treatment is that there are instances of depression where we should leave people alone and there are kinds of depression where it is necessary to take charge of the patient. Where suicide is a serious risk, we cannot afford to throw back any responsibility on to the individual. We, as professional workers, have to take responsibility ourselves, and set in motion some process which leads to the form of treatment which is the most appropriate or the most effective at that particular stage.

I have dealt with depression at some length, but I want to return to the fact that the changes in middle age, even including depressive illness, have, within certain limits, a positive function in adapting individuals to a new status in life. A new status can be satisfactory, and some people do find fulfilment in their work and in the personal relationships in middle age at a level that hadn't been possible for them before.

We can think of any individual as having some particular aim in life and some appropriate image of himself or herself at every stage. There has been in our culture, perhaps, an exaltation of youth or of early adult life as being that part of life that matters. Other stages of life have been thought of as being either the stage of "becoming" or the stage of "having been". We should, instead, look for the new levels of maturity which are achieved for the first time in later life.

NEW LEVELS OF DEVELOPMENT

We have been accustomed to thinking that all growing stops at the end of adolescence. It is true that height cannot increase once the bony structure is complete. Perhaps it was on the analogy of this that it was thought that intelligence reached its maximum before the beginning of adult life. Psychologists now are prepared to think of further stages of intellectual development, and there is no structural limitation for this such as there is for physical growth. Ideas about *emotional* growth have never been able to be expressed in precise language, but it seems credible that every relationship with another individual can add something to one's personality. This is part of the process of growing-up which can continue even into the stage of life when we must admit to growing old.

VALUE IN EACH STAGE OF LIFE

Each stage of life has its separate importance. Childhood has an identity of its own and is not the stage of being an immature adult; adolescence has been prolonged to the extent of being more than an in-between stage; and adult life has received an extension into and beyond an active middle age. Therefore, there could be new subdivisions of the adult phase according to functional capacity, self-image, and cultural expectations. Each change of function can have some element of growth, but this growth should not conceal the reality of degeneration of some of the tissues, with consequent diminution in some kinds of performance. Growth is represented by more effective use of the existing and remaining capacities.

Some people preserve the image of youth too long, as when men and women well past middle age refer to themselves as "girls" and "boys" and where, in places of entertainment patronised by the elderly, the conveniences are gaily labelled "Lads" and "Lasses".

Growth takes place through parenthood, grandparenthood, and in more indirect contacts of younger colleagues at work.

Melanie Klein describes how the personality characteristics laid down in infancy can still influence the adult interactions at every age; she deals with the origin of envy and greed in the infant. Greed makes demands which exceed anything which can be received, but envy is worse because the coveted object has to be spoiled to prevent any other person's enjoyment of it. When, however, good experiences predominate over the bad, it becomes possible to work through primitive anxieties; and the processes of reparation and of gratitude come into operation. "If gratitude for past satisfactions has not vanished, old people can enjoy whatever is still within their reach. Furthermore, with such an attitude, which gives rise to serenity, they can identify themselves with young people."[*]

* M. KLEIN, *Our Adult World, and other Essays*, Heinemann, 1963.

CHAPTER 19

Old Age

OLD age is frequently discussed not as a stage of life but as a problem of residential accommodation, social amenities, and medical attention. It is as if at some arbitrarily chosen age, 60 or 65, people cease to be ordinary members of the community, and become a special group for whom the community has to make provision. Even with regard to provision, it is rare for this to be discussed from the point of view of the feelings and deliberately chosen desires of the individuals concerned.

POPULATION TRENDS

The social impact becomes important, and even more so because of the increasing proportion of old people in the community. At the beginning of this century only 1 in 21 of the population consisted of those over the age of 65. In 1963 the proportion was one-ninth, and the calculation according to present trends is that 1 in 7 of all people in 1975 will be over that age.

The widespread policy of enforced retirement at the age of 65 means that such people have to be maintained out of their own savings which were accumulated in their productive years, or, alternatively, they have to be maintained by the efforts of others who are at present in the productive stages of life. The responsibility becomes either a personal one within families, or a communal one when provision is made through financial contributions in the form of pensions or Social Security. The community provision can also include residential services or various kinds of supportive case-work or nursing.

RESPONSIBILITIES AND BURDENS

Thus the care of old people can be regarded as a burden for which provision has been made by their own selves in an earlier stage of their lives, or by others at the present time. If we consider that increased

225

longevity makes this period of old age much longer than it used to be, and if we also consider that the dependent stage of childhood and adolescence is being made longer than used to be the case, it will be seen that there is a considerable increase in the responsibilities of the able adult population, who carry also responsibility for the care of those who are temporarily or permanently disabled through illness or inherent defectivenesses.

Perhaps members of the adult population have come to regard themselves as representing the whole of the community and as a race apart. Individual adults at times feel and act as if they personally had never had a childish dependent state, and as if they have no intention of becoming dependent in their old age. Thus, at times, it seems that there are three races of man—children, adults, and old people—rather than a people in which each individual has a series of stages of the same life.

In less cynical moments one might comment on the extent to which the community is in fact prepared to provide for those who are no longer capable of looking after themselves. There is a good deal of feeling of compassion and concern for those who are dependent, but we must be aware at the same time that there are two aspects of feeling about carrying the burdens of others. Resentment and hostility is the other aspect of the ambivalent picture. Occasionally people can conceal their ambivalence by being able to express their wish for provision to be made for old and other dependent people, but make it clear that this care should be carried out by "The Government". Their concern and hostility can be expressed simultaneously in criticism of existing provision.

Sometimes we hear people speaking resentfully or in a hostile way of some burden that they are carrying themselves, and in this case the hidden part of feeling is the tenderness which makes them able to do it at all. Others conceal the hostility under elaborate care which over-protects their dependent relatives and which restricts their freedom of action.

Some of the problems with regard to old people are related to the conflict between the generations. It is implied that problems at the present time are greater than formerly, yet there always has been some distinction between the elderly and the young adults. In some cultures, old people have been venerated to an extraordinary extent as the carriers of wisdom, and treated with almost religious adoration.* Perhaps it was their scarcity value, in cultures where most people died young, that allowed this special treatment. Those who survived must indeed have had some special qualities!

CARRYING THE CULTURE

Some old people in our culture are able to express themselves well, and are carriers of the culture of their youth and may have added some appreciation of contemporary culture to their personal experience of previous generations. Some old people convey to their intimate family this feeling of being somehow special. An eighteenth-century writer said, "Old age is such a charming condition. What a pity it lasts such a short time"—and perhaps there was something personal in the feeling. One remembers that George Bernard Shaw, on reaching his ninetieth birthday, was very concerned at the idea of mortality, and felt that at least for a few selected people there should be some lengthening of the ordinary span of life.

Many people are reluctant to let go of life itself, and some are unwilling to let go of a particular position which they have held in life. This may be the position of power or authority in a family, where a woman is reluctant to let go the burdens of housekeeping, or a man to let go the responsibility for making the important decisions which affect the lives of other members.

Problems arise on an economic level when men are able to maintain their positions and block the promotion of younger people. Such individuals, if in a managerial or ownership position, may hold on to power and financial responsibility, and not only impede other people's advancement, but also to hamper the progress of the concerns which they are directing. This may happen also in voluntary organisations where a chairman holds on to his position for a period long past his full usefulness to the committee.

* Felix Post points out (1965) that man stands out in the animal kingdom by reason of his capacity to store and elaborate life experiences mentally, and to transfer them by speech to other members of his species. In a wider sense than the merely biological one, he remains useful to his race after his reproductive role is over. (*The Clinical Psychiatry of Late Life*, Pergamon Press, 1965.)

RELUCTANT ABDICATION

It may happen that an individual gives up his wealth or his position but yet still wants the disposal of it in his own hands. We may think of this as a modern practice which has grown up to save the payment of death duties, but a similar story occurs in Shakespeare's *King Lear*. In this play a whole range of human conflicts is depicted with a depth of understanding which goes far beyond that which modern psychiatric writers are capable of revealing.

One facet of the story concerns Lear's decision to divide his kingdom between his daughters. Two of the three daughters express their love for him in suitable words at his request, and are correspondingly rewarded. But the third is unable to deny the complexity of her intense feelings—her share is therefore refused her and divided between the other two. When ex-king Lear arranges to stay, in turn, with the two daughters who are his inheritors within his lifetime (much as an elderly parent of today stays with his married children in turn), the daughters begin to feel that he is still competing with them for the authority that he gave away. His very vigour disturbs them. His daughters plead with him to accept the consequences of his new status and obey the orders of those who know better than he does what is good for him (or them).

> "O Sir, you are old;
> Nature in you stands on the very verge
> Of her confine : you should be Rul'd, and led
> By some discretion, that discerns your state
> Better than you yourself,"

says Regan. Later she says "Being weak, seem so"! His family cast him out into the storm, which he defies, and he fights impotently against the elements. It is a matter of our choice whether we think of his madness as coming from the degenerative processes of old age in which his behaviour becomes troublesome, or whether we think of him as justly rebelling against, and being driven mad by, the ingratitude of his daughters.

None of the problems of old age—personal, family or communal—are new. What is new is the fact that more people live to a greater age, and therefore any problems which exist are multiplied. The economic aspects have to be faced, and it may become more important than ever to find value in the capacity and competence that old people still have in family, social and occupational life.

DEGENERATION OF TISSUES

It is still appropriate to deal with the life of old people in the different aspects—physical, intellectual, emotional and social. The physical changes include the continuation of degenerative processes, or wear and tear of various tissues. There are changes which are to be expected and which we call normal. The rate of metabolism is reduced, i.e. the tissues work at a lower rate and chemical interchanges go on more slowly. Some tissues may shrink, and many old people find it convenient to eat less and become thinner. This may happen imperceptibly as, when the output of energy becomes less, the food intake may be reduced, and appetite, which is partly a matter of habit, becomes less. Many people accommodate themselves very well to the metabolic change by slowing down many of their activities, and yet finding themselves able to preserve some interest in restricted fields. There may be a change in the rate of working and even a change in the rate of thinking about one's work.

Changes take place in the central nervous system, particularly in relation to the cells in the brain tissue, and the total amount of mental activity is reduced. Thus, amongst the normal changes, there is some deterioration in intellectual capacity. The deterioration seems less marked in those of high intelligence, and it is one of the unfair aspects of nature that those who have more, have it longer!

MEMORY CHANGES

There are some characteristic patterns of mental life in old age. Memory for recent events may be lost while the recollection of events long passed may still be preserved. A man may forget what he has had for his meal that day, or even whether he had a meal at all, and yet remember quite clearly what happened at his place of work on a particular day twenty years ago. Sometimes the difficulty of conversation with an old person is that particular topics of long ago become repeated time and time again, and interest is lost in their conversation.

EXCLUSION FROM FAMILY DISCUSSION

Old people sometimes become separated from members of their family on account of their lack of capacity to enter into the day-to-day life of the home. Sometimes this lack of capacity is increased by the reluctance of other members of the family to share the knowledge of day-to-day events with the old person, perhaps because he is slow to grasp them. There may be a tendency to exclude him from family councils, to make decisions without consulting him, and, sometimes, without conveying the decision. Important events occur in a household, and the old person has no foreknowledge of them. This can lead to a feeling of confusion, of uncertainty, and to the expression of a belief that he is no longer valued in the household. He comes to feel that he is disregarded, talked about behind his back; and one has only to exaggerate these feelings a little, and we have a complete picture of the mental disturbance which we call a "Paranoid State". In a more severe form there is a feeling that the individual is being persecuted or being denied rights to which he is entitled. Paranoid states of varying degrees become frequent in old people, and perhaps form the characteristic mental disturbance at this stage of life, just as depressive illnesses are characteristic of the period of involution during middle age.

MENTAL DISTURBANCES, ORGANIC AND FUNCTIONAL

Many other types of mental disturbance can occur during old age. Depressive illnesses can occur from endogenous or from exogenous causes in the same way as in middle age. These can be variations of mood or exaggerations of ordinary feelings that people of all ages can have from time to time. Sometimes there is an exaggeration of personal characteristics which had been present previously in a milder form. It is no longer easy to conceal various personality traits, which differ from individual to individual, when the older person is no longer in complete control of his faculties. Meannesses, hatred, maliciousness, and a variety of minor or major anti-social tendencies become revealed. An older person may sometimes become a caricature of the self which he seemed before, when the lifting of controls and inhibitions reveals that which had previously existed but which had been kept within what appeared to be the normal range.

Physical, intellectual and emotional characteristics thus become linked with one another in the changing nature of behaviour which results from the degenerative processes. There are the social implications, too, with regard to the various aspects of care and treatment. Some of the mental changes might be thought of as due to organic or structural changes, and many of the mental illnesses are ascribed to senile degeneration and are labelled "Senile Psychosis".

Many of the changes, however, seem to be "functional" rather than structural, and they are not necessarily permanent mental disorders. This is important as there is a tendency to look upon the mental changes in old people as irreversible, and therefore to seek permanent residential placement for those who become mentally ill. Some patients improve rapidly when transferred to hospital. There may be a degree of benefit from the very fact that in a psychiatric hospital the individual has *permission to be abnormal.* He is allowed to be himself. He can be confused and is not forced to fit into the pattern of his younger self that he can no longer equal. He then becomes able to make a new adaptation at a level which actually is within his capacity.

PROBLEMS OF RESIDENTIAL ACCOMMODATION

There is, nevertheless, a serious clinical as well as social problem with regard to the fact that residential accommodation is sought for the elderly person with mental symptoms. Provision is made under a variety of medical and social services. A large proportion of the hospital beds in the country in general, and psychiatric hospitals in particular, is occupied by patients over the age of 65. Some patients are there for the purpose of receiving active medical and nursing treatment, and some are there because there is nowhere else for them to be. A patient suffering from some limitation of function as a result of mental or physical illness may need long-term treatment, but the time may come when the actual treatment is less important than the general care. It is one of the functions of the 1959 Mental Health Act to place responsibility for social, rather than medical, care on to local authorities instead of the hospital boards, and it is expected that some people who have had a long stay in hospital should be returned to the community. It may, however, be impracticable to discharge people from hospital, which is their only home and which is the home which they have known for many years. Perhaps the most that we can do is to see that this type of hospital population is not added to, and we can consider alternative types of residential accommodation to prevent new admissions of this type to hospitals.

VARIETIES OF HOSPITAL, HOSTEL AND HOUSING PROVISION

Apart from psychiatric and general hospitals there are some hospitals which specialise in the treatment of chronic and disabling illnesses, and there are geriatric wards especially for old people. Outside the hospital system, Welfare Departments of the local authorities have the responsibility of providing homes for old people who are unable to provide homes for themselves and who have no relatives who find it possible to provide a home for them. In addition, Housing Departments make special housing provision where old people can live independent lives with the minimum of supervision. Finally, one of the new duties of the Health Departments of local authorities* is to provide hostels for elderly people who have mild mental illness which may not call for, or be amenable to, general medical or psychiatric treatment.

There is an increasing demand for all these different kinds of accommodation, and it is a frequent topic of social workers that families of old people are no longer willing to take responsibility for them. Nevertheless, a recent survey shows that by far the largest proportion of old people live in their own homes with their families, and often quite happily and on good terms. Difficulties can occur, and some of these are due to the changing patterns of living and technical "progress". The very nature of progress in housing can present a difficulty. Slum clearance and the rebuilding of houses in new suburbs is often carried out in a manner that fits the nuclear family consisting of a father and mother with two or three children. The two- or three-bedroomed house or flat becomes the most frequent unit. Spare bedrooms are less frequent, and the demands for higher standards of accommodation and hygiene make it more difficult to fit in an old person as an extra resident within

---

* From the 1st April, 1971, this responsibility was transferred to Social Service Departments of the local authority.

the family. Even where there is a spare bedroom it may be of a kind which is lower in status, size, and amenities than the principal bedrooms.

The fittings of a modern house, with its streamlining and electrification of cooking and working equipment, form a different setting from the homes in which many of the old generation were brought up. It is difficult for an old person to find a place where he is comfortable and does not damage valuable furnishings. Kitchens have become workshops and not living rooms, and, where furniture is precious and easily damaged, the old person is less acceptable in the home. In some cases, as a result of rehousing, the bathroom becomes a sign of the new status and of the improved standards of living. A chamber pot is looked upon as something archaic and if, as a result of the difficulty of finding the way to the bathroom at night, accidents happen, the old person feels ashamed and may be subjected to criticism or abuse.

In the smaller family the physical burden of looking after an old person who becomes feeble is greater than in the large family where the duties are shared. If husband and wife go out to work there may be no one at all to take the responsibility for an aged parent or relative. There are, therefore, a good many reasons why there seems to be pressure to get special places for old people, and yet in many families all that is asked for is some help in order to maintain and keep the old people within the family circle.

In some localities it has been the experience that when help is given at an early stage, before distress and conflict have reached a high level of intensity, the integrity of the family can be maintained. In some cases a short admission gives relief to all concerned. Sometimes an old person is admitted for the weekend to give the family a rest; in other cases, during the week, when the family are out at work. There are day hospitals where patients can find occupation, as well as treatment, and return home to sleep, and there are night hospitals where people can sleep and go out to work in the day-time if they are still able to do so.

The structure, architecture and siting of the various types of residential accommodation is a matter of controversy. There are mansions in the country where provision is made for old people on a grand scale but in complete isolation from their families or from the community in general. There are small blocks of houses on the fringe of housing estates, or special types of accommodation scattered amongst ordinary housing. There are old people's homes in which there are resident wardens and provision for some medical supervision; and it has been said, partly jocularly and partly seriously, that the ideal site for an old people's home would be one with a public house at one corner, a Woolworths' store at another, and a fish and chip shop at a third corner! Amongst the considerations for siting of such homes are the arguments as to whether old people should intermingle with the younger ones or not; whether they would lose patience and be disturbed by the noise of young children, or whether they would wish to see them running about.

DEPENDENCE AND INDEPENDENCE WITHIN THE FAMILY AND COMMUNITY

When all these considerations have been discussed are we not taking responsibility, even with the best intentions, for the way that old people *ought* to feel, without giving them an opportunity to work out what they *actually do* feel? We arrive at the best decision that we can, and expect the old people to be grateful. "Being *old*, seem so!" we say. The question arises as to whether it might not be possible for old people to have a more independent life of their own, productive, and with emotional satisfactions appropriate to their needs and capacity.

In many homes the grandparents still serve as a stabilising influence, receiving, and therefore justifying, respect, and building up a special kind of relationship with grandchildren or great-grandchildren.

Perhaps it is the suddenness of change of function which leads to loss of status and loss of self-respect within the personality of the old person before other people begin to share in this process of devaluation. Perhaps the industrial pattern may need to change if this self-respect is to be preserved. Mental disturbances in middle age are more frequent in women than in men, and, in middle age, the menopause is a more clearly marked and sudden change of status in the woman than in the man. The change is marked by the cessation of menstrual periods. At later stages, mental disturbance is more frequent in the male, and it is the man who has the more clearly marked and sudden change of status here. The woman usually continues with her housework and her responsibility for the home, and she continues to get her status from this. The man gives up his occupation with voluntary or compulsory retirement,

and there is a day when he is working and a day following when he is
no longer at work. If he owes his self-valuation, and his valuation by
others, to his work, he suffers a serious loss on that particular day.

RETIREMENT, SERENITY AND DEATH

Discussions on the preparation for retirement are often carried out
by people who themselves would have no problem. The interests they
suggest by way of preparation for others are the interests which would
give themselves satisfaction. We are apt to judge what is good for other
people by our own appreciation of our own needs. We have to recognise
the variety of levels of intelligence and of types of social satisfactions,
and we cannot arrange that other people should enjoy the activity that
would give us pleasure.

Once again we are reminded of the fact that we have an image of
what people *ought* to be like, and we try to fit them into this pattern.
We begin this process when we have our children, and we judge them
as successful and unsuccessful, and even as good or bad, by the degree
to which the actuality fits our fantasy. The patients or social casualties
who come for help are expected to fit a particular existing image that
we have of them in their particular role. We continue to do the same
with old people.

Once again we are left with the problem of trying to find a way to
help individuals to live at a level of expression which is within their
capacity at a particular time, and to help them into participation in the
process if they have that ability. The simultaneous processes of the drive
towards independence (and separation) and the need for dependence
(and joining in with other people's lives) is something which begins
before birth and which continues to the end.

There are limits to the duration of life which are genetically determined.

The potentiality for longevity is linked in some ways with the sex
chromosomes, and females live longer than males. The increase in
longevity in a population is due to the fact that more people attain the
possible span of life than before and it is not an increase in the total
span of life available.*

* F. J. KALLMANN, *Genetic Factors in Ageing,* in *Psychopathology of Ageing,*
by P. H. HOCH and J. ZUBIN, Grune & Stratton, New York, 1961.

Consideration of the subject of death is often restricted to death that takes place in the aged. Children ask about the facts of death as urgently as they ask about the facts of life, and the answers to the questions on death are often more incomplete than the information that is given about sexuality and birth. There is a reluctance in those who are in early adult life to contemplate their own death or the death of young children, but these deaths occur. It seems difficult to come to terms with a universe in which death can come through the chance of injury or disease, and not through the inevitability of reaching the limit of life. Doctors and social workers are hesitant in discussing the topic of death even with those suffering from incurable illness at the terminal stages, yet the dying need professional care and the involvement of their families; and the relatives of those who die, whether suddenly or after long illness, need some preparation and consolation.

Hinton has challenged some of the traditional taboos and discusses topics such as speaking of death with the dying and the way that awareness of approaching death can be accepted or denied.*

Death itself is something which is feared at many stages of life. At some stages the fear can be denied, but there are times when this fear takes a greater intensity, and people become concerned about leaving some effect or trace of themselves as a living immortality. They seek to influence their children during their lifetime, or afterwards, by instructions and conditions which they can lay down. Sometimes this wish becomes frantic when the capacity for present-day activity and influence seems to be becoming reduced. Many people, however, achieve a serenity during old age and feel they can afford to let go of life and be content with what they have given and received.

---

* JOHN HINTON, *Dying*, Penguin Books Ltd., 1967.

Further Reading

(supplementary to publications referred to in the text)

BELL NORMAN W. and VOGEL E. F., *A Modern Introduction to the Family*, Routledge & Kegan Paul.

BENEDICT R., *Patterns of Culture*, Routledge.

BLACKBURN J., *The Framework of Human Behaviour*, Kegan Paul.

BLACKBURN J., *Psychology and the Social Pattern*, Kegan Paul.

BOWLBY J., *Child Care and the Growth of Love*, Pelican.

BOWLBY J., *Maternal Care and Mental Health*, World Health Organisation.

BURLINGHAM D. and FREUD A., *Infants without Families*, Allen & Unwin.

CAPLAN G., *An Approach to Community Mental Health*, Tavistock Publications.

CAPLAN G., *Concepts of Mental Health and Consultation*, U.S. Dept. of Health, Education and Welfare.

CAPLAN G., *Prevention of Mental Disorders in Children*, Tavistock Publications.

CARSTAIRS G. M., *This Island Now*, Penguin Books.

ENGLISH O. and PEARSON G., *Emotional Problems of Living*, Allen & Unwin.

ERIKSON E. H., *Childhood and Society*, Norton, N.Y.

FAIRBAIRN W. R. D., *Psychoanalytic Studies of Personality*, Tavistock Publications

FERARD and HUNNYBUN, *The Caseworker's Use of Relationships*, Tavistock Publications.

FLUGEL J. C., *Psychoanalytical Study of the Family*, Hogarth Press.

FRAIBERG S. H., *The Magic Years*, Scribner, New York.

FREUD A., *Introduction to Psychoanalysis for Teachers*, Allen & Unwin.

FREUD S., *An Outline of Psycho-analysis*, Hogarth Press.

FREUD S., *The Psychopathology of Everyday Life*, Pelican.

GLOVER E., *Psychoanalysis*, Staples Press.

ILLINGWORTH R. S., *The Normal School Child*, Heinemann.

ISAACS S., *The Nursery Years*, Routledge & Kegan Paul.

KAHN J. H. and NURSTEN J. P., *Unwillingly to School*, Pergamon Press.

KLEIN M., *Our Adult World and other Essays*, William Heinemann.

KLEIN M. and RIVIERE J., *Love, Hate and Reparation*, Hogarth Press.

LELLO J., *The Official View on Education*, Pergamon Press.

LEVY D. M., *Maternal Overprotection*, Columbia University Press.

LINTON R., *The Cultural Background of Personality*, Kegan Paul.

LURIA A. R. and YUDOVICH F. IA., *Speech and the Development of Mental Processes in the Child*, Staples Press.

MEAD M., *Cultural Patterns and Technical Change*, UNESCO.

MILLER E., *The Generations*, Faber & Faber.

MILNER MARION, *A Life of One's Own*, Penguin Books.

PEARSON G. H. J., *Emotional Disorders of Children*, Norton, N.Y.

238   FURTHER READING

PIAGET J., *The Child's Conception of Number*, Routledge & Kegan Paul.
PIAGET J., *The Moral Judgement of the Child*, Routledge & Kegan Paul.
PRITCHARD D. G., *Education and the Handicapped*, Routledge & Kegan Paul.
READ H., *Education Through Art*, Faber & Faber.
RIESMAN D. and others, *The Lonely Crowd*, University Press.
SEGAL H., *Introduction to the Work of Melanie Klein*, William Heinemann.
SCHAFFER H. R. and EMERSON PEGGY E., *The Development of Social Attachments in Infancy*, Society for Research in Child Development.
STORR A., *The Integrity of the Personality*, Pelican.
TINBERGEN N., *Social Behaviour in Animals*, Methuen.
THOMPSON S. and KAHN J. H., *The Group Process as a Helping Technique*, Pergamon Press.
WINNICOTT D., *The Child and the Family*, Tavistock Publications.
WINNICOTT D., *The Child and the Outside World*, Tavistock Publications.
Growing up in a Changing World, World Federation for Mental Health.

General Literature

The Bible : Book of Job.
ALBEE E., *Who's Afraid of Virginia Woolf?*
BELLOW S., *Herzog.*
BARSTOW S., *A Kind of Loving.*
ELIOT GEORGE, *The Mill on the Floss.*
IBSEN H., *The Wild Duck.*
OSBORNE JOHN, *Look Back in Anger.*
PINTER HAROLD, *The Caretaker.*
SHAKESPEARE, *King Lear.*

Index